English Language Teaching

A Modern Approach

Chief Editor

Shravan Kumar

Editors

Harleen Kaur

Savithri Swaminathan

ATLANTIC

PUBLISHERS & DISTRIBUTORS (P) LTD

Published by

ATLANTIC

PUBLISHERS & DISTRIBUTORS (P) LTD

7/22, Ansari Road, Darya Ganj, New Delhi-110002
Phones : +91-11-40775252, 40775214, 23273880, 23275880
Fax: +91-11-23285873
Web: www.atlanticbooks.com
E-mail: orders@atlanticbooks.com

Reprint 2018, 2023

Printed & bound in India by Atlantic Print Services

From the pen of editor...

Dear Readers,

We are truly happy to bring out the Conference Proceedings of a three-day International-cum-Annual Conference organized by the English Language Teachers' Association of India (ELTAI) at Raj Kumar Goel Institute of Technology & Management formerly Raj Kumar Goel Institute of Technology for Women (RKGITW), Ghaziabad, Uttar Pradesh, India from 9th to 11th July 2015. About 400 + delegates from all over the country and abroad took part in the conference. This conference's highlights were four plenary talks, two symposiums, two panel discussions and a creative writer's session—eminent educational administrators, academics, media personnel, heads of NGOs, creative writers and ELT specialists participated in this three-day conference. Three parallel paper presentation sessions and 14 parallel workshops were also organized on these three days. Members of Faculty, research scholars and ELT specialists of international and national repute took part in these deliberations.

This book comprises of thirty-one papers which focus on the problems and solutions of standards of English which we have been discussing for decades. The achievement of standards in English in the midst of problems such as large classes, dearth of teachers' commitment, lack of infrastructure, centrally prepared textbooks/course books, divergences in the levels of linguistic proficiency among urban and rural learners and so on is extremely difficult but extremely significant as well. The broad areas covered in this collection include the following areas:

- Setting learning outcomes for English as a language of communication
- Standards-driven approach to teaching and learning of English
- Assessment standards of English for various levels of education
- Quality provision in English education
- Charting and tracking an academic revolution in respect of English education
- Quantity versus quality in language education
- Strategic directions for teaching and learning of English
- Views of Stakeholders on the quality of teaching and learning of English
- Trends in teaching and learning of English
- Transnational experiences in setting standards
- Status and preparation of English teaching personnel
- Role of ICTs in achieving learning outcome standards
- Use of English literature to improve language skills

The book is coming before the readers with the collaboration of Atlantic Publishers and Distributors (P) Ltd. and English Language Teachers' Association of India (ELTAI). We hope it will open up new vistas for improving the standards in teaching and learning of English and prove to be beneficial for those who could not attend the conference. The articles in the book attempt to weave together some of the techniques and strategies employed by the experienced and innovative teachers to enhance the standards of English in our country as the deteriorating standard of the language is of our primary concern.

Finally, I would like to thank all the delegates who attended the conference and made this event a meeting of minds and hearts. I consider it an opportunity to express my deep gratitude to all those persons without whose help the conference and the publication of the articles would not have been possible. I hope you will enjoy reading through this anthology and your valuable suggestions are always welcome for the betterment of teaching and learning of English in our country at all levels of education.

I am grateful to all team members of Atlantic Publishers and Distributors (P) Ltd. and express my special thanks to Mr. Harjeet, Harendra and Mr. Sanjeev Kumar for seeing the book through the press in record time.

Shravan Kumar
Chief Editor

About ELTAI

The largest Network of Teachers of English in India (An Associate of IATEFL, UK) The English Language Teachers' Association of India (ELTAI) was founded on August 7, 1974 by the late Padmashri S. Natarajan, a noted Educationist. We bring out *The Journal of English Language Teaching*, a bi-monthly, and it is given free to all the members of the Association. Our consultancy services offer Teacher training packages and organize bi-monthly meetings on current ELT themes relevant to the Indian context.

We host annual conferences and regional conferences on specific areas relevant to the ELT scenario today. Delegates from all over the country as well as the world outside participate in them, present papers and conduct workshops.

MISSION

We provide a forum for teachers of English

- To meet periodically and discuss problems relating to the teaching of English in India
- To help teachers interact with educational administrators on matters relating to the teaching of English
- To disseminate information in the ELT field among teachers of English
- To undertake innovative projects aimed at the improvement of learners' proficiency in English
- To promote professional solidarity among teachers of English at primary, secondary and university levels and strive promote professional excellence among its members in all possible ways

VISION

ELTAI envisions making India a hub of ELT related activities and to conceptualize the experiences of English language teaching-learning and symbiotically share them with others.

ELTAI shall develop into a movement spreading across the length and breadth of the country empowering teachers to make every learner of English globally competitive. ELTAI shall aim at becoming a recognized leader, a catalyst.

Contents

List of Contributors

Pradip Sharan. Associate Professor of English, Motilal Nehru College (Eve), Delhi University, New Delhi.

Roma Karanjkar. Faculty in English, ELTIS, Pune.

Vidya Vati. Lecturer [English], Directorate of Education, NCT of Delhi.

Shailesh Kumar Mishra. Assistant Professor of English, Government Vedram College, Malkharoda.

Bhupendra Kumar Patel. Assistant Professor of English, Government Navin College, Nawagarh.

Naziya Hasan. Assistant Professor, Dept. of Teacher Education, Manipur University, Imphal, Manipur.

Ramana Prasad. Assistant Professor, Dept. of English, Vasai Engineering College, Hyderabad.

Priyanka Sharma. Associate Professor, Dept. of English, K.I.E.T., Ghaziabad.

Soniya Verma. Assistant Professor, Dept. of English, R.K.G.I.T., Ghaziabad.

Jayadeb Sahoo. Lecturer in English, Govt. Auto. College, Bhawanipatna Kalahandi, Odisha.

Reena Singh. Assistant Professor, Applied Sciences, Krishna Institute of Engineering and Technology, Ghaziabad.

Gandi Sobhan. Ph.D. Scholar, Department of English, Andhra University, Visakhapatnam, Andhra Pradesh.

A. Babu Rajendra Prasad. Asstt. Professor, Ideal Institute of Technology, Ghaziabad.

Archana Sharma. Asstt. Professor, ABESIT, Ghaziabad.

Noor Rizvi. Research Scholar, Department of English (ELT), A.M.U, Aligarh.

Koel Hazra. Research Scholar, Department of English, BHU, Varanasi.

Yogita Bhamare. Faculty in English, ELTIS, Pune.

Gopal Krishna Dwivedi. Associate Professor – English & Communication Skills, Institute of Technology and Science, Mohan Nagar, Ghaziabad.

Purnima Tiwari. Teacher, Govt. H.S.S. Sakri Bilaspur, Chhattisgarh.

Ripunjoy Bezbaruah. Assistant Professor of English, Bongaigaon College, Assam.

M. Vanisree. Associate Professor, Department of English, S.V. Engineering College for Women, Tirupati.

Sahab Uddin. Associate Professor, Dept. of English, Haji Anfar Ali College, P.O. Doboka, Nagaon, Assam.

T. Kranthi. Asstt. Professor of English, MVSR Engineering College, Hyderabad, Telangana.

Muhammed Ali Chalikandy. Al Buraimi University College, Sultanate of Oman.

Nizara Hazarika. Associate Professor, Dept. of English, Sonapur College, Assam.

Piku Chowdhury. Assistant Professor, Satyapriya Roy College of Education Kolkata, West Bengal.

Manju Gautam. Vice-Principal, G.G.S.S. School, No. 2, Dr. Ambedkar Nagar, New Delhi.

Vinita Dhondiyal Bhatnagar. Associate Professor, Department of Humanities, UIT, RGPV, Bhopal.

Shyam Ji Dubey. Assistant Professor (English), Galgotias University, Greater Noida, Gautam Buddh Nagar, U.P.

Ravi Bhushan. Ph.D. Assistant Professor, Department of English, Bhagat Phool Singh Mahila Vishwavidyalaya. Khanpur Kalan. Sonepat, Haryana.

Sonia Gouri. Assistant Professor, A S Dept, KIET, 13 KM Stone, Ghaziabad-Meerut Road, Ghaziabad.

Kartikey. Centre for Language Studies, Teerthanker Mahaveer University, Moradabad.

Varsha Vats. Dept. of Humanities, Teerthanker Mahaveer University, Moradabad.

Neha Anand. Assistant Professor, Center for Language Studies, Teerthanker Mahaveer University, Moradabad.

1

Politics is the Cause of Disastrous Decline in the Quality of Teachers and the Teaching of English in India

Pradip Sharan

Abstract

"English has been part of our education system for more than a century. Yet, English is beyond the reach of most of our young people, which make for highly unequal access..., school-leavers who are not adequately trained in English as a language are always at a handicap in the world of higher education." The statement quoted above is from the report of the Knowledge Commission 2006. This statement supports my contention that the teaching of English in non-urban schools in India is in a pathetic state. I also contend that the status of English in the functional domain is similar to a foreign language in non-urban domain, whereas, its status shifts to a second language and an international language in the urban/metropolitan context. So, it is a 'pedagogues nightmare' (the term used by Braj B. Kachru) to propose a uniform pedagogy to achieve the desired result with respect to the proficiency in English of the Indian learners.

The Teaching of English in India at Present

We can perceive India with a Janus like face—one of the urban India and the other, rural India. In the urban India, we find schools especially private, teaching English from class one. On the other hand, in the rural areas the government schools start teaching English from class 1, 3 or 5, varying from state to state. Moreover, the teaching is done by ill-equipped teachers and the syllabuses designed are not appropriate to the context in which teaching of English is done. Furthermore, a teacher has to teach English, a foreign language, in a negative environment like a large class, where pupils are without textbooks, there is lack of motivation among the students towards learning English. In addition to this traditional, outdated and ineffective teaching methods are some of the causes for low level of proficiency among the school students and graduates. The other important pitfall is that the only teaching aid available to the teachers of the English language is the blackboard. Mushroom like growth of public schools in India, especially in cities and towns, without any regulatory body to check the quality of teachers and their teaching, add to the pathetic state of affairs with respect to the teaching of English in India. It is found that the teachers who are appointed to teach English in rural schools are Matriculate with no training or knowhow about the teaching of English. They are ignorant about the techniques, methodology, pedagogy, etc. relating to English language teaching. The books prescribed for the primary school children consist comprise of literary pieces difficult for them to understand and appreciate. The attitude is far from language teaching. They do not have any idea that the second language pedagogy would be different from the foreign language pedagogy—a situation prevalent in non-urban India. Here, I would like to corroborate my contention with the views expressed by Rama Mathew (Mathew 2008: 5) regarding the state of affairs in schools in India. She gives the two main reasons for the present scenario in the non-urban/ non-metropolitan India.

1. "Teachers' poor language proficiency.
2. English is tested and therefore taught as a content subject: a large part of the test/exam tests the memorized understanding/knowledge of the texts in the prescribed textbooks and not the skills of language, i.e. what the learner can actually do in terms of reading, writing, speaking and listening in new situations."

Regarding the situation prevailing in India with respect to the teaching of English Robert Slaterry observes in his article "Can our Students Learn English (Fortell 2010: 3-4) that in our primary and secondary schools more than 50% teachers are para teachers i.e. they are untrained and normally have passed the Board examinations. He further complains about the situation that—"...are the trained government school teachers capable of teaching English well". He says that many of them have passed English in the Board examinations by memorizing answers to questions—the system prevailing in India where unsuitable textbooks and unsuitable methods of teaching are in vogue.

According to S.C. Sood (Fortell 2009: 8), "Inequalities are created by our education policy: We have regional medium schools and English medium schools, private expensive schools side by side with ill-equipped state schools,... and what not to cater to the diverse needs of our people.... We can only make an effort to reduce inequalities and help those in the lower rung to move upward!" He further observes that the "existing teacher training courses are heavily loaded in favour of allied theoretical subjects with a comparatively little component of teaching of English".

Regarding the learners of the English language his comment is, "most of our learners cannot, therefore, practice conversation in English outside the classroom for want of a suitable interlocutor in their immediate surroundings in day-to-day life."

Falguni Chakravarty and A.L. Khanna observed (Fortell 2009: 13) that "The desire for learning a new language notwithstanding, a critical situation confronting the NGOs and government schools today is the non-availability of competent teachers to teach English. It is a well-known fact that a very large number of teachers who are responsible for teaching English, lack proficiency in those very skills of English which they are expected to build among their students".

They further observe that many of the teachers of English in schools in rural areas have not gone through the formal Teacher Training programs and they do not speak English in the class, though they can read and write in English but cannot comprehend difficult and complex sentence structures. Their vocabulary is very limited.

The situation has not changed much in India even after five decades have passed since the time the above-mentioned educationists expressed concern over the then prevailing situation with regard to English Language Teaching. It is pertinent to mention that during the 1960s and '70s much research and effort was put on the English Language Teaching in the US and the UK. New methods of teaching English as a foreign language were developed. Teacher training programs incorporating micro-teaching and practice teaching in schools were implemented. According to Brian McGarvey (1986), in the UK micro-teaching technique was developed for the in-service training of experienced teachers at Lancaster University in 1972. Micro-teaching has been a valuable addition to the methods used in teacher education and training. It has to be remembered that micro-teaching is an additional technique and is not intended as a substitute for school based experience. The micro-teaching experience had strong links with practice teaching to help the students to transfer the skill to ordinary classroom situations. As per the Hargie and Maidment survey of 1975 there were 113 UK universities using micro-teaching in teacher education. There was a great change in the attitude of the practicing teachers of English there. They realized the importance of English language teaching and considered it as a separate discipline in a number of universities there. The teachers of English have to obtain a degree in MA-Teaching, MA in TESOL, ELT, ESL, EFL etc. as a pre-service qualification there (in the US and the UK). This prerequisite qualification was in force in the past too.

The shortsighted education policy in India has caused a skewed educational growth disadvantageous to the underprivileged class and to the underdeveloped regions of India. It is no doubt that there is a growth in education sector in our country. There is a tremendous growth with respect to the number of schools, colleges and teachers. It is estimated that a whopping 220 million children are enrolled in schools in the country. According to the World Bank report based on the International Conference on "PPP in Secondary Education", August 2011 there are 159,703 secondary schools and 75,000 private schools in India. According to one estimate there are around 3,640,000 teachers of English in India. Eighty per cent of all recognized schools at the elementary stage are government run or supported, which make it the largest provider of education in the country. The darker side is that due to the shortage of resources and lack of political will this system suffers from major ailments like high pupil-teacher ratio, shortage of infrastructure and poor level of teacher training. According to the latest DISE survey the percentage of untrained teachers (para-teachers) is 54.91% in private schools compared to 44.88% in government schools. According to the National Knowledge Commission report, English is offered as a second language in 19 states of which 16 introduce it in class I, one in class III and two in class V. According to the National Curriculum Framework 2005 (NCF)—26 out of 35 states and union territories introduced English as a language from class I and the remaining states introduced the language either from class III or V. It is also observed that India today has 92.07% schools at the primary stage teaching through mother tongue. With respect to the teaching/learning of English, there is a qualitative decline among the teachers and students alike. In this regard, I again quote the observation of Rama Mathew when she says "...do teachers have adequate proficiency so that they can provide the learners with exposure to the English language?.....have we moved away from treating English as a content subject i.e. looking at the textbook and the 'lessons' as an end rather than a means to provide practice in the use of the language.... Teachers are also largely unaware of ESL pedagogy." Now the question arises that whether the teaching of English is needed in our country or not and if yes, then what would be the nature of English teaching—as a foreign language or as a second language. I have already explained that in India both these situations exist. So, the need of the society determines the language policy.

It has been observed that the teachers of English are of two types. There are those who are teaching in the urban public schools catering to the privileged class children and there are those who are teaching in government schools for under privileged society in cities and the rest of the country. Those who teach in public schools are well educated graduates from universities with B.Ed. degrees (in many cases). But there are other untrained teachers teaching in government schools with no opportunity and facility to update and upgrade themselves in English language teaching. In many cases, it has been found that the teachers of English, teaching in rural government schools are not even matriculate and also not proficient enough in English language. The Focus Group on teaching of English in the 2005 National Curriculum Framework has mentioned that, "the teachers of the regional government schools often have extensive passive knowledge of English but find it difficult to transact English lessons effectively because they do not speak the language with confidence...nor having much opportunity to use English in their daily lives". In its report the 'clrindia' mentions that the principle cause for the inadequate command of English of high school leavers is that their teachers themselves have very limited knowledge of English. Consequently, little English is spoken or transacted in the classroom. Moreover, neither their pre-service training nor the limited opportunities for in-service training has equipped teachers to teach English as a second language. There are a large number of untrained para-teachers teaching English in non-urban schools in India. In this situation one cannot expect much about the quality of teaching English in schools. The students passing from such schools find great difficulty to cope with the subject—'English', which is a literary study at the university stage. Therefore, with this scenario in the education sector in India, it is high time for all educationists, English teachers and policy-makers to think seriously about the urgency of an effective policy with respect to a focused teacher training program, both short-term and long term, so as to train teachers and thus reinvigorate the teaching of English language in schools and colleges in India.

Here, I would like to present the experience of Robert Slaterry, a Jesuit teacher teaching English in schools in Jharkhand for the last 35 years. He says that the teachers are untrained and they resort to unsuitable methods for teaching English and inculcate among the students rote learning strategy to pass the examinations. Moreover, he observes that most of the time students listen to Hindi rather than English. A large number of words are taught to the pupils without using them in sentences. This methodology is in no way is profitable for the students to learn productively and to use in day-to-day life. So, the suggestions proposed by Robert Slaterry is that the syllabus and the textbooks should be prepared by the teachers of English who teach in ordinary Jharkhand board schools rather than the university professors or teachers in English medium schools. The syllabus for the teacher training colleges has to be revamped by incorporating more practical teaching activities rather than theory. He also suggests, in his article, for the periodic in-service training for the teachers employed in schools and regular monitoring of the teacher training programmes. The other suggestion made by him is to revamp the methodology of teaching English. The students should get ample opportunities and exposure to speak English in each class and the teachers should be familiar with cooperative learning in groups or in pairs.

The concern expressed by Robert Slaterry in his article regarding the inferior quality of teachers teaching English in schools in India is again reiterated by S.C. Sood in his article (Sood 2010: 9-11). He also, expresses concern about the ill-equipped teachers of English language teaching in schools in India. He stresses on the need for in-service teacher training programmes and the establishment of a permanent agency to work for the development of the teaching skills of English language teachers. He argues that the main concern of this agency would be the curriculum development for the teacher training programmes and the implementation of various short and long courses for the teachers of the English language in schools and colleges in respective states in India. He observes "Hence, what is needed is a longer training and practice which can be given by a local agency. It is also seen that without a sound theoretical background knowledge of ELT, teachers resort to making inferences about new principles which may result in elaborations and distortions (innovations/adaptations to suit the environment in which they teach?) of the CLT principles to which they are introduced." He argues that the short-term in-service teacher orientation/refresher courses by teacher training institutions such as DIETS, SCERTs, RIEs, NCERT, departments of education, university departments/academic staff colleges for teachers in the past have not been very effective in developing the teaching skills and theoretical knowledge of ELT among the participants. He also cites two projects (Madras Snowball aimed at training 27000 teachers of English in Tamil Nadu in 1959 and CBSE-ELT curriculum renewal exercise in secondary schools in India 1988-94), one of them a colossal failure and the other yet to be evaluated. That is the reason why he strongly argues for a local unified agency for in-service teacher education and research, and the development of curriculum renewal for English teacher trainers. He expresses concern that there is a serious shortage of trained teachers in India. The result is that the fresh recruits do not have any mentor to guide them. There is also lack of suitable environment for self-development in the present school education system. There is also no facility available for research and self-development. He sums up his article with a suggestion that "education in India is on the concurrent list and both the center and the state governments can frame rules but if there is one fixed agency responsible for curriculum renewal in English language…it will equip itself with the expertise required to undertake the job keeping in mind the local resources, customs and practices either on its own or in collaboration with other agencies, it will initiate the cycle of curriculum development from time to time. Creation of such an agency would also obviate chances of any rivalries that often crop up among various agencies and institutions dealing with in-service teachers' education…thus mar effective implementation of projects" (Sood 2010: 9-11).

Many people have raised questions regarding the linguistic competence of the teachers of English and the pedagogy/ methodology and the ELT issues with respect to the teaching of English in India. Thus, it very well supports my contention that the ill-equipped teachers in schools need to undergo intensive teacher development programmes to be thorough in ESL/EFL pedagogy, second language theory and the research findings related to the teaching of English to young learners. So, it is the need of the hour to move from the traditional memory test to a proficiency test. Here, I would like to quote Rama Mathew's views again regarding the development of the proficiency among the teachers in schools as follows:

1. "Recruit (hereafter) only those who have the level of required proficiency...."
2. "The existing teachers should be asked to undergo a proficiency course (to be made available face to face and online) and then pass the proficiency test.... The course should also be such that they enjoy doing the course and find it a fun activity. Since there is no shortcut to improving ones language competence and needs time, it should be an ongoing activity for teachers.... Apart from this, in-service pedagogy courses should have a built-in mechanism to improve teacher proficiency." (Mathew 2008: 5-7)

Regarding the teaching of English in India, Rama Mathew says that because of the strong international pressures on governments for making the teaching of English from lower grades in schools, many states in India have now begun the teaching of English from class I itself. The reason is that English provide an enhanced status and ensures social and economic benefits such as access to higher education, increased job opportunities and social mobility.

Before I proceed further, I would like to clarify and distinguish between a foreign language situation and a second language situation. A foreign language situation is one in which the target language is not the native tongue of the people in that country and it is not used for the purpose of the internal communication function in that community. The purpose of learning the foreign language is to communicate with the speakers outside the country. According to Littlewood (1984: 2) "...a 'second' language has social functions within the community where it is learnt (e.g. as a lingua franca or as a language of another social group), whereas a 'foreign' language is learnt primarily for contact outside one's own community". And according to Nunan (2000: 3) the foreign language situation is when the target language is used within the ambit of school or institution where it is taught and no opportunity is available to the learner to use it in social life. Wilkins in his book "Linguistics in Language Teaching" observes that "...Second language situation is that the language being learned (L2) is not the mother tongue (L1) of any group within the country but that it does have some internal, social functions". He further states that "the scale and variety of use of the second language differs enormously. It can encompass part or all of the government administration, politics, law, medicine, industries, internal trade, in newspapers, general publishing and education. As a result, in education it may become the medium of instruction at any level from the primary school upwards" (Wilkins 1972: 150-51). Regarding a foreign language situation he states "A foreign language learning situation is one in which the target language is not the mother tongue of any group within the country where it is being learned and has no internal communication function either. The aim of teaching the language is to increase the ease of contact with foreign language speakers outside the country" (Wilkins 1972: 153-54). Relating to Indian situation Wilkins observes that "India is a country in transition. English is using its status as second language and in some states has already become a foreign language. It is now been felt that the regional languages can cope with all aspects of education except technical and scientific subjects at the university level.... Only in southern India does English remain a second language, because it can serve as a more acceptable lingua franca than Hindi." Thus, I feel that the status of English in most parts of India other than big cities and towns is as a foreign language.

I feel that the teaching does not contribute to the pupils' exposure to English. The effectiveness of language teaching techniques of teachers plays an important role. A teacher of English in a second language situation, as in the case of India, is primarily a teacher of English literature and so he cannot prove to be an efficient teacher of language unless re-trained in this discipline. The most striking difference between EFL teaching and ESL teaching with respect to the methods and materials used, is the cultural and situational context of learning. In a second language the characters in texts, the vocabulary used and the context created are all drawn from the children's own background and not from the culture of the language it is associated with, because the content of learning is associated with the daily life and the language has the functional role in its own country. In course of time, the second language is used in the development of awareness about its own culture like Indian-English writings or African writings. In the case of foreign language learning, the learner needs it to form contacts with community other than its own. The context of learning is not his own culture but that of the community to which that language belongs to. The foreign language teaching is typically directed to an older age group that means it starts at the secondary school level. Moreover, the methodology recommended for EFL teaching is on inductive approach to learning. In a foreign language situation, as in the case of non-urban India, the language teacher is the only person to provide exposure to his/her students in the target language, and that only for an hour per day in a week (5 days). It means that the number of hours spent in the learning process is very low and the practice in that language is dispensed with, resulting into a slow progress.

The status of English in urban areas is a "Second language" for all practical purposes. In a second language situation the language is in use in various domains like education, administration, commerce, judiciary, journalism, as well as, in social interaction. Now, on the basis of the above-mentioned statements, I would like to say that both the situations exist in India i.e. a foreign language situation in the non-metropolitan/rural/semi-urban and a second language situation in the urban/metropolitan domain. Thus, the methodology of teaching would also change with the language situation. The teaching, in a foreign language situation, has to be language oriented with structural-functional syllabus, which we do not find in practice in India. According to the research finding of Vai Ramanathan (1999: 211-31), the teaching instruction in English in neither place—school or college—in Gujarat, India prepared the students to use English in the real world. According to the students, their teachers were themselves poor speakers of English and it was therefore not surprising that the students found English difficult. The reason for this state of affairs at present is the result of the ignorance and lackadaisical attitude of the policy-makers towards English during the post-independence era.

Language Policy in India Since Independence

During the colonial period, the teaching of English, in schools and colleges, was given priority over other language studies and it was a matter of prestige for people to learn English because it opened the doors of opportunity and status in society. It also gave the learners the opportunity to find jobs as clerks in government offices.

The perusal of the education policy in India since independence would explicate the causes for the present state of affairs in respect to the teaching of English in India, especially in rural areas. The teaching of English language was introduced in schools and colleges during the British colonial rule. This was the beginning of western education in India in the medium of English. At the same time, it inculcated the taste for English literature among the elite. This system continued till the era of independence movement in India. After independence our leaders tried to give due weightage to the regional languages of India as the medium of instruction, which were neglected by the British regime. There were people in those days who were strongly opposed to the idea that English remained the language of instruction, as they were against anything that symbolized British imperialism. They were also wary of the fact that if English continued as a medium of instruction or the language for imparting knowledge to the people in India, they would never psychologically free themselves from the British hegemony. During the post-Independence era, the policy makers tried to reduce the influence of English on the Indian people by downplaying its importance in all spheres of life through the language policy.

The constitution of India places education in the concurrent list, which empowers both the state and the center to provide education to the citizens of India and enact laws and formulate policies in this regard. The 8th schedule of the constitution enumerates the official languages of India and mentions "English language" as an "associate official language" for 15 years. It also empowers the center to enact laws to extend it for a further period of 15 years if the need arose. Due to this provision in the constitution, the provinces in India had their own policy regarding the teaching of English in their respective states. Consequently, according to the attitude of the policy-makers towards English, the teaching of English was considered as an optional subject in the curriculum and subjects like Sanskrit, Hindi and the regional languages received the main focus. The native tongue became the medium of instruction at the school stage. In case the English language got a place in the curriculum, it was in the form of a literary study,—a continuation of the colonial education system. In the year 1953, the Secondary Education Commission recommended English as a language to be taught in educational institutions in India because it had been the source of bringing national unity. The 'States Reorganization Commission' had asked the Union Government to elucidate a policy outline for education in mother tongue at the Primary school stage. Then in the year 1956, the Central Advisory Board gave its three language formula as the National Policy of Education at state level schools. The English language got its place in the three language formula but its status was not the same as during the pre-independence era. The Kothari Commission of 1966 gave English an important place in the modified three language formula, but the teaching of English got affected as it was not a compulsory subject in the school curriculum. Rather, the regional languages or Hindi became the medium of instruction. English was not taught in the lower primary stage except in public schools. There was no uniform policy in India, which still continues to this day. In some of the states in India the teaching of English in schools started from class three, four or six as per the policy there. Even at the higher secondary level also the teaching of English was not a compulsory subject. It was no longer a compulsory subject at graduate level either. In some of the states students completed their post-graduation the medium of instruction being their mother tongue without acquiring the basic knowledge of

English. In the absence of any uniform policy of the government since independence, the teaching of English in India suffered a lot. This had turned into a vicious cycle in the course of six decades since independence. We find, now-a-days, that students pass out of schools without acquiring the basic structure of English language. Even though consciousness among the people regarding the importance of English has improved slightly in the non-urban sector, there is not much change in the quality of teaching in schools.

In many states in India not much change took place at the college level or in universities, with respect to the role of English since pre-independence era. The English language remains a medium of instruction at the college stage and is also mandatory for students to pass in this subject. In the past, this caused a great strain on students because they were not taught English in schools properly and they were not competent enough to cope with the standard of English prescribed to them at the college level. This scenario of the decline in the teaching of English because of the apathy of the policy-makers caused great concern among a few conscientious educationists and teachers of English.

Way back in 1960's the educationists, such as, Gokak and Siddhanta realized the gravity of the situation and expressed concern. They were of the opinion that the English language should be taught in a different way, as English language has a place in the International arena. They felt that the English language was needed to be taught in schools so as to keep pace with the world but the nature of teaching had to be language teaching rather than literary studies. To substantiate this point, I quote the views of Bruton, Gokak and Siddhanta.

Bruton opines, "there are a great many people in India who refuse to accept the view that today for the large majority of Indian children English is as much as, a foreign language as it is, for example, for the average French or Japanese child". He further says "there has been a disastrous fall in standards of achievement in English in schools and colleges. The average Indian child of today learns English under much less favourable conditions, beginning much later at the age of 11 or 12, studying the language only for perhaps 5 periods a week for a total period of 5 or 6 years, in large classes with a teacher who may be a mere matriculate in English" (Bruton 1961: 15-17).

According to Gokak, "...There is a dilemma in the teaching of English at all levels because of the changed context in which it is taught and the partial reform that we have implemented with regard to the medium of instructions...the replacement of English at the secondary level by the regional languages and the continuation of English as medium at the university level without providing, at the same time, for a more intensive study of English at the secondary level" (Gokak 1964: 60). Gokak further says, "many of them do not even have a mastery over even a thousand words and they cannot handle even simple structures correctly" (Gokak 1964: 100).

Regarding the teaching of English in India, Siddhanta opines, "We have to recognize that we cannot have a leisurely way of teaching English that we had in past.... With the widening of the curriculum and the introduction of new compulsory subjects to give General Education, the teaching of English can occupy fewer years in school and fewer hours in the weekly time-table. New methods of teaching have, therefore, to be introduced to ensure quicker mastery of the spoken and written language, keeping the objectives of the training in view" (Siddhanta 1961: 4).

According to Sharan, "The old, traditional methods of teaching English (followed previously) should be discarded in favour of 'new' methods of language teaching" (Sharan 1981: iv) and to sum up, I quote Bruton again who says, "In my experience in India, the greatest difficulty lies in convincing the teacher of this necessity for control...of the fact that English is a foreign language. This situation may change when Indian Universities realize the necessity for including some treatment of the English language in their courses instead of devoting all their time to the study of English Literature" (Bruton 1961: 17).

Conclusion

The politics is that the policy-makers for the Universities and schools are themselves ignorant of the fact that English language teaching is a separate discipline just like English literature or Linguistics and the teachers of English Language have to undergo specialized training for teaching language skills (Reading, writing, speaking and listening). The teaching of English literature is content-based teaching, whereas the teaching of English language is a longitudinal language learning process. As a result, the content-based teaching of English in schools has led the students to resort to rote-learning. Students get good grades in English because they depend on memorized learning, but they lack language skills to use in different domains as per their need. They are unable to write applications, memos, notices, reports, etc., which are required in their daily lives.

At the University level the policy-makers, who are on the panel as experts, propose English literature (to be taught) with the assumption that the students at the college stage would be proficient in English language and would appreciate literature like poetry, drama, novels and prose. They prescribe classics and the writings of great writers to the students to read, but the reality is that the majority of students are not proficient enough to appreciate poetry, drama or novels. As a result, at the undergraduate level they resort to rote-learning from keys available in the market. In majority of cases the students never read the original texts prescribed. This only shows the apathy or ignorance of the stakeholders regarding the situation prevalent in our country with respect to the teaching of English language in schools and colleges.

The policy-makers/professors in the universities in India do not give importance to the training of teachers of English in ELT at the college stage. The politics may be that they are ignorant of the ELT discipline and the need of developing language skills of students by creating specialized courses like (English for Specific Purpose, English for Academic Purpose, English for Science and Technology, English for Law, and Commerce, etc.) for developing the language skills of students. The reason is that the majority of teachers in colleges throughout India have expertise in English literature as they have BA, MA, PhD degrees in English literature. They do not have knowledge about English language teaching nor do they want that ELT discipline should in any way challenge their monopoly in higher education. Some teachers at the University/College level do understand the importance of ELT teaching at the under-graduate stage and the need for the development of various courses for the students, and also, the importance of training the teachers of English in ELT, but are unable to voice their concern against the majority of teachers professionally qualified in English literature. For those who would like to know the courses required for specialization in ELT (BA, MA degrees), I'm enumerating them as follows: Curriculum development, syllabus design, material production, lesson plan, practice teaching, micro-teaching, language teaching methodologies, pedagogy, linguistics, developmental psychology, psycholinguistics, etc. The teachers of ELT should undergo specialized training in this field. The expertise in this field would help them to decide what to teach, how to teach and whom to teach what? to the learners, similar to what the professionals in English literature do for teaching different genres of English literature (novels, stories, poetry, drama, etc.).

So, the policy-makers/professors in the panel should have the expertise/specialization in ELT, so that they frame uniform policy for the whole country with respect to teacher education, curriculum development/syllabus design. If professionals and educationists work with earnestly then the decline in the overall education system and specially the teaching of English language in schools and colleges could be arrested. One has to understand that English language is important for students seeking higher education and also for the opportunity in the job market.

Suggestions

S.C. Sood in his article, "In-service English School Teachers' Education Programmes: Need for a Permanent Agency" (Fortell 2010: 9-11) argued cogently for the establishment of a local unified agency for in-service teacher education and research, and the development of curriculum renewal in English. He further expresses his concern over the situation in India where the requisite environment for self-development of the teachers of English does not exist in the present school education system.

His suggestion in this paper is that "Education in India is on the concurrent list and both the centre and state governments can frame rules but if there is one fixed agency responsible for curriculum renewal in English language, an important tool for empowering the common man at the centre and the states, it will equip itself with the expertise required to undertake the job keeping in mind the local resources, customs and practices either on its own or in collaboration with other agencies to initiate the cycle of curriculum renewal and development from time to time."

Thus, how to improve the situation in India, Slattery suggests that "It is surely possible that with a proper syllabus, suitable textbooks, a well thought-out examination pattern, regular in-service training of teachers, serious pre-service training of future teachers, monitoring by heads of schools and education department officials, we can in ten years, enable a good majority of our Hindi medium school students to get to a competency in English."

Regarding the teachers of English, Sood (Fortell 2009: 8) suggests that "it is necessary to produce teachers dedicated to teaching English language with qualification like PGDTE, DELTA or similar other certificate/diploma qualifications with the main focus on teaching English to speakers of other languages...".

According to Donald Freeman in his review "Teacher Learning and Student Learning in TESOL" (TESOL Quarterly, Vol. 35, 2001: 608-09) teacher education has been identified as the central variable in the transformation and reform of educational systems at the national and the local levels. This argument is grounded on the common sense and research that teachers are central mediators in what and how students learn in their classrooms, so teachers must engage in their own professional learning to improve student learning. He further argues that the teacher learning occurs formally through pre- and in-service teacher training and professional development. He further says that the teacher learning becomes the critical link in supporting cultural linguistic diversity through educational reform and systemic improvement.

The philosophy of Freeman is strengthened by the argument of Bailey (Tesol Quarterly, Vol. 35, 2001: 609-11) when she says that English is taught by a variety of people around the world, that is, trained and untrained, native and non-native speakers so the appropriate initial teacher preparation and the continued professional development of teachers throughout their careers is imperative. She further argues that the demand for appropriately prepared teachers require appropriate initial preparation of language teachers. The standard of target language mastery attained by non-native English speaking teachers working in varied contexts, and the nature of the evolving knowledge and skill bases are needed by all teachers.

Greta J. Gorsuch in the article "EFL Educational Policies and Educational Cultures; Influences on Teachers' Approval of Communicative activities" (TESOL Quarterly, 2000: 675-80) observes that the educational policy is actually a political symbol. According to Elmor and Sykes (1992) the curriculum policy makers are essentially political people dealing at the state and national levels with educational issues. The educational policy in the form of curriculum documents serves the symbolic function. The policy statement addresses content not instruction. Policy-makers want short term results. Thus, the policy statements are adopted for the sake of political expediency. Gorsuch further says that 'The Course of Study' as a curriculum statement focuses on content, ignoring instruction. According to Lincicome (1993), the politically inspired educational reform effort culminating into 'The Course of Study' is filtered through many layers of bureaucracy. And Cuban (1993: 274) rightly observes that the educational policy-makers must understand that for teachers' instruction to change, teachers' beliefs must be transformed.

It has been observed by LoCastro, 1996 that the reform in foreign language education is a top-down affair where the input is generated by high-level bureaucrats and university consultants. Gorsuch further observes that 'The Course of Study' focuses on content, not making any systematic reference to instruction.

The issue of social justice and educational and linguistic rights have become important throughout the world in this century. So, my suggestion is that language policies and the rights of learners are important issues to be considered by policy-makers in India.

Roland Schmidt, Sr., in his article "The Politics of Language in Canada and the United States: Explaining the Differences," (Tesol Quarterly, 2000: 626, 629) argues that language conflicts are not about language *per se* but about ethnic conflicts and power relationships. He further argues that language acceptance is about politics rather than about language itself.

According to Lia D. Kamhi-Stein (Tesol Quaterly, Vol. 34, 2000: 426), "Yildirum and Kiraz suggest that teacher education programs integrate technology into the curricula of courses other than those designed to teach computer literacy". Moreover, "Irujo and Johnson (1997) argue that CMC tools should be integrated across the curricula of TESOL teacher preparation courses and that students should be given specific direction in how to use such CMC tools."

So, we educators/English language teachers have the responsibility to identify the audience as policy-makers to educate them through different forums, the issues like social justice and rights of learners, language planning and language policy to other members of teaching community, government officials, media, the public, academics in various fields and the policy makers. They have to provide historical information (i.e. the development of language attitudes and policies in India and the politics of language conflict in the country).

References

Bailey, Kathleen M. (2001). Teacher Preparation and Development. *TESOL Quarterly*, 35, 609-11.

Bruton, J.G. (1961). "Some common misconceptions about the English language and about language teaching current in India." *Central Institute of English Bulletin*, No. 1.

Chakravarty, Falguni and Khanna, A.L. (2009). Capacity Building of Teachers of English; An Intervention in Non-formal Education Centres in Rajasthan. Fortell, 16, 13-17.

Clair, N. and Adgar, C.T. (2000). "Sustainable Strategies for Professional Development in Education Reform." In Teacher Education. ed. Karen E. Johnson. 29-49. Virginia: TESOL Inc.

Freeman, Donald (2001). Teacher Learning and Student Learning in TESOL. *TESOL Quarterly*, 35, 608-09.

Gokak, V.K. (1964). English in India. Calcutta: Asia Publishing House.

Hafernik, J.J. (2000). Language, Literacy, Politics and Access. Reviewed. *TESOL Quarterly*, 3, 625-27.

Littlewood, W.T. (1984). Foreign and Second Language Learning: Language-acquisition research and its implications for the classroom. Cambridge: C.U.P.

Mathew, Rama (2008). "Teaching English to Young Learners: Need for Introspection." *Fortell*, Issue no. 13 (January 2008): 5-7.

Mathew, Rama (2010). "Equal Education Opportunities for Children: The Case of English and Mother Tongue for the Marginalized Children." *Fortell*, Issue no. 17 (January 2010): 6-7.

McArthur, T. (1983). *A Foundation Course for Language Teachers*. Cambridge: C.U.P.

Nunan, D. (1989). *Designing Tasks for Communicative Classroom*. Cambridge: C.U.P.

Prabhu, N.S. (1987). *Second Language Pedagogy*. Oxford: O.U.P.

Ramanathan, V. (1999). "English Is Here to Stay: A Critical Look at Institutional and Educational Practices in India." *TESOL Quarterly*, Vol. 33: 211-31.

Schmid, Carol (2002). The Politics of Language; Conflict, Identity, and Cultural Pluralism in Comparative Perspective. Reviewed by Theresa Wise. *TESOL Quarterly*, 36, 115.

Sharan, P.B. (1981). *Contrastive Linguistics and The Teaching of English*. Vol. 1, Patna: Progressive Printers.

Sharan, Pradip (2011). "English in India: Some Situational and Pedagogical Considerations." *Fortell*, Issue no. 21 (May 2011): 14-16.

Siddhanta, N.K. (1961). English studies today. *Central Institute of English Bulletin*, No. 1.

Slaterry, R. (2010). "Can Our Students Learn English?" *Fortell*, Issue no. 17 (January 2010): 3-5.

Sood, S.C. (2009). Teaching English to Young Learners. *Fortell*, 16, 7-10.

Sood, S.C. (2010). "In-service English School Teachers' Education Programmes: Need for a Permanent Agency." *Fortell*, Issue no. 18 (May 2010): 9-11.

Wilkins, D.A. (1972). *Linguistics in Language Teaching*. London: Edward Arnold. http://knowledgecommission.gov.in/downloads/recommendations/LanguageLetterPM.pdf

2

S for Stimulus: The Effect of Audio and Audio-Visual Stimuli on Writing Skills [The Role of ICTs in Achieving Standards]

Roma Karanjkar

Abstract

Writing has always been one of the most challenging skills for a teacher to teach and a learner to learn. Teachers have often found it difficult to motivate their learners to write. Rather than asking them to put pen to paper, giving them a stimulus to guide their thought process might be a better idea. Many teachers bank on the lecturing method to teach writing. However, such classes become teacher oriented. Therefore, using the Language Laboratory, the presenter wishes to show how audio and audio-visual aids work as stimuli for the learner and produce the desired response. She will do this by conducting an experiment on a class of international students of a proficiency course (basic level) at ELTIS. This study analyses the kinds of changes seen in learners' writing—both before and after the two kinds of stimuli are used.

Keywords: Writing, Stimulus, Audio-visual, Response, Learning Preferences, Language Laboratory.

Introduction

> Between stimulus and response there is a place where we chose our response.
>
> —Stephen Covey

Both teachers and students feel that writing is important. The question one can ask is, "How do teachers make students better writers?" I believe that teachers can help students to become better writers by providing them a stimulus.

Initially, I had been very complacent with the age old method of teaching writing in a classroom. After some preliminary brainstorming on the topic, I used to ask my students to write a letter, recount, narrative and other writing tasks. However, I came to realise that students were struggling with basic concepts in writing such as vocabulary, spellings, organizing ideas, creativity. On the whole, I realised that my students found it difficult to pen down their ideas, as it was easy to express in one's mother tongue but very difficult to do the same in a foreign language.

I wanted to reach out to my students and get them motivated enough to write. Hence, I pondered upon the thought of using the language laboratory for my writing classes. Since with the advent of technology classes can be made interesting and fruitful, I decided to put this idea into practice.

I surveyed some teachers at ELTIS and found that most of them who taught writing complained that it is difficult to motivate the learners to write. Ms. Mukul Ahmed said, "It also takes a long time to help them to develop meaningful content." Ms. Mala Hinduja said, "Getting students to write longer pieces of writing like letters and recounts can be challenging. Moreover, lack of vocabulary hampers writing exercises." Others felt that perhaps students did not think that writing was so important, and so this is why they were not motivated to write. Since I wanted to know how students viewed their problems with writing, I conducted a survey.

Students' Survey

A survey was conducted on 17 students studying the basic level of the six-month certificate course at the English Language Teaching Institute of Symbiosis. The learners were students from countries like Iraq, Yemen, Afghanistan, Saudi Arabia and D.R. Congo.

A table showing number of learners who agreed to each item follows:

Sl. No.	Item	Number of learners who agreed
1.	Do you think writing is an important skill?	17
2.	Do you think writing is difficult?	6
3.	Do you enjoy writing on a topic given to you by your teacher?	12
4.	Do you think you face problems while beginning your writing task?	9
5.	Is vocabulary important for a writing task?	17
6.	Which amongst the following is important for writing?	
	Introduction	4
	Main body	10
	Conclusion	3
7.	Do you think ideas are important for writing?	16
8.	Do you think you have enough new ideas for writing?	4
9.	Choose the option that describes your problem out of the options given below:	
	Poor vocabulary	8
	Wrong Spellings	9
	Organizing ideas	2
10.	Where do you look for creative ideas when you write?	
	Use your own imagination and past experiences	11
	Get them from your teacher	3
	From the environment and the people around you.	4

Interpretation and Analysis of the Results

The results were analysed both qualitatively and quantitatively. The most popular items were considered and were connected to their beliefs about writing.

In contrast to what teachers felt, all 17 learners agreed that writing was an important skill as it will form a basis for their academic career. Since the learners never had to write in English in their respective countries, they said that they found it difficult to write or meet the expectations of the teacher. The survey showed the following three main areas of difficulty faced by students.

Vocabulary: 17 learners agreed that vocabulary was important for a writing task. Although writing tasks are made up of ideas, they could be completed without sufficient vocabulary. Being unable to find the right words resulted in their losing the flow of writing.

Spellings: More than half of the learners (9) felt that they had problems with spellings.

Ideas: Regarding creativity in writing, while most of them (16) thought that ideas were indeed important, only a few (6) felt that they had enough ideas. Two of them felt that they had problems with organisation of ideas.

Finally, more than half (10) felt that forming the main body is also one of the problem areas. 4 said that framing an introduction can be tedious since it has to capture the reader's attention. Lack of vocabulary or inadequate exposure to reading disables them from forming an attention-grabbing introduction. 11 agreed that the only way to put pen to paper was to depend on their meagre imagination and past experiences.

Although the three problems deal with different aspects of writing, there is a common thread in them. These problems could arise because of lack of exposure, lack of interest in reading newspapers or novels, and lack of supplementary material used in the classroom to develop vocabulary or promote new ideas.

Learners are intrinsically motivated to write but the ghosts of vocabulary, spelling, and creativity haunt them, thus crippling them from writing further.

In conclusion, the results show that students are willing to write, but need help in vocabulary, new ideas and spellings. What follows is description of my experiment.

Strategies to Stimulate Effective Writing

Based on the results of the survey, I thought of using the language laboratory to deal with my learners' writing conundrums. I decided to explore what kind of effect a stimulus would have on their writing in these three areas. ESL learners learn the target language better using their aural skills, while some learn better through their audio and visual intelligence. "Teachers have always known that their students have different strengths. In the language teaching field, some of the differences have been attributed to students' having different learning or cognitive styles" (Larsen-Freeman 169).

"Everybody likes to look at pictures, their use in the classroom provides a stimulating focus for students' attention" (Raimes 27). At ELTIS, teachers do use visual aids like cartoon strips and realia to develop vocabulary in writing. They also use the whiteboard to list out vocabulary words, but students are not always able to gauge the context and use the words appropriately. The main purpose of the language laboratory remains largely to teach listening and speaking skills. Unfortunately, using the language laboratory to include audio-visual stimulus to develop students' writing is still under-exploited.

The Experiment

The students were taken to the language laboratory and made to listen to a wide range of audio and audio-visual clips. The main aim was to make them write using the 3 Cs of writing —cohesiveness, coherence and content. Students were evaluated on these parameters at ELTIS. One of the teachers, Ms. Archana Bhagwat, says, "It is difficult to teach writing as the learners struggle with coherence and cohesion."

The first two activities began with guided writing since it was a basic class. The aim was to encourage them to write on their own, or what is more commonly referred to as scaffolding in pedagogy.

A total of 6 tasks were done with the learners. There were two audio inputs and four audio-visual inputs. Based on these inputs, learners were given a corresponding worksheet which would help them to grasp the structure of a text, for example, a recount. They were also given some scaffolding to help them organize their thoughts.

(a) **The Little Pianist (audio aid):** The students were made to listen to a narrative 'The Little Pianist'. They were given a worksheet, wherein, they were given the beginning words of each paragraph and the learners were expected to complete the rest of the paragraph.

One of the students, Mustafa, who had trouble forming basic sentence structures, came up with some sentences that were worth noticing. For example, "He loved and dream of become pianist", "Every Sunday, before going to bed he practice playing piano", "Really he wanted to be not just a good pianist He wande to be a great pianist in the word" *(sic)*.

(b) The First Well (audio-visual aid): The second experiment was also a narrative where the students were made to watch the video with subtitles. The aim behind choosing a video with subtitles was to make the students aware of the structure, make the learning integrated where the students read and listen at the same time, and also help them retain at least the basic spellings with the help of the subtitles.

After watching the video, the learners were given a worksheet with less scaffolding than the previous task. One of the learners, Mohammed Taib, came up with a very well-structured story. He used phrases like 'the generals searched high and low'. He could retain most of the words from the video and hence could include necessary details like 'loaded the ice,' 'gazed,' 'harvest,' 'vanished,' 'dwindled,' and so on. His conclusion read: "The whole village lived happy and they harvest plants and life came back to the village" *(sic)*. This conclusion was original and not from the video. The use of the word 'harvest' in the conclusion shows that he was able to use the vocabulary in the right context.

(c) A World without Water (audio-visual aid): The aim was to expose students to the water crisis the world is facing. The video had only static images with slogans and students were asked to write creatively on the topic.

First, the students were made to write their thoughts on the same topic without a stimulus. One of my students, Omar Abdullah wrote, "I will start my paragraph with a question. Can imagine the world without water? What would happen if it is? Water is needed for many things. It's the precious gift of nature. It has no smell no test and no coulor. A world without plants is no plants no farms no life. That's a world without water" *(sic)*.

It's quite evident that he started off well but could write only a few lines. There was no structure and most of the points were repetitive. However, after the stimulus, he was able to pen down an essay of about 200-300 words. Here is an excerpt from what he wrote:

> "Water is life. It's the most precious gift of nature. Every drop counts. There are many people they take water for granted like they keep the tap on while bathing or brushing. They don't realize this grace.
>
> What will happen if we do not save water? What if we have to pay for every drop? We should save and conserve this precious so as to protect this grace. We shouldn't waste water by playing with it. We are responsible for it.
>
> I think we should have to think about this grace and save it. We should advise others who doesn't care about it because life is water." *(sic)*

Here we see that Omar's essay has a better structure. He followed the guidelines on the worksheets and used the words and one-liners extensively from the video. To some extent even his punctuation improved compared to his previous writing.

Another student Wardi Esmail, wrote, "Industries wasted millions of, later of water to get money" (*sic*). This line too, was from the video. By '*later*' he meant litres. However, he could communicate his ideas effectively.

(d) Kaelyn's Scary Experiences (audio-visual): In this experiment the students were shown a video where a girl recorded a live feed of her "scary experiences" of paranormal activity in different places. Some students refused to write and complained saying that they did not know what to write since they do not believe in ghosts as it is not a part of their culture.

After showing the video, a student, Mawlood Khalid, who struggled more than others, came up with a wonderful recount. Since he could not narrate his own experience, he actually imagined himself in Kaelyn's position and wrote a recount.

He could differentiate between the parts of a recount—Introduction, Event 1, Event 2 and conclusion. These are some of the lines he wrote:

Event 1: "I was cook in the kitchen and listen to music but suddenly light switch off and all house become dark" *(sic)*.

Event 2: "I was standing in my place but does not able to move because I was afraid. I heard sound of water is open but nobody in the house jues me" *(sic)*.

Conclusion: "After 1 hour the light is came. I feel good after light came and I complete cook the dinner." *(sic)*.

Mawlood did not have a scary experience in the past. However, the video helped him to create one. The video also helped in bridging the cultural gap between the students' beliefs and the events that took place in the video.

(e) **"Imagine" John Lennon (audio):** Considering the students' background, I thought a free writing exercise would be the best way to pour their feelings out. The students were made to listen to a song called 'Imagine' by John Lennon. This is a song about imagining a world where people live in peace, a world where there is no violence and a world where everyone lives as one. Later, they were asked to write about their feelings without worrying about grammar or spelling.

Mohammed Sadeq, a student from Yemen, struggled with several problems like sentence construction, bad spellings, and organization of thoughts.

After the audio stimulus what he came up with was quite touching:

> "Sometimes ask myself why the war in life? In the war kill poor man and weak. I want to see the world be as one. (Idea from the song)
>
> I see people kill or end. People dishonest make war. I want peace in my life. People like to revenge and make war. My letter (message) for all make war stop and rumour and greed. And change your think." *(sic)*

Here we can see that in spite of this being a free writing exercise, he could show some change in the organization of thoughts towards the end.

(f) **Advertisements (audio-visual):** For this experiment the students were made to work in groups to break the monotony and encourage collaborative learning. They were shown three advertisements in English of 31 seconds each. One was an advertisement for tooth paste, another for Horlicks, and the third for cornflakes.

They were asked to write a persuasive essay where they had to persuade a troubled customer to buy their product. Since advertisements use persuasive techniques, I chose simple advertisements to prod them into the concept of persuasive writing at the basic level.

Each group consisted of four members. The weaker learners were paired with the stronger ones. The members themselves nominated one member to write the essay and one to take notes while watching the advertisement. Every member of the group contributed towards the essay. Here are some samples of what they wrote:

Group 1 Oral B 3D: "Oral B 3D white toothpaste removes 90% surface stains in 5 days. You will get a new smile. After use you will feel something change in their teeth. All the problems to your teeth will find a solution. This product is available everywhere."

"Our company is definitely the best company in the world. Also the product is useful for each age. You will get a good teeth and nice breathe also a nice personality" *(sic)*.

Group 2 Junior Horlicks: "It's a product for toddlers. We specialize food for kids. Children will never reject eating this food. Your fussy eaters will like our products. It has right nutrition for complete grow and energy. It's reasonable. Your children will always be active. It will improve their mind. Junior Horlicks 1-2-3 is available in different flavour. You should buy our product because you can solve your problems" *(sic)*.

Group 3 Kellogg's cornflakes: "Kellogg's cornflakes are easy to make. You can make it tasty and healthy by add your special touch like almonds. There are good fats in the product that help you to feel full for a long time. It gets the family on one table And it is very easy to make it. You will not spend your money or time to make it. It is the right way to start your day. A great breakfast makes a great day" *(sic)*.

Words and sentences like (surface stains, fussy eaters, toddlers, nutrition. A great breakfast makes a great day) were used from the original advertisement. Even though the clips were of approximately 31 seconds each, they added many ideas and words on their own.

Conclusion

After these experiments with my class, I found that exposing students to auditory and visual stimulus did in fact improve their vocabulary. It helped in developing unique ideas and also played a very large role in exposing them to various ways in which the English language can be used.

Using the language lab to enhance writing skills in students also helps cater to their different learning styles. Sitting in a classroom may not benefit auditory or kinaesthetic learners. Making use of the language laboratory can enrich the teaching process tenfold.

It is true that spellings did not see much improvement during this experiment but the focus was mainly on encouraging vocabulary and creative ideas in writing. Different techniques like online spelling games, drilling, using flashcards and introducing spelling patterns can be used to improve spelling while still in the language laboratory.

The most prominent effect that using audio/audio-visual stimulus in the language laboratory has had is allowing students to use new vocabulary in a meaningful context, rather than just reading a word and passively knowing its meaning. A language laboratory is all about using the available resources to provide a stimulus that is more than just a topic and a format for students to follow. Providing this stimulus to students learning English as a second language, would go a long way in making process-oriented writing more effective than product-oriented writing.

References

Larsen-Freeman. *Techniques and Principles in Language Teaching.* Oxford University Press, 2000. Print.

Raimes, Ann. *Techniques in Teaching Writing.* Oxford University Press, 1983. Print.

3

Teaching Language through Literature: Theoretical and Practical Perspective

Vidya Vati

Abstract

This paper aims at emphasizing that literature may be a powerful tool in English Foreign Language classrooms. Language skills i.e. Speaking, Listening, Reading, Writing and other areas of language like vocabulary, grammar and pronunciation can be taught in a integrated manner through literature. The concept of teaching language through literature can be implemented organizing various activities in the classroom from text in English. The texts mentioned in the paper are prescribed in Delhi schools at Secondary and Senior Secondary level. On the basis of classroom experience the author is making a point that literature provides ample opportunities for developing and practicing speaking, listening, reading and writing. Reasons for using literary texts in foreign language classrooms are analyzed. It is suggested that selection of texts and activities should be according to the needs of learners to facilitate language teaching and learning.

Keywords: Language, Literary Texts, Learners, Activities.

Introduction

There has always been a debate on methods and approaches throughout the history of foreign language teaching. The objectives of teaching language have influenced approaches and methods of teaching L2. Previously any foreign language was taught the way Greek and Latin languages were taught. The goal of language learning was to appreciate Literature. The second language was learnt through the Grammar Translation Method. Literary texts were translated as these texts were assumed to represent models of good writing. But in the era of approaches like Audio-lingual, Suggestopedia, Total Physical Response literature was relegated to the background. Linguists such as Topping (1968) argue that literature should be excluded from foreign language curriculum because of its structural complexity and lack of conformity to standard grammatical rules. But recently the educationists began to rethink on whether literature can be a source of L2 learning.

Povley (1967) says that linguistic difficulty of literature has been overstated. Literature with its extensive and connotative vocabulary and its syntax can expand language skills. Duff and Maley (1990), Brumfit and Carter (1986), John McRae (1994), Widdowson, Gillian Lazar favor literature as an effective tool for language learning. According to these scholars literary texts provide ample opportunities for a number of activities in classroom to enhance language competency. "Literature consists of some lexical items and expressions which cannot be found in the linguistic texts. Literary texts contextualize and socialize language items and lead to the use of actual words and expressions in real situations" (Widdowson). Literature is rooted, so far as the foreign language learner is concerned, in the oral basis of language learning; rooted in lively and meaningful oral drills, in spoken and acted dialogues, in simple dramatization of stories; indeed in those very procedures which make for successful and interesting learning of the language. Brumfit and Carter have emphasized the role of literature as 'an ally of language'.

Reasons for using Literary Texts

Collie and Slater (1990: 3) cite four reasons for using literary texts in a foreign language classroom.

(i) Authentic material: Literature provides authentic material in real life contexts (travel timetable, pamphlets, cartoons, advertisements, and newspaper or magazine articles). Brumfit and Carter (1986: 15) assert the point that "a literary text is authentic text, real language in context to which we can respond directly".

(ii) **Cultural enrichment:** Every foreign language learner cannot visit the country of language. Literature mirrors, cultural, aesthetic, moral values upheld by the native users. Through characters the reader has fair idea of how the natives speak and how they behave. This helps the learner to feel the codes and norms that shape a society.

(iii) **Language enrichment:** Literature provides learners lexical, syntactic items, structures, ways of connecting ideas. These items can be used to enrich writing skill.

(iv) **Personal involvement:** Since literature offers authentic material in real life situation, a reader lives the text as the story develops and events unfold.

Maley (1989) also gives seven reasons for regarding literature as potent source of language learning.

1. **Universality:** Literature deals with themes like death, love, envy, bitterness, religious/social strictures which are common to humanity. Only treatment of themes differs from person to person and society to society.

2. **Personal reference:** Since literature offers universal themes and real life settings, learners easily relate to them.

3. **Variety:** Learners come across language of various hues, language related to law, medicine, sermon, ball-dance, and pubs, colloquial language which help learners to understand specific language also.

4. **Economy and suggestive powers:** Literature is storehouse of myriad ideas that go beyond what is apparent. Suggestive power generates language discussion.

5. **Socio-linguistic richness:** Language in literature changes from one group to another. The learners find formal language, informal language, regional dialects, and jargon. This richness enhances competence in target language.

6. **Ambiguity:** Literature has ambiguity which leads to varied interpretations and different perceptions.

7. Interest: Literature is stage of human drama. It is intrinsically interesting.

Literature and Teaching Language Skills

Literature can be a good resource for teaching the four language skills—speaking, listening, reading, and writing—if taught in an integrated manner.

Literature and reading skill—Reading skill may be developed provided student centric approach is adopted. It may be a collaborative learning [group learning]. Students may be asked to read a section of short stories, fiction, drama and direct questions related to setting, character and plot may be asked.

Literature and speaking skill—Literature reading can enhance communicative reading. After reading task is over, learners may be asked to discuss in groups, every group frames some questions and elicits answers from peer groups. In reading poetry the learners know stress, pitch, and intonation thus increasing their speaking skill. In drama they can assume role play and simulation.

Literature and listening skill—Reading aloud of poetry and retelling of stories enhances listening skill of learners.

Literature and writing skill—The students may be asked to pick up any word or phrase or sentence to write anything in the beginning. This is called free writing. Literature helps learners to develop writing skill through controlled the writing like rewriting of any passage or story.

Using Novel in Teaching Language

"Short fiction is a supreme resource for observing not only language but life itself. In fiction characters act out all the real and symbolic acts people carry out in daily lives and do so in a variety of registers and tones." (M. Hismanoglou). Gillian Lazar has given following reasons for using novels in L2 classroom:

- A novel, if selected carefully, may provide a more involving source for pedagogic activities for learners than course books.

- Novel addresses complex situation and adult dilemmas. It can provide the basis for variety of classroom activities ranging from extensive reading tasks to close textual analysis.
- Novel gives glimpse of another culture.

The teacher has to identify some features of the novel which provide opportunities to the learners to increase language competence. I have selected "Silas Marner" by George Eliot for discussion and I hope principles of activities would be applicable to other novels also.

(i) Widdowson (1984: 246) has drawn attention to that creative force which he labels 'language capacity'. "The struggle to make meaning is further intensified in the novel because as a fictional construct it does not refer in any direct or obvious way to the real world" (Widdowson, 1984: 165). In the creative process of 'making meanings', language capacity of learners increases. By encouraging learners to make predictions the teacher helps them to enhance their capacity for making meanings.

(ii) A novel opens a storehouse of words. Some words recur throughout the text to create a web of meanings; some words have symbolic meaning. In textual analysis the teacher can teach how language items acquire meaning and show how a particular effect is being created.

Some examples from Silas Marner:

- It (Raveloe village) was nestled in a snug well wooded hollow.
- Marner's inward life had been a history and a metamorphosis.
- His trust in man had been cruelly bruised.
- His insect like existence.
- Marner's gold gathered his power of loving together into a hard isolation like its own.

(iii) When we teach novel in language classes, learners develop a fair perception of communicative language. Students may be assigned homework the reading of one chapter and teacher can devise activities around the chapter. Next day the class can be divided into groups. One group may discuss the chapter and other groups write their impressions about their classmates.

(iv) As pre-reading task the teacher gives a list of unfamiliar words in advance and learners are supposed to know the dictionary meaning. This habit will enhance their dictionary skill. But tell the learners that reader is not expected to understand every word in reading a novel. One has to guess the meaning of some unfamiliar words in the context.

(a) Silas Marner had cured Sally Oats of rheumatism.
(b) He invited none to step across his door-sill.
(c) I must hand over the rent to the squire.
(d) His trust in man had been cruelly bruised.
(e) He was suspended from church membership.
(f) Silas was deceived by his friend William Dane.

[In the sentences given below we can tell learners why these cannot be changed into passive voice or active voice is better.]

(a) He weaved like a spider.
(b) Gold became an end itself.
(c) He rose and placed his candle on the floor near his loom.
(d) He went to the door and followed her footsteps.
(e) The coins seemed irrelevant to him.

"...for the villagers it (Marner's appearance) had mysterious peculiarities which corresponded—the exceptional nature of his occupation, and his advent—an unknown region called 'North'ard'. So had his way of life: he invited no comer to step—his door-sill, and he never strolled—the village to drink a pint—the rainbow or to gossip—the wheelwright's: he sought no man or woman, save—the purpose—his calling or—supply himself—necessaries. Jem Rodney saw Silas leaning—a stile—a heavy bag—his back, instead of resting the bag—the stile.

Answers: ....with, from, across, into, at, at, for, of, in order to, with, against, with, on, on

(v) The learners are to write summary of the chapter or events. Word-limit must be given.

(vi) The teacher can prepare **work sheets** with sentence completion or a chronological ordering of event.

(vii) The students have ample scope to learn Active Voice and Passive Voice. If sentences are picked up from text, the learners' knowledge of events and themes of the novel will be reinforced along with increased language competence. Students can have some practice in change in voice.

(viii) After reading the text all groups write about characters which appear in the novel. Each group selects one character. They can make a diagram writing adjectives that are used to describe the characters and then they can make a presentation in the classroom. Here peer opinion can be elicited.

(ix) Another grammar based activity may be using cloze tests. The teacher will select extracts from the novel and delete some grammatical items. The learners are to fill the gaps. The teacher would inform them whether the deleted word is a noun or a verb, a preposition or a connectors.

(x) The groups may write true or false statements from selected chapters as class work. Then each group asks/ brainstorms other groups.

Using Poetry in Teaching Language

Poetry also provides good material for practice in developing correct pronunciation and intonation. Rhythms and rhyming not only develop language skills, they also add fun and enthusiasm. I have taken 'Aunt Jennifer's Tigers' by Andrienne Rich. It is a short but suggestive poem.

Here is the Text:

Aunt Jennifer's tigers prance across a screen,
Bright topaz denizens of a world of green
They do not fear the men beneath the tree
They pace in sleek chivalric certainty.

Aunt Jennifer's fingers fluttering through her wool
Find even the ivory needle hard to pull.
The massive weight of Uncle's wedding band

Sits heavily upon Aunt Jennifer's hand.
When Aunt is dead, her terrified hands will lie
Still ringed with ordeals she was mastered by
The tigers in the panel she made
Will go on prancing, proud and unafraid.

A number of activities can be designed to enhance language skills like speaking skill and listening skill.

(i) The visual prompts may be shown to the learners and they guess the theme of the poem. Different responses can be written on the blackboard.

(ii) The groups are asked to write some unfamiliar words or phrases and arrange them according to the parts of speech. Then each group gives a response. Since responses are short, hesitant learners can be encouraged to speak.

(iii) They may also be asked to transform those words into another part of speech. They discuss vocabulary. In the poem we find words like chivalric, certainty, terrified, proud etc.

Chivalric ---- adjective; Chivalry ---- noun
Terrified ---- adjective; Terror ---- noun
Certainty ---- noun; Certain ---- adjective
Proud ---- adjective; Pride ---- noun

The learners may make sentences using these words in pairs and responses can be sought. Even antonym/synonym can be discussed. First, we take **antonyms:**

Chivalric ----- coward/deserter
Certainty ----- unsteadiness/shaky
Proud ----- humble/submissive
Terrified ----- confident/assertive

Now **synonyms:**

Chivalric ----- brave/valiant
Certainty ----- sureness/authority
Proud ----- pleased/satisfied
Terrified ----- threatened/frightened

(iv) The teacher takes first reading with rhythm and rhyme and learners repeat in chorus.

(v) The teacher reads the second time with rhythm and rhyme and learners write, stresses, pauses and end word—rhyme pattern. In the poem for example—screen-green; band-hand; made-unafraid. This task enhances their listening skill.

(vi) Learners can act the characters speaking one or two lines. In Aunt Jennifer's Tigers they can act the role of Aunt Jennifer, Uncle Jennifer, tigers. The teacher can help students write dialogues. This activity will increase speaking and writing skill. The students have lot of fun.

(vii) The poetry is full of literary devices and underlying meanings. These literary devices like simile, metaphor, alliteration, pun, personification are used in everyday life or proverbs like, 'Where there is will, there is a way'.

(viii) Poems can be summarized to enhance writing skill.

(ix) Concept formation may be attempted around a word. This can be a noun, verb or a phrase. In the poem the following words/phrases may be given to the students for forming concepts and discussed in the class:

> Prance, bright topaz, fluttering, wedding band, massive weight, ordeal.

Challenges

There are some difficulties in using literature as a resource for teaching foreign language [here English].

(i) Text selection is the biggest challenge for a teacher. Text should relevant and interesting to the learners. Success in using literature greatly depends upon a selection of text. The text should not be difficult on either a linguistic or conceptual level.

(ii) Text should be appropriate matching the linguistic ability and comprehension level of the learners.

(iii) Text should not be too lengthy. Lengthy texts might pose the question of how to maintain the students' interest.

(iv) Cultural background of the text needs to be comprehensible to the learners.

(v) One of the biggest challenges is too much new vocabulary. It becomes an obstacle for students in understanding the text.

(vi) Archaic language and local dialects also pose problems for the foreign learners.

Simple, interesting and relevant text will motivate the learners not only to read literature but also analyze them from the language point of view. The teacher will have to give idea about the era in which the novel was written, and the socio-economic and cultural influences on language used by the writer.

Conclusion

Literature is a potent tool in the language classroom. But the teacher's role as a facilitator is very crucial in using literature as a resource for language. The success of language teaching also depends on the selection of text, and methods and techniques used by the teacher. Of course aims and objectives of teaching literature also count. Novels have dialogues and authentic language which open wide vistas for learners in enhancing linguistic competence. The learners will find poetry and other genres of the literature a useful resource to develop their language skills. For foreign learners theme in some texts in English may be topically different but it may be thematically same as they find in literature of their native language, as literature of every language deals with both universal and topical themes.

References

Brumfit and Carter as quoted by Koutsompou Violetta-Irene: The Use of Literature in the Language Classroom: Methods and Aims. *International Journal of Information and Education Technology*, Vol. 5, No. 1, January 2015.

Collie J. and Slater S. (1990). *Literature in the Language Classroom: A Resource Book of Idea and Activities*. Cambridge: CUP.

Hismanoglou, M. "Teaching English through Literature", Journal of Language and Linguistics, Vol. 1, No. 1, April 2005.

Lazar, Gillian: Using Novels in Language Learning Classroom, Internet

Maley, A. 1989. "Down from the Pedestal: Literature as Resource" in Literature and the Learners: Methodological Approaches. Cambridge

Widdowson, H.G. "Talking Shop", *ELT Journal* 37(1): 30-35.

4

Idioms in English: Meaning More than Words

Shailesh Kumar Mishra and *Bhupendra Kumar Patel*

Abstract

A language of a society is a carrier of its socio-cultural elements. Like the other languages, English too conveys meanings that are not only textual and denotative but also contextual and connotative. Sometimes it communicates more referentially rather than textually. If a language acts only on the basis of its grammar and content vocabulary, it loses its power of communication as it does not, then, include figurative and referential implications and indications to convey the complete sense. An Idiom is a phrase or sentence that has some referential and figurative meaning than the composite verbal meanings of the words it has. The characteristic of an idiom is referentially symbolic, thematic or contextual. Idioms are used in English, like many other languages, to convey the traditional and cultural learning and its expressions of a society in figurative and aphoristic ways. Idioms are formed and developed by the varied formal domains of a language utilizing almost all the content-elements and subject-matters of the daily life.

Keywords: Society, Carrier, Vocabulary, Implications, Indications, Domain, Expression.

Introduction

The knowledge of a language and its 'skills of communication' is not complete without the exquisite mastery over the grammar, content vocabulary and idiom vocabulary of the language. The language consists of its own colors and shades. If the language functioned only on the basis of grammar and content vocabulary, it would cry over the loss of its cause and effect. An Idiom is a phrase or sentence that has some referential and figurative meaning than 'the composite verbal meanings' of the words it has. The feature of an idiom is referentially symbolic, thematic or contextual. Idioms assimilate the traditional and cultural learning and its expressions in figurative and aphoristic ways in them. Idioms are shaped and formed by the different standard areas of a language using almost all the content-elements and subject-matters of the daily life. Idioms are the subsequent outcomes of the development, heightening and enhancement of a language that is a pivotal role in culture. They are found in a language that keeps a solid traditional and cultural background. The total control over idioms is attained from their repeated and frequent use. The coherent use of idioms in communication is possible only when the language speakers know the subject and its salient references. There are idioms and phrases found in all the languages of the world. As English is spoken throughout the world, it has a big hoard of Idioms. It is full of idioms varied in contexts and conditions because of its usages and presence in various parts of the world. English is proud of its rich treasury and long list of idioms. In English, usually the use of idioms for native speakers is of no concern whereas the non-native speakers of English may face troubles and constraints, if they want to use idioms indiscriminately. If the thematic and contextual idea behind an idiom is properly understood well in advance by the non-native speaker of English, it enhances the effectiveness of his language when the same idiom is used in the similar situations.

Importance of Idioms English Language Learning

English is one of the richest languages of the world hoarding more than 1,000,000 words. Its rich vocabulary and varied versions make this language a bit hard and confusing to learn and use masterly. At the same time, it is known to be the most flexible language too in the world. It is to be understood well that knowing only the denotative meaning of a word will not serve the purpose. One has to know the connotative comprehension of that word also. Understanding the exquisite meanings of English words requires more than knowing the denotative meaning of words. It demands from its speakers to have the connotative word comprehension too. In other word, it may be said that one must understand the figurative language as well. Because of the dependence of English on the denotative and connotative meanings, the learning of and mastery over idioms is vital in Learning of English. The adequate knowledge of idioms is a pre-requisite for both the native and the non-native speakers of English. But in the case of latter, it is more essential as they don't have the knowledge of the cultural and historic background of the birth or the appearance of a particular idiom. For example, there are many idioms in the American English those are related to golf, basketball, football, baseball and rugby. For people who don't understand American baseball, the expression, "He struck out," may have little or no sense. Native speakers will know this is a reference to someone who was failed in achieving a coveted goal. As the Americans people usually know better about these games, they use the idioms related with these games comfortably and commandingly whereas it might be difficult to understand these words usages especially for people who come from countries which are not familiar with these games.

"In linguistics, idioms are usually presumed to be figures of speech contradicting the principle of compositionality. This principle states that the meaning of a whole should be constructed from the meanings of the parts that make up the whole. In other words, one should be in a position to understand the whole if one understands the meanings of each of the parts that make up the whole."[1]

Idioms share cultural, traditional and historical information and learning and enrich people's understanding and the referential manipulation and implication of a language. The term 'Idiom' has been defined in various ways and with varied words. Some of the definitions are as follows:

(1) The language peculiar to a country, a class, a community, the people or 'sometimes to' an individual.

(2) "A construction or expression having a meaning different from the literal one or not according to the usual patterns of the language."[2]

As there are lots of idioms there in English, it will be almost impossible to know the meanings of all the expressions, but with the enhancing of knowledge of English increases the comfortable understanding of the idioms that come across in one's learning process. Idioms are elusive. Usually Idioms cover all the sorts of expressions we use that are peculiar to English, including clichés and slang.

"Prepositional usage is also a common part of idiomatic expressions."[3]

They become the part of our language without realization that they are the part and parcel of our communication. They belong to the different parts of our life. Some categories into which they fall are: food and cloths, education and career, games and sports, recreations and hobbies, arts and music. Idioms are pervasive. They are used in both formal and informal languages. Their use in formal language ascertains the height of knowledge and proves the subtleties of communication. Now the use of idioms in education, business and media turns to be the sign of depth of knowledge in the undertaken subject and that of command over the language of communication. Idioms covertly introduce the communication skill of the speaker. They transmit a good deal of information about the speaker. Speakers who efficiently communicate in English that is enriched with idioms show the high understanding of the language. Navjot Singh Siddhu, the ex-test player of Indian Cricket Team, is regarded highly by the world of media, social sites and that of sports for his commendable knowledge and tremendous skills of using idioms, phrases and proverbs. With the start of the use of Information and Communication Technology (ICT) being used in the fields of science, education and commerce; the significance of verbal communication has started increasing day by day. The language adequately assimilated with idioms, phrases and proverbs is gaining ground, being regarded and paid handsomely. The speakers who can proficiently use idioms get better prospects and opportunities in their working areas and in the society. It is expected from the L2 (Non-native language) learners that they should understand and use a variety of common idioms in discourses. It may be highly advantageous for those who are planning to work anywhere in the global world that uses English as the language of communication.

"L2 learners are expected to understand a variety of common idioms, which is advantageous for those planning to work in a world that increasingly uses English as the language of communication and commerce. Whether it is working in one's native country or in an English-speaking country, idioms are important as part of the shared knowledge among English speakers."[4]

Idioms are important carrier and medium of communication of the shared culture and its knowledge among speakers. Unless one understands idioms, they cannot understand the cultural references and it may create a chasm between their understandings and expressions that may mar the very spirit of communication. The level of understanding of a language is high in those speakers who have sufficient knowledge of idioms of the target language. In that case they understand the language deeply and may communicate better than others.

"The wider meaning consists of a definition where lexical usage shows a deeper understanding of the target language and culture. Since vocabulary and culture are intertwined, L2 speakers can gain more vocabulary through idioms and conversely, can learn more about idioms from being exposed to the target culture."[5]

The idioms are born as the result of the understanding of a situation or a fact keeping in view a particular culture. The culture is the decisive factor in the creation of an 'Idiom'. It may be said that an idiom is an expression of a culture in nutshell about a particular situation or on a particular matter.

"Idioms consist of new meanings attributed to existing words or of wholly new words, generally accepted as lying outside standard polite usage. It usually passes out of usage in time or is accepted into standard usage."[6]

It is usually difficult to understand the meaning of an idiom if the learner does not use it time and again.

"Ideally, vocabulary shouldn't be learned in a vacuum, and this is especially true for idioms. There are a variety of idiom dictionaries for those who wish to learn more about idioms."[7]

The learning of idioms is facilitated well when the learners have good reference materials.

"Role-playing, writing and interactive activities such as matching the parts of idioms are some activities that can help L2 learners to expand their knowledge and use of idioms. Knowing which idiom should be used when comes with practice and time."[8]

Types of Idioms

Idioms can be categories in two ways: (1) On the basis of formation and (2) On the basis of the function. Idioms can be a single word, a phrase or clause, or a complete sentence. Usually idioms, if seen on the basis of the compositionality, mean nothing. They have to be seen in contextual and cultural totality.

"The most common types of idiom are polysemes. They are words—often verbs—and phrases with multiple, somewhat related meanings. An example is the verb "run;" to "run with a smart idea" or "run a computer program" are related to, but quite different from running a foot race."[9]

There are idioms in English for almost all the spheres of our life. We can hardly come across any area of our daily life where no idiom or idiomatic expression found. On the basis of different facts of our daily life, idioms are categorized as follows:

(1) Age: Act one's age (To be mature)
Example: You must act your age, stop being childish.

(2) Numbers: Nine to five (working hours)
Example: He is busy working nine to five.

(3) Life: Dog's life (a miserable existence)
Example: After the death of his wife the old man lives a dog's life.

(4) Death: Kiss of death (something that looks good but that actually brings ruin)

Example: Their business treaty with Simon's company is a kiss of death.

(5) Animals: Back the wrong horse (to support wrong person or promote wrong concept of idea.)
Example: Don't back the wrong horse! You know she cannot win the competition.

(6) Men and women: A man of few words (A man who does not speak/a man of action)
Example: Sachin Tendulkar is a man of few words but his bat speaks a lot.

(7) Colors: Feel blue (to feel sad)
Example: They felt blue after their defeat in the election.

(8) Clothe: Laugh up your sleeve (to be secretly amused)
Example: They're quite before their boss but they laugh up their sleeves.

(9) Food: Go bananas (to become very angry)
Example: He went bananas when he saw him sleeping.

(10) Health: Alive and kicking (to continue to be healthy)
Example: You should not worry; your grandma is alive and kicking.

(11) Money: Dime a dozen (easy to get, available anywhere)
Example: He should not be proud of his talent. People like him are a dime a dozen these days.

(12) Relationship: Raw deal (said when someone is ill treated)
Example: He has got a raw deal. He is innocent, but he has paid a heavy penalty.

(13) Home: The home stretch (The last part of a difficult work)
Example: He is in the home stretch after a weak of hard work.

(14) Law: Read the riot act (warn someone forcefully)
Example: The coach will read the riot act to the disobedient players.

(15) Love: Puppy love (A childish infatuation with another person)

Example: Don't be angry, your son in the puppy love.

(16) Music: All that jazz (Everything else related to something)
Example: They enjoyed the treat: drinks, foods, dancing and all that jazz.

(17) Nature: Get into deep water (to be in trouble)
Example: They got into deep water when the engine of their jeep got stopped.

(18) Science: Blow a fuse (lose your temper)
Example: Hey, don't blow a fuse.

(19) Religion: Devil-may-care (careless or defiant)
Example: She has a rather devil-may-care attitude to her cousin's illness.

(20) Parts of the body: At your mother's knee (when you were a child)
Example: He learned this prayer at his mother's knee.

(21) Sport: Walk the talk (To do what one said one could do)
Example: To make your plan succeed you have to walk the talk.

(22) Time: Under the wire (At the last minute)
Example: He submitted his paper just under the wire.

(23) Travel: Paddle one's own canoe (to do something by oneself)
Example: Mohan has to paddle his own canoe after his father's demise.

(24) War: Keep your powder dry (Be prepared for the worst)
Example: To succeed in life, keep your powder dry.

(25) Weather: Have a face like thunder (To be angry about something)
Example: His boss had a face like thunder when he came to know about his report.

(26) Work: work your fingers to the bone (to work extremely hard)
Example: They work their fingers to the bone to develop their business.

How to Teach Idioms in ELS

The teaching of Idioms is very significant with regard to 'Teaching of English as Second Language'. It has already been discussed that Idioms play very decisive role in learning of English as second language. The knowledge of idioms provides the speaker profound mastery over communication skills. Considering the value and importance of idioms for a language learner, the duty of a teacher of English (as second or non-native language) becomes more challenging and difficult. The teaching of Idioms in ELS is tougher as they mostly mean connotatively and the learners have to know the cultural references of the idioms and their contexts. Only literal and contextual meanings may lead to confusion and lack of understanding.

The teacher of English has to provide maximum information about the idiom being discussed. The teacher should provide the background story of the genesis of the idiom. It enhances the students' understanding of the idiom. The examples which are referred while teaching the idiom should be familiar to students. The use of such examples facilitates the process of understanding of the function of the particular idiom by students. The role of ICT may do wonders in this case and it may facilitate the teaching and learning process (TLP). In this regard, the spiral approach in TLP may bring better results. The practice activities should incorporate the spiral approach in formulating exercises. The role-plays based on the idiom-theme may also accelerate the learning process. The role of the teachers of English is very pivotal and vital in all of these suggested activities and methods because they have to facilitate the TLP wherever and whenever the need arises. Here the competency of the teacher counts a lot.

"If you keep an open mind and play your cards right, your proficiency in English will soon be something to crow about."[10]

Conclusion

One who has attained mastery over the uses of English idioms is treated as an effective speaker who is conferred with 'the gift of gab'. At the same time if a speaker of English fails to have the command over using English idioms, he mostly finds his efforts going to dogs. This life becomes a fortune for the speaker who masterly uses coherent idioms on the different situations in the day-to-day interactions. It is expected from a teacher of English as second language that he himself has a rich vocabulary and treasury of idioms, phrases and proverbs. If the teacher enjoys this coveted position, he may accelerate the best possible learning efforts of the students. It is proved that the good knowledge of idioms facilitates the TPL of ESL. It may finally be said that idioms enrich the effective language experiences.

Notes

1. http://en.wikipedia.org/wiki/Idiom dated 14/04/2015
2. *New Webster's Dictionary and Thesaurus of the English Language* (1993). Connecticut: Lexicon Publishers, Inc.
3. Princeton Review (1998). *The Princeton Review: Grammar Smart, A Guide to Perfect Usage*. New York: Random House.
4. http://lib.chdu.edu.ua/pdf/zbirnuku/7/37.pdf dated 14/04/2015
5. *Ibid.*
6. *New Webster's Dictionary and Thesaurus of the English Language* (1993). Connecticut: Lexicon Publishers, Inc.
7. http://lib.chdu.edu.ua/pdf/zbirnuku/7/37.pdf dated 14/04/2015
8. *Ibid.*
9. http://www.wisegeek.com/what-are-the-different-types-of-idioms.htm dated 14/04/2015
10. Laflin, Shelley Vance (1996). *Something to Crow About: A Concise Collection of American English Idioms for Everyday Use*. Washington D.C.: United States Information Agency.

5

Mobile Learning for ESL Students: A Modern Approach

Naziya Hasan

Abstract

The present paper describes the conceptual background, advancement and advantages of mobile learning along with its shortcomings in the light of the pilot study conducted by the researcher on the small sample of 50 secondary students and 10 teachers of Kendriya Vidyalaya. The records of interview were analyzed qualitatively which clearly depict that students have a positive attitude towards the use of mobile phones in and outside the classroom for second language learning in the current era of modernized and digitalized heads, hearts and hands. But on the other hand, mostly teachers are not supporting its use in the classroom as it will impede proper learning and will negatively affect the teaching learning process. Even some teachers are favouring the supervised, restricted and modified use of mobile phones in language learning. Supported by the result, this paper tries to explain the role of mobile aided language learning with its proper and rational implementation.

Introduction

In the current era of modernized and digitalized heads, hearts and hands, the conventional and traditional path of education has taken a new turn to prepare human recourses according to the needs and requirements of the ever moving and developing society. Nowadays, definition of education is rapidly changing with the passage of time which intentionally or unintentionally brings changes in aims of education, objectives of education, methodology, teaching and learning practices, tools and techniques for imparting education, teacher-taught relationship, agencies of education, etc.

Advancement in digital technologies has smoothened as well as hindered the path of education. But the obstacles and hurdles can be crossed easily, if its positive effects are worth consideration as compared to its negative counterparts. Various technologies like computers, laptops, projectors, digital libraries, software, etc. are being used at large level because of its productive and effective functionality. But when the matter of mobility comes to the fore, these technologies lag behind because of its not being accessible, affordable and portable to everywhere by everyone. Education is not only meant for selected area or population but it is the fundamental right of each and every child irrespective of caste, creed, race, gender, socio-economic status and other so-called man-made criterion. We should think of those equipments or techniques which can be accessible and affordable for the larger concerned population. One can easily encounter the public using mobile phones, tablets, smart phones, palm tops, etc. Its proliferation and emergence caused all of us to understand and realize the effective power of these devices for and in learning. These are the most flexible, accessible, movable, portable and affordable means of communication. Have you ever thought of using this technology in the field of learning and teaching English as a second language? Various scholars, educationists and psychologists have made much effort to start it as an approach in the field of language education. This kind of teaching and learning is basically being supplemented by the use of mobile phones, smart phones, tabs, etc. We cannot deny or underestimate the place and importance of teachers by use of electronic gadgets but can supplement and assist the teachers so that better learning and innovative and effective teaching may emerge.

Mobile Learning

The use of mobile devices, which is often accompanied by learner mobility across diverse contexts and settings, puts a spotlight on learners and their experiences. According to Tony Bingham (In Chad Udall's Mastering Mobile Learning), "If you have ever used your smart phone or mobile device to look something up, you have experienced mobile learning." Sharples, et al. (2009) define mobile learning as "the process (both public and personal) of coming to know through exploration and conversation across multiple contexts among people and interactive technologies".

Desmond Keegan in his "Mobile Learning: A Practical Guide" has cleared the concepts of e-learning and m-learning which depict functionality and mobility. "In defining mobile learning one confronts tensions between functionality and mobility. There is a continuum from the point of view of functionality in the devices used for e-learning and m-learning. This continuum goes from desktop computers to laptop computers to PDAs or handhelds or palmtops to smart phones to mobile phones. In the definition of mobile learning the focus should be on mobility. Mobile learning should be restricted to learning on devices which a lady can carry in her handbag or a gentleman can carry in his pocket. I, therefore, define mobile learning as "the provision of education and training on PDAs/ palmtops/handhelds, smart phones and mobile phones".

FUNCTIONALITY	MOBILITY

COMPUTERS	LAPTOP COMPUTERS	PALMTOPS	SMART PHONES	MOBILE PHONES

E-LEARNING	M-LEARNING

Fig. 1. Functionality and mobility in definition of mobile learning*.

* Taken from Desmond Keegan 'Introduction'.

One of the characteristics of mobile learning is that it uses devices which citizens are used to carry everywhere with them, which they regard as friendly and personal devices, which are cheap and easy to use, which they use constantly in all walks of life and in a variety of different settings, except education. It offers a supportive and conducive environment in which learner prepare for second language communication outside the classroom and receive helpful personal freedom of expression. These tools free teachers from the mundane tasks of grading rote memorization and provide immediate feedback for parents along with students. Frankly speaking, mobile technologies expand and extend the territory where language may be rehearsed and practiced. These devices allow students to connect, communicate, collaborate and create using rich digital resources.

Recent studies have shown the divergent and innovative use of mobile devices in and outside the classroom. In their study, Chin-Hing Chen and Shih-Hsun have described the personalized intelligent mobile learning system for supporting English learning. N. Hockly (2012) has demonstrated the SAMR (Substitution, Augmentation, Modification and Redefinition) model of Puentedura (2010) while using mobile devices. G.M. Chinnery (2006) has described the common features of technological devices which help in messaging, video-conferencing, video-recording emailing and internet accessing. It enables communicative language practice, access to authentic content and task completion. While keeping in mind the true advantages of mobile learning approach, the present research focuses on the views of students and teachers towards the use of mobile devices for second language learning and teaching.

Definition of the Term Mobile Learning

Mobile learning here means the use of mobile devices for more than having phone calls in teaching learning process of English as a Second Language.

Objectives of the Study

The present study has following objectives:

- To find out the innovative use of mobile devices for learning English as a second language.
- The study the views of teachers towards the use of mobile devices for learning English as a second language.
- The study the views of students towards the use of mobile devices for learning English as a second language.

Methodology

The researcher has selected 50 students and 10 teachers purposively from Kendriya Vidyalaya, Jagdishpur (Uttar

Pradesh) to collect data for her study. It is a qualitative study which has used unstructured interview for collecting data from teachers as well as students. Researcher has personally interacted with the students and teachers. Their records were maintained in the form of written notes and analyzed qualitatively.

Result

The researcher has collected data from 50 students and 10 teachers of Kendriya Vidyalaya by using unstructured interview.

The following questions were asked to the selected students and teachers:

- Should mobile phones be allowed in school premises?
- If yes, Why? If no, Why?
- What are the advantages of using phones in school?
- How can it help you in second language learning?
- What are the disadvantages of using mobile phones in the classroom?

Among students, 48 were having positive view towards the use of mobile devices for studies in and outside the classroom. Rests of the students are found that possessing a mobile phone in classroom was against the rules of school and the sole factor of indiscipline among them. But the majority considered it easily accessible and flexible device. It can provide them immediate feedback which is beneficial for improvement in their performance. As language learning is a skill subject, it needs individual attention and proper training which can be made easy by using mobile devices.

When asked for its advantages, 90% students said that it can be used as a tool for language learning just as learning writing skill (They learn the format of letter writing, essay writing, article writing etc. by different authors), speaking skill (They follow and practice several activities, especially for pronunciation, online and for that they get feedback too), enhancing reading skill (They use to read novels online and get help by the use of online dictionaries at the same time without wasting time) and making grammatical points and rules strong and clear (They use several sites for practice papers and online tests for clearance of grammatical points and rules).

For second language learning, it is considered very productive and fruitful. More than 90% students were supporting the introduction of mobile learning for language learning. It is analyzed that various social networking sites can also be used in this field. Most of the students nowadays are having practical knowledge of facebook, twitter, whatsapp, etc. Students can easily and freely share their ideas on these apps and sites. It helps them overcoming their confusion regarding the topic of study. Even British Council has introduced several apps which can be used in language learning at each level.

From the collected data, it was analyzed that 40% teachers were finding it quite hectic. They thought that it would hamper their privacy as students might text them after school hours. It is like taking the job inside the home. Sixty per cent teachers found it as a favourable technique for better performance in scholastic as well as co-scholastic areas. Hundred per cent teachers thought that by introducing these devices, students will become friendly and interact freely without hesitation. It is more beneficial for shy students who generally don't participate actively in the teaching-learning process. One teacher said, "As modern day students are more techno friendly, it may be implemented as mobile phones are definitely more attractive to students than books. But phone lingo might impede proper learning if discretion is not practiced."

Nowadays, in every school or institution, teachers are focusing and giving attention on identifying the bright students and late or slow bloomers of their schools. Its selection is easy but implementation of the remedial measures needs refinement. In the class of 45 students, individual attention cannot be given to each and every child according to their needs and demands. By use of mobile devices, this problem can be tackled. Interesting and effective teaching can be brought forward. They can be reached anytime easily by the teacher and can be instructed accordingly and immediately. Slow or weak students are shy in nature and feel humiliated very soon. They need extra attention and care by teachers' side. So this device may prove fruitful with enduring commitments. Feedback discussion among students is possible by this device. And discussion of the strong and weak points of the students are one of the most important and productive techniques of overcoming the problems and bringing improvement in their performance.

Conclusion

On the basis of the analyzed results, it can be concluded that students are having positive attitude towards the use of mobile phones in and outside the classroom whereas teachers are not supporting its use in the classroom as it will create problem of discipline and students will not focus on their studies. Some teachers favoured its supervised, revised and restricted application. This technology can be proved a boon only when it is being supervised by the teachers so that originality of students will not suffer due to excess data available on internet. Technologies should be used without compromising the quality of teaching and learning.

References

Alley, M. et al. "Use of mobile technology to train ESL adults", Canadian Council on Learning.

Chinnery, G.M. (2006). "Emerging Technologies: Going to the MALL: Mobile Assisted Language Learning". Retrieved from http://llt.msu.edu/vol10num1/emerging/

Hockly, N. (2012). "Mobile Learning". Retrieved from http://eltj.oxfordjournals.org at Manipur University on 10 June, 2015.

Levy, M. (2009). "Technologies in use for second language learning". Retrieved from http://www.jstor.org

Mentkowski, M. and Associates (2000). "Learning that Lasts". San Francisco: Jossey-Bass Publishers.

Puentedura, R. (2010). "SAMR and TPCK: Intro. to advanced practice" available at http://goo.gl/78UJn.

Sharples, M. et al. (2009). "Mobile Learning: Small Device, Big Issues" in N. Belacheff et al. (eds.), *Technology enabled learning: Prnciples and Products*. Dordrecht: Springer.

West, D.M. (2013). "Mobile Learning: Transforming Education, Engaging Students, and Improving Outcomes" Retrieved from http://www.brookings.edu/research/paper/2013/09/17 on 13 May, 2015.

6

Developing Collocational Competence of Engineering Students through Authentic Materials

Ramana Prasad

Abstract

A large number of engineering students face difficulty in using English language due to deficiency of collocations in their mental lexicons. In spite of possessing technical skills, lack of collocations knowledge reflects in their speaking and writing which could affect their chances of getting placed in reputed firms. This paper aims to highlight the importance of teaching collocations to develop students' fluency and confidence in using the language. It suggests ways to promote their awareness of lexical chunks by exploiting carefully-chosen authentic materials for language input. By designing a variety of interesting exercises and tasks from the chosen material and encouraging the students to notice and place and use words in acceptable ways, teachers can develop their collocational competence to the desired level. This will help the students to use language in a natural and fluid way in professional as well as in social situations.

Introduction

The curriculum and syllabus for students studying in engineering colleges is understandably dominated by technical subjects. English is taught mostly in the first year to improve their language and communication skills so as to get them 'placement-ready' in their fourth year. Within the limited time available, the syllabus designers need to slot in all the four language skills of Listening, Speaking, Reading and Writing in addition to Grammar, Vocabulary and Pronunciation activities. As a result, it is virtually impossible to cover any component thoroughly. My experience with the students has shown that although they are technically sound, some of them find it difficult to express their knowledge in writing and speaking due to their inability to string 'chunks of words' together. In other words, they lack 'collocational competence', which, according to Jimmie Hill (2000) is the ability to "combine words in predictable ways". This deficiency makes them fumble and search for words which they do not possess in their mental lexicons thereby affecting their language production.

This paper begins by quoting a few examples of erroneous use of language by the engineering students in their writing and speaking activities. It explains the role of collocations in language use and why it is necessary for teachers to teach collocations. Then it shows how an authentic text (newspaper article) can be used to create awareness of collocations and how some simple exercises can be designed and used in classroom to benefit students. It also highlights the importance of collocations dictionary in teaching and learning. The paper concludes by reiterating the importance of teaching collocations to engineering students.

Mis-collocations

During the course of my teaching, these are some of the mis-collocations that I have observed in some students language:

He thinks that he has *chosen a wrong decision.*

1. I am sorry I *did a mistake.*
2. Overflowing garbage bins are causing *very inconvenience.*
3. He apologises and *makes sorry* to him.
4. The author *makes the readers confused.*
5. I am *owning* the system.

Grammatically, these sentences may be correct. However, for a language-proficient listener, these utterances will certainly sound odd and out of place. Unless corrected explicitly, they get fossilised and become very difficult to correct subsequently. Hence, the importance of collocations needs to be demonstrated to the students to produce language appropriately.

Need for Teaching Collocations

Research has shown that collocations play a major role in language production. Firstly, the manner in which "words combine in collocations is fundamental to all language use" (Hill 2000). A customer desirous of having tea at a café will ask for a *cup of tea* and not a *glass of tea* or a *bowl of tea*. However, if he wants to have soup, he will ask for a *bowl of soup* and not a *cup of soup*. A *handsome man* is not the same as a *beautiful man* as is a *pretty woman* not the same as a *handsome woman*. One *rides a bicycle* but *drives a car*. So, the choice of vocabulary is often pre-decided and predictable.

Secondly, collocations make our language fluent (Hill 2000). Native speakers are able to speak quickly and efficiently because ready-made chunks of language are stored in their mental lexicons which can be immediately recalled for use. They do not process language word-by-word but in multi-word units. This enables them to process and produce language quickly.

Thirdly, collocations help us to express complex ideas in a precise and quick manner. We can focus less on the form of words and more on the ideas. Adequate knowledge of phrasal verbs, idioms and collocations of different kinds will enable one to use language in a natural and fluid way. On the other hand, lack of this knowledge will lead to erroneous combinations, pauses and hesitations which will ultimately affect fluency.

Finally, knowledge of collocations will help one to depend less on grammar (Morgan Lewis 2000). Lack of collocations knowledge will force a student to use longer utterances to communicate something which a proficient user can do with precise lexical phrases. This increases the chances of grammatical errors and needless work on grammar when the focus needs to be on building vocabulary.

What should Teachers do?

In view of their importance discussed above, it is necessary for teachers to devote a reasonable part of their class time for teaching collocations. Instead of individual words, teachers should focus on teaching language chunks which will pack more power and meaning when they are used in speaking or writing. Knowing a word should mean "knowing something about its collocational field" (Hill 2000). The first step is for the teachers to make their students aware of their mis-collocations. Then they should guide them to look for two- or three-word expressions and notice acceptable collocations. This should be followed by some interesting exercises used in conjunction with a collocation dictionary.

Since they deal with co-text, collocation dictionaries are extremely useful in finding a range of common collocates of words. Students should be encouraged to browse through these dictionaries and record *verb + noun*, *verb + adjective + noun* and *adjective + noun* collocations and learn familiar words in new combinations.

Game 1 (Adjectives)	Game 2 (Verbs)
1. Court	1. Express
2. Criminal	2. Conceal
3. Legal	3. Voice
4. Divorce	4. Avoid
5. Impeachment	5. Feign
Answer (noun): proceedings	Answer (noun): disappointment

In order to make the learning interesting and useful, authentic materials such as newspaper articles, magazines, technical journals, etc. can be used to create awareness and teach collocations. Students should be exposed to subject-specific collocations to develop confidence in using their subject knowledge for various purposes. For the purpose of this paper, I have used an article titled *World football rocked* from *The Hindu* dated 28 May 2015 to design some simple collocation exercises from the same article.

COLLOCATION EXERCISES

I. The Collocation Game

In this activity, the teacher reads out a list of adjectives/verbs one by one. Students need to write them down and give the noun which collocates with all the adjectives/verbs. The order of the words chosen should be from general words to stronger collocates.

II. Odd Verb Out

One verb in each line does not collocate with the noun. Cross out the one which does not fit.

1. await, avoid, accept, seek, face, fight, order
   EXTRADITION
2. audit, check, make, keep, block, submit
   ACCOUNTS

III. Phrase Match

Match the following collocations without looking back at the original text.

1. sponsorship	turmoil
2. presidential	extradition
3. awaiting	reports
4. plunged into	rights
5. dogged by	vote

IV. Fill in the blanks using the clues given below. You may change the form of the word as necessary.

undulating, risky, doing, build, biggest, foster, owning, uneven

"As charged in the indictment, the defendants' ________ a culture of corruption and greed that created an __________ playing field for the __________ sport in the world," said FBI director James Comey. "Undisclosed and illegal payments, kickbacks, and bribes became a way of _________ business at FIFA."

V. Fill in the blanks without looking back at the text. The first letter of the collocation is given as a clue.

Separate from the U.S. investigation, Swiss prosecutors said they had **o**____________ their own criminal proceedings against **u**___________ people on suspicion of mismanagement and money laundering related to the **a** ________ of rights to host the 2018 World Cup in Russia and the 2022 World Cup in Qatar.

Data and documents were s__________ from computers at FIFA's Zurich headquarters, the Swiss prosecutors said. Officials said that following the a_________, accounts at several banks in Switzerland had been blocked.

VI. Write an essay in about 300 words on "Corruption in the IPL".

Use the following nouns to write about the topic. Look up your collocation dictionary and choose nouns, adjectives and verbs needed to express your ideas. Choose useful phrases to write a good essay.

greed, bet, bribe, cheating, law, power, punishment

Recommendations

The exercises given above are by no means exhaustive. Teachers can design a variety of exercises and activities suitable in their contexts and depending on the needs of their learners. Exercises can be designed for any kind of authentic materials. However, the teacher needs to study the text carefully and notice the collocations himself first before using them as a language input for his students. It is important that the text is subject-specific, has an engaging content and possesses a variety of collocations for vocabulary learning and language production. Teachers need to encourage students to not only notice collocations but also "select those collocations which are crucial to their particular needs" (George Woolard 2000).

Conclusion

If engineering students need to exhibit their technical skills, they need to develop good language skills including knowledge of collocations. The paper demonstrated how an authentic text (newspaper article) can be used to create awareness of collocations and how some meaningful exercises can be designed from it and used in classroom in tandem with a collocations dictionary to develop collocational competence. This will "allow students to read more widely, understand more quickly and speak more fluently" (Hill 2000), which will make them communicatively competent.

References

Hill, J. (2000). Revising priorities: From grammatical failure to collocational success. In M. Lewis (Ed.), *Teaching collocation: Further Developments in the Lexical Approach* (pp. 47-69). Hove, UK: Language Teaching Publications.

Lewis, Morgan (2000). There is nothing as practical as a good theory. In M. Lewis (Ed.), *Teaching Collocation: Further Developments in the Lexical Approach* (10-27). Hove, UK: Language Teaching Publications.

Woolard, G. (2000). Collocation: Encouraging learner independence. In M. Lewis (Ed.), *Teaching collocation: Further Developments in the Lexical Approach* (28-46). Hove, UK: Language Teaching Publications.

7

Educational Technologies and Concepts: A Study on Blended Learning and Emerging Trends in Teacher Education Programs

Priyanka Sharma and *Soniya Verma*

Abstract

These days teacher's education system is facing problem of inaptness and irrelevance. There is a visible gap between how students live and how they learn. Schools and colleges have struggled to keep the pace with the rate of change in students' lives inside and outside the educational institution. Students and scholars spend their adult lives in multitasking, multifaceted, technology-driven, diverse and vibrant world. India has a large system of education. There are nearly 5.98 lakh Primary Schools, 76 lakh Elementary Schools and 98 thousand High/ Higher Secondary Schools in the country, about 1300 teacher education institutions for elementary teachers and nearly 700 colleges of education/ university departments preparing teachers for secondary and higher secondary schools. Out of about 4.52 million teachers in the country nearly 3 million are teaching at the primary/elementary level. A sizeable number of them are untrained or under-trained. As far as in-service education is concerned the situation is not very encouraging. In this scenario it has been observed that teacher educators are not professionally committed and overall competencies of teachers leave much to be desired. This paper aimed to provide a conceptual framework to address the critical emerging issues in teacher's education in India and other developed part of the world.

A good teacher's training programs must have teachers working continuously with expert master teachers in a traditional classroom or virtual setting to enhance the knowledge and experience base. Some trends are opportunities, others disruptive, a challenge or threat; some turn out to be a short-lived novelty (an innovation can develop into a trend, or die out), others slow-burning, even barely noticeable but seismic and enduring over the long term. However expert teachers are also imparting knowledge about how students learn, how to assess their learning and about effective teaching strategies to provide them a platform to build repertoire.

Keywords: Education reform, Teacher education, Professional-Teaching strategies, Trends.

This paper explores how the theory and practice of globalization impacts teacher education and role of faculty in preparing educators for the same. Meaning of this context fact is understood differently by the people involved in activities related to global economies. Globalization and education is a rapid resource aimed at providing varied perspectives on conduct in which education is being shaped by global processes. We begin with the nature of globalization within modernity, and modernity's characteristic as that of steady transformation. In many contexts, globalization is associated with technological innovation and the salvation of the Third World by advanced capitalist societies. The teacher is fundamental in supporting such educational transformation. Only the teacher can develop those skills and capabilities required for building a knowledge society. Therefore, the teacher needs to be changed first by orienting him in the latest pedagogies and empowering them to develop appropriate competencies and capabilities among learners. The perception of teaching as a profession is fairly new; most teachers in modern nations today are college or university educated. In this paper, we also view education and educators as involved agents in the construction of a just social world, and contend that this implies infusing the curriculum and teacher education with multinational sensibilities, frequently, through critical theory and aspects.

> "If you educate a boy, you educate one individual,
> If you educate a girl, you educate a teacher.
> If you educate a teacher, you educate a community."

It is correct that in earlier days, teachers were only the males from higher community such as brahmin community and kshtriyas teaching the rich, but now the entire system is changed. Now we have female teachers with highly qualification and also imparting knowledge skills and others activities. Today's overall education is totally depends on the quality of teachers and that a sound program of professional education of teachers is essential for imparting desired type of education. Dating back to the olden days, feedback of teachers form students were not taken by higher authorities, but in this cut throat competition it has become very difficult to maintain an Education system. As Francis Bacon remarks that Knowledge is power, this also implies that teaching is an art that can be acquired through a series of well designed series of activities, it's essential, therefore due to prominence should be laid on the education of the teachers. According to the encyclopedia of Educational Research (1941), Walter S. Monroe, defines teacher's education as:

> The total education experiences which contribute to the preparation of a person but the term is completely employed to designate the program for the courses and other experiences offered by an educational institute for the announced purposes of preparing persons for teaching and other educational services and for contributing to their growth in competency for such service. Such Teacher Education Programs are offered in teacher colleges, normal schools and colleges and universities.

Teacher education institutions have been proliferating and mushrooming all over the Country with profit motives until the National Council for Teacher Education (NCTE) with its headquarters in Bangalore, came up with and insisted on mandatory norms and standards for these institutions. As a result of their intervention, many institutions have constructed buildings with classrooms and procured infrastructure to meet their standards. These institutions were even been forced to increase the salary of teacher educators to the basic amount in the government scale. But later, the effectiveness of NCTE intervention reduced and the powerful lobby of private education institutions had their way in running their teacher education shops.

The Education Commission (1964-1966) said, "...a sound program of professional education of teachers is essential for the qualitative improvement of education." India has one of the largest Higher Education System in the world. Main players in the higher education system in the country are: University Grant Commission (UGC) is responsible for coordination, determination and maintenance of standards, release of grants. Over the last half a century and particularly, in the recent decades, teaching learning has been undergoing drastic changes. There has been a shift towards student centered classrooms with teacher's role more as facilitator of learning rather than an autocratic master. Unlike in the past when the teacher was entrusted with transferring the contents of curriculum to a passive audience of students, today new experiments are being tried out in the classroom that includes project based learning, development of thinking skills, and discovery learning approaches. As part of Sarva Shiksha Abhiyan (SSA) the textbooks have also been modified (in my opinion, to make them worse than before in many respects).

Professional Councils are responsible for recognition of courses, promotion of professional institutions and providing grants to undergraduate programmers and various awards. The statutory professional councils are: All India Council for Technical Education (AICTE), Distance Education Council (DEC), Indian Council for Agriculture Research (ICAR), National Council For Teacher Education (NCTE), Rehabilitation Council of India (RCI), Medical Council of India (MCI), Pharmacy Council of India (PCI), Indian Nursing Council (INC), Dentist Council of India (DCI), Central Council of Homeopathy (CCH), Central Council of Indian Medicine (CCIM).

Teacher Education program is one which plays an important role in acquition of today's qualification framework. Teachers Education program is the process of providing teachers and potential teachers with the skills and knowledge necessary to teach effectively in a classroom environment. Most teacher education stats with initial training such as a degree program at a college or a university, through other paths are available for a candidate to begin teacher's education program. "Teachers education may assume a leader; one day all children in this nation will have the opportunity to attain an excellent education." This statement appears on the wall at the TFA headquarters in New York and also on the organization's letterhead and the opening words—One Day, All Children, are the title of Wendy Kopp's (2003) book about the founding of this enterprise. It is a motto that works on two levels to make the case for TEP as an exercise in altruism ship role in the transformation of education or to be left behind in a swirl of rapid technological change UNISCO-2002.

A teacher must complete some sort of teacher education before becoming a full-time teacher. In most cases, a teaching candidate will enroll in a teacher training program at a college or a university, thus allowing them to opportunity to earn a bachelor's degree in education. A student then may choose to continue his or her teacher's education by obtaining a master's degree in education. Teacher-Education Programs is considered to be the hub of entire education because it is believed that as is the B.Ed., so will be secondary and higher education system. The Teacher Education program is differing from other educational programmers in the sense that it trains the student teachers for a profession. A teacher shapes the style of thousands of youth during his tenure. According to the Dictionary of education—C.V. Good (1973), teacher education is defined as "All formal and informal activities and experiences that help to qualify a person to assume the responsibility most effectively." Basically Teachers Education Program provides grants to institutions of higher education to fund doctoral students to conducing by research in other countries in moderns foreign languages and area studies for period of 6 to 12 months. Teacher's education refers to the policies and procedures designed to equip prospective teachers with the knowledge, attitudes, behaviors and skills they require to perform their task effectively in the classroom, school and wider community. Continuing education courses, seminars and professional development activities are all considers part of ongoing teacher training. The Teachers Education program differs from other educational programmers in the sense that it trains the student teachers for a profession. Yet teacher education aims at providing opportunities to their students with necessary knowledge, skills and value system for evolving market places, common living environment and to prepare good citizens for lifelong learning. A teacher must complete some sort of teacher education before becoming a full-time teacher as they are the main pillars of a sound and progressive society. They bear the weight and responsibility of teaching, and apart from parents, are the main source of knowledge. Basically Teachers Education Program can be broken down into these blocks:

- Foundation knowledge and skills
- Content area and methods knowledge
- Practice at classroom teaching or at some other form of educational practice
- Field observations
- Student teaching
- Internship
- Should be able to develop content and make quality of the content.
- Excellent written and verbal communication.

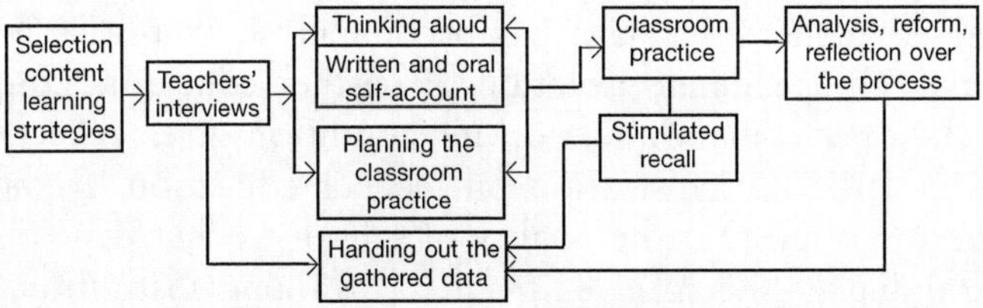

Teachers for lower primary classes are trained in Teacher Training Institutes (also called junior basic Training Institutes or primary Teacher Colleges) attached to state departments of education. These types of course usually last for two years and leads to a diploma or a teacher training certificate. Upper primary school teachers are trained in two years and the course leads to a diploma. They must have passed the higher secondary education. The evidence on open and distance learning for teachers goes back two generations. In 1963, nearly 200,000 children of Palestinian refugees were in primary or lower secondary schools, where they were taught by 4,648 teachers. But of these only 450 had received any teacher training; most had done a course of secondary education and nothing more. Thus, with a team of faculty, predominantly females, with high qualification and submissive and with meager remuneration that challenges even their self-esteem, the teacher education is carried out. The B.Ed. course is a single year course. The syllabus itself is riddled with problems of content irrelevance, poor standards, and absence of focus on essential areas etc. Even though the number of academic days is few, all sorts of co-curricular activities are carried out including a number of celebrations such as union day and festivals and even all India tour program.

There is no substantial research going on in improving the education or evaluation of the existing programs. The evaluation of teacher trainees in the teacher education institutions is another big joke. The difference in the marks between high achievers and low achievers is minimal and the faculty members are least bothered in either encouraging the trainees to score high or to punish the lazy with low marks. Thus, most trainees who enter these institutions come out with flying colors. As a result of all these, teacher education has become close to a farce in the country. The academic isolation of teacher educators coupled with their poor salary and working conditions itself reflects the neglect of the administration on teacher education. It should not be forgotten that the quality of school teacher depends on the training he/she receives from the training institution and allowing teacher education to rot adversely impacts education sector. Hope that the Education ministry will start focusing on the B.Ed. education, where the roots of the education system lie. Improving the teacher education would positively impact the education sector as a whole. The United Nations Relief and Works Agency looked at the problem and saw that it could not be solved by the classic method of pre-service training: if you took the teachers out of the schools to train them, you would have to replace them with less experienced, and no better qualified, teachers. So it was necessary to devise a kind of in-service training that was as good as pre-service. Any state embarking on this type of reform will need to provide financial resources to ensure that institutions of higher education can recruit faculty and increase their capacity to prepare qualified teachers. However, the results of this study would indicate that some consideration must be given to the form of the financial support that is provided to teacher preparation programs. In the case of New Jersey, grants enhanced the ability of institutions to hire new faculty, but they also may have led to the dramatic variability that was found in student-to-faculty ratios among institutions. Grants are a notoriously unstable method of funding, which can lead some schools to rely on part-time and adjunct faculty. Because the research indicates that faculty-student relations are critical to nontraditional students succeeding in teacher preparation programs, policy-makers should consider a more permanent financial commitment for the development of programs.

In conclusion, developing a high-quality system of teacher preparation requires the coordination of human and financial resources so that there is equity and quality in the programs offered by institutions within a state. This coordination is particularly critical in preschool education because the workforce is extraordinarily diverse in qualifications, knowledge, and experience, and the workforce is located in a range of settings that have historically been regulated differently. As the New Jersey context has indicated, most states probably have the leadership and much of the expertise needed to develop high-quality programs, but without coordination and support, it is unlikely that states will be able to transform the early childhood workforce in the way that research indicates is necessary. In short, the potential for creating a high-quality system is there—it is now up to teacher educators and policy-makers to work together to make it happen.

References

Studying teacher education: the report of the AERA Panel on Research; By AERA Panel on Research and Teacher Education, Marilyn Cochran-Smith, Kenneth M. Zeichner.

Teacher Education Program Accountability: in search of meaningful outcomes evidence by Susan, J. English.

Making a difference in teacher education in self study, Edited by Clare Kosnik, Clive Beck.

Socio-culture and influences on teachers education program by Dennis M. McInerney.

Teachers education program; policy, narratives, study and cases by Hendrik D. Gideonse.

8

Preparation of English Teachers for Effective Language Learning

Jayadeb Sahoo

Abstract

English Language Learning, a challenge in the field of English Language Teaching, has been an international issue. The role and status of the English teacher is although undisputed, under-performance of the teacher has been a core issue to be addressed. Because of the diverse backgrounds of teaching and needs of the ELLs, educators need specialized preparation to work effectively with them. It is clear that all teachers with ELLs in their classes need to know about second language development, cross-cultural issue and methods to teach both language and academic content. To achieve teacher quality in educational system, educators are to be prepared with the knowledge, skills and dispositions to work effectively with ELLs. Achieving this goal calls for improved preparation programmes for teachers and administrators, and appropriate coherent professional development for practicing educators. The paper presents the need, problems and solutions of preparation of English teachers to create the best possible environment for ELLs.

Successful English language learning is closely related with the successful and effective English teachers round the globe. English is an important international language; it is learnt in most of the countries of the world in the different capacities such as first or second language. The success of language learning is indebted to the qualified and well-trained teachers who are capable of educating the learners of the diverse backgrounds.

The teachers of ELLs need to know about second language development, cross-cultural issues and methods to teach language and academic content. The language learning may fail if teachers fail to understand the methods and environment of English language teaching to the ELLs. Teachers who perform inadequately not only fail to achieve their own performance standards, but they can also affect the performance of those with whom they come in contact e.g. other staff, pupils.

Inadequate knowledge about language, needs of ELLs will lead to the incomplete learning of English language. It is a fact that an adequate number of specialist teachers who need to know strategies for teaching linguistically and culturally diverse students are essential. From one of the studies in the United States, it is found that only 2.5% of teachers who instruct ELLs have an academic degree in ESL and only 30% of the teachers have received some training in the field. The example of U.S. is applicable to all the countries with regard to qualified teachers of English.

We don't have enough expert English teachers for imparting English language teaching in spite of efforts of states, educators and administrators. The need of the hour is to prepare a force of well trained English teachers on a priority basis to ensure the successful acquisition of English language.

But the issue of preparing English teachers involve a number of questions which should be taken into consideration while devising methods of the preparation of English teachers to ensure teachers' quality.

Ensuring Teachers' Quality

1. Before recruitment to ensure teachers' quality, we need know what kind of teacher is best suited to teach English learners.
2. How can we recruit and keep highly qualified teachers?
3. How do specialists (bilingual and ESL teachers) differ from other classroom teachers in their preparation needs?

4. What should be content of pre-service and in-service professional development?
5. How can we ensure that all teachers know what they need to know about language?
6. What pathways can we identify that can lead to the creation of highly qualified teachers?

The answers to these questions help the administrators and educators to establish systematic institutions to recruit and train the English teachers.

It is discovered that presently a number of ELD teachers are not prepared to work with a culturally and linguistically diverse students population. They fail to achieve expertise on the job. Such teachers are stressed due to lack of success, and they can 'burn out' quickly and leave the profession. Even if they don't quit the job, they can't motivate the ELLs and can't provide quality education.

In order to address the issue and to retain quality in English language teaching, it would be right to examine into the deeply rooted problems in the way of preparation of English teachers.

Problems in Preparation of the Teachers

1. Motivation: It plays a vital role in a teacher who is inspired and dedicated in educating learners. But it is seen that most of the teachers who are in-service don't volunteer to enhance their knowledge in their teaching career due to different reasons. This kind of unmotivated teachers can't motivate and instil learning in the ELLs.

2. Lack of incentives: Teachers must be rewarded with some incentives like promotion or financial benefits to encourage and motivate them to join different professional development programs, workshops and seminars. It is found that teachers don't take initiatives to join these programs as they don't get any incentives. Even Government sponsored programs are ignored by most of the teachers. Of course sometimes institution does not encourage the teachers for enrichment of teachers' knowledge. Teachers neither get leave nor financial support from thc organisation.

3. Defective recruitment policies: Candidates from different academic backgrounds join schools as teachers and teach English although they do not have the right temperament for teaching English language. It is seen that there is no special recruitment policies to attract the candidates with English Honours background to join the profession. Any graduate with bachelor of education degree is entrusted with ELLs which is really unfortunate.

4. Unsystematic training policies: The pre-service training of the teacher candidates doesn't strengthen the knowledge and command of English language of the teacher candidates as very little content of English is taught in training. In India, in B.Ed. Degree, the candidates with English methods are taught a little about the language by educators who are not competent enough to train the candidates.

In-service teachers also don't receive consistent and comprehensive training to deal with the ELLs in their classes. No designated institutes are there which equip the teachers to update knowledge and skills. In India NCTE, SCERT, ELTI and some other institutions have come forward to train the in-service teachers but are not able to cover all the teachers of English for various reasons.

5. Low paid job: Teachers have low spirit because of Government policies regarding their salaries. They are not paid up to their expectations. Good students with English language background are discouraged to join the profession as they are appointed somewhere else with high salaries.

All these along with some other reasons contribute to the English teachers' under performance. The other reasons like inadequate leadership, indifferent management practices and defective systems and procedures are also responsible for under performance.

Although recruitment and preparation are important issues with respect to strengthening the teacher corps for English learners, the reality is that most teachers who will be teaching these students in the foreseeable future have already completed their training and are in the schools. For these teachers the key to strengthen their skills is professional development. A number of studies have demonstrated that good professional development increases teachers' sense of competence and provide them with tangible strategies for better meeting of their students needs (Gracia 1992, Herman and Swigert 2003).

It is found that after entry into the workforce, teachers have limited opportunities to update and enhance their knowledge and skills throughout their careers. This stands as a barrier in the way of effective language learning of the students as the success of the learners depend much on teacher's knowledge and applications of effective teaching in the classroom.

Preparation of English teachers can't be done only at the time of entry into the profession. The pre-service training needs to be reinforced in the teaching career frequently. Teachers need to continue renewal and extension of the skills, knowledge and awareness to be effective in multilingual dynamic environment. Potential and existing teachers need the professional development where they can explore their beliefs about their students and increase their repertoire of linguistic and cultural relevant pedagogy (Caldoon 1998, 2000). This helps the teachers to have their needs which include institutional mission and goals, student performance data and teacher support mechanisms.

The institutions assigned the task of giving training to the English teachers need to give special attention to the development of four skills of teachers which are very often neglected by the teacher education. The institution should also make provisions for theory, research, modelling of demonstration of instructional methods, coaching during practices into teachers' active teaching repertoire (Joyce and Showers 1998).

To achieve quality in teacher training the following points should be taken care of:

(i) The teacher should be provided with theory and practices on how to work in collegial teams.

(ii) The training should add the analytical, creative and practical learning to teachers' teaching and assessment method.

(iii) Summer coaching of 2-4 weeks on lesson plans and year-long curriculum should be provided by summer institutions to accomplish the task of the teachers.

(iv) The needs of teachers like teaching resources, lesson plans, teaching tips, methodology articles, access to the latest thoughts and debates on English language teaching, professional development resources and communication practices (CoPs) should be addressed to by providing these resources for teachers' knowledge through free websites. British council has several useful websites which can support the teachers to be well-equipped.

Continuing professional development (CPD) is extremely crucial in teaching because the pre-service and induction training are highly inadequate. But response of the in-service teachers to CPD is very discouraging. They view professional development as a movement from a mere teacher to a researcher, trainer, speaker, academic writer and teacher educator. As professional development is purely teachers' own responsibility, It is a personal journey and it depends on the interest of the teachers. Only motivation can motivate the teacher to take part in the professional development programs conducted from time to time by NCTE, other Govt. Organisations and NGOs like British Council, The Regional English Language offices and different teacher associations like ELTAI.

Preparation of English teachers in India: Preparation of English teachers in India is a major challenge for educational thinkers and administrators. It will not be inappropriate if one claims that there is no ELT specific teacher education in India. The pre-service teachers are given one year general teaching in which very less importance is given to English teaching through teaching methodology containing hundred marks only. Care is not taken to give training to develop all the four skills of the teacher candidates. The pre-service training, thus, is ineffective and inadequate.

The in-service teachers of English language of high schools do not receive effective training as well. In Odisha, although agencies like NCTE, SCERT and RAMSA try to equip teachers, the training is of short duration of three to four days. ELTI, Bhubaneswar of course imparts training for one month which can be very much helpful for teacher development.

In spite of efforts to update English teachers, the mission has failed due to various reasons as described in the earlier part of this paper. The aim of the preparation of English teachers is to produce accomplished English teachers. An accomplished English teacher is supposed to be/have the following qualities in him:

(a) Self-reflective and self-critical.
(b) An excellent communicators, clear articulators and responsive to others.
(c) A strong background in the field of English language and English teaching.
(d) An active involvement in English teaching within the whole school and beyond the school.
(e) Thorough understanding of English as a subject.
(f) Knows how language is developed through all four models.
(g) Prepares classroom materials of high quality.
(h) Makes learning accessible and motivates challenges and stimulates pupils.
(i) Understands language as a system, knows components like phonology, syntax, semantics etc.
(j) Understands the role of culture in language.
(k) Understands planning, implementing and managing instruction.
(l) Understands Assessment and professionalism.
(m) Ability to draw instructional program that includes ample opportunity for speaking, reading and writing.
(n) Knows how learning takes place both within the learner and through social interaction.
(o) Understands his role in the larger professional sphere of English language education.

But, till date, an accomplished teacher is far from reality. The teacher preparation agencies need to be revised and modernised to accomplish the task of producing well-trained and qualified teachers.

Conclusion

Training English teachers is not as easy as it seems, as many hurdles lead to difficulties on the way to reach the goal. The present initiatives of institutions, Govt. and educators are not enough. The teacher education syllabuses need to be revised and give more emphasis on the theory and practices of English language. The duration of pre-service training i.e. one year (B.Ed.) course is not admirable and is not effective. The current situation in India is that at present the duration of B.Ed. course has been increased to two years. In spite of this, English language training is unsatisfactory. The duration of pre-service teacher training should be increased and special training on Reading, Writing, Listening and speaking should be imparted to teacher candidates for one whole year to achieve proficiency in each of the four skills. Candidates with English Honours background must be recruited as they have the motivation to develop professionally and they can prove as better teachers of English. Attractive salary packages should be given to attract the meritorious and inspired candidates to become teachers. Incentives for attending workshops, seminars, summer courses, orientation or refresher courses must be given to encourage the English teachers to participate in the programs for professional development in large scale.

The pre-service and in-service programs for English teachers should be integrated for better results of training. These should be continuous training programs for English language teachers to update their knowledge and skills for effective English language learning, as success of teachers is linked to students' achievement.

References

Tellez Kip, Waxman C. Haresh. *Preparing Quality Educators for English Language Learners*, Lawrence Erlbaum Associates, Publishers, Mahwah, New Jersey, 2006.

Green Andrew. *Becoming a Reflective English Teacher*, McGrahill, Open University Press, Berkshire, 2011.

Goodwyn Andrew. *Developing English Teachers*, Open University Press, Buckingham, 1997.

Wright Trever. *How to be a Brilliant Mentor*, Routledge, London, 2010.

Gunasekhar Paul, Padwad Amol, Pawalec Daphne. Starting, Stimulating and Sustaining English Language Teacher Education and Development, British Council, 2011.

9

Honing English Communication Skill of Techies through the Various Genres of Literature

Reena Singh

Abstract

In the developing countries or rather say third world countries where English is not the first language it becomes a great challenge for the teachers to impart the knowledge of English Language especially to the students of technical courses. Thus it becomes really significant to initially grab the attention of the students to while beginning with the process of education. The English Language Teachers of technical students develop a sense of frustration, alienation and insignificance due to the student's attitude towards the subject. In this paper I have tried to discuss broadly on the areas firstly, challenge of teaching English language that too, to the technical students, secondly, the remedy to teach through modules of Literature developed especially for them and lastly to expose the students and motivate them to participate in various genres of literature to enhance their skill of vocabulary, expressions and word order used in literary texts. In this I have tried to incorporate the process and methods of Language teaching to enhance their skill of being a better professional to become successful string of corporate Instrument.

Introduction

In the Third World countries where English is not the first language it becomes a great challenge for the teachers to impart the knowledge of English language especially to the students of technical courses. This Paper aims at emphasizing the use of literature as a popular technique for teaching both basics of English language skills (i.e. reading, writing, listening and speaking) and language area (i.e. vocabulary, grammar and pronunciation) to the students of technical courses for whom communication or languages learning as a subject is unable to create any interest or importance. English language learning or communication is very significant for the professional world but they don't realize it.

For the students it is the subject which is least important and it is enough if they study it the night before the exam. The test of the teacher begins when s/he has to grab the attention of the students at the time of imparting knowledge. Language teaching with its core devices of grammar modules seems dull and dry for the techies. It also becomes difficult to catch their attention. By the time they understand its significance they are left with no time for learning language is a gradual process. So the use of literature in the ELT classroom is mandatory I believe as it is rejuvenating and also a revival for a number of reasons. Having formed part of traditional language teaching approaches, literature became less popular when language teaching and learning started to focus on the functional use of language. However, the role of literature in the ELT classroom has been re-assessed and many now view literary texts as providing rich linguistic input, effective stimuli for students to express themselves in other languages and a potential source of learner motivation.

Although incorporating literature in language class is a difficult task for various reasons firstly the teacher should have atleast sensibility of both Literature and Language. Secondly, the proper assessment of what to included of literature part in language rather become overenthusiastic while the selection that to follow one's own passion rather seeing the students' perspective. Thirdly, time factor for technical curriculum is a major hurdle in following this pattern. Though according to Fitch O'Connell "the key point is that literature can be a very flexible tool for any language teacher:

it requires no specialist training;

it can be brief, contemporary and relevant;

it can be used to enhance, supplement and complement the curriculum;

it can aid students' speaking as well as reading skills;

it can engage the class in aspects of critical thinking that textbooks rarely do and open minds onto the world;

it can assist with specific language learning and it is an ideal tool for revision purposes."[1]

So when selecting the literary texts to be used in language classes, the language teachers should take into account needs, motivation, interests, cultural background and language level of the students. However one major factor to take into account in whether a particular work is able to reveal the kind of personal involvement by arousing the learners interest and eliciting strong, positive reactions from them. Reading a literary text is more likely to have a long-term and valuable effect upon the learner's linguistic and extra-linguistic knowledge when it is meaningful and amusing. Choosing books relevant to the real-life experience, emotions or dreams of the learners is of great importance. Language difficulty has to be considered as well. If the language of the literary works are simple, this may facilitate the easy understanding of the literary text though this by itself is not the most crucial criterion. Internet, appeal and relevance are also prominent, enjoyment: a fresh insight in to issues felt to be related to the heart of peoples own thoughts or situations exemplified clearly in a work of art; the other, equal pleasures of noticing those same thoughts, feelings, emotions, or situations presented by a completely new perspective; all these are motives helping learners to cope with the linguistic obstacles that might be considered too great in less involving material.

For the language learners, the ideal way to increase their understanding of verbal/non-verbal aspects of communication in the country within which that language is spoken, just not probable for the diversified language user in India. So, the English learning becomes difficult due to the influence of their native language so the best way is to combat this problem for such learners is literary works, such as novels, plays, short stories, etc. facilitate understanding how communication takes place in the country. The world of a novel, play or short stories is an imaginary one, it presents a full and colourful setting in which characters from many social/regional backgrounds can be described. A reader can discover the way the characters in such literary works see the world outside (i.e. their thoughts, feelings, customs, traditions, possessions, what they buy, believe in, fear, enjoy hours they speak and behave in different settings.

The various genres of Literature are Poem, Short Stories, Fictions or Novels, Plays and Song Lyrics. An increasing number of stories in English are written specifically for learners of other languages. As English teachers, Literature that is the literary text is one of the tools ready in our hands to offer them language acquisition and contribute cultural knowledge and understanding. It acts as a catalyst to acquire and stimulate learning. It at once appeals to the feelings and to their thoughts which in turn pave the way for the student's language enhancement and growth. It makes aware of:

- The broadening of students' horizons by giving them knowledge of the classics of literature. The student's improvement in general cultural awareness
- The students' creativity and literary imagination and to develop their appreciation of literature
- The psychological stress and attitude of the mind
- The historical truths of life
- The philosophy of life
- The innate, inborn goodness of man
- The required changes in individual, society and even in history.

There are times when teachers are challenged daily with students who do not fit into the curriculum. In a classroom, there are many students with special needs, language differences and with different learning styles. It is in the hands of the readers to make their sources interesting. As such, Literature is an amalgamation of prose, poetry and dramas. Prose text will be used to teach language, vocabulary, phrasal verbs, contemporary issues, theories like psychoanalytical issues, communicative skills which further facilitates to discussion among peer members and most probably reading.

Among the literary genres used in language teaching, poetry is one of frequent appearance. Due to their short length, perfectly suitable for a single classroom lesson, their peculiar structure, and their characteristic linguistic features (unusual syntactic patterns, polysemy of words, alliteration, etc.) poems become favourite tools for language teachers. The evocative character of poetry, its imagery, its appeal to feelings and personal experience make it very interesting and enjoyable for the second language learner. The language teacher should exploit the deviancies of the poetic language in order to heighten the language awareness of the learners towards the way in which language can be adapted or changed to fulfill different communicative purposes. Saraç (2003: 17-20)[2] also explains the educational benefits of poetry as follows: It provides readers with a different viewpoint towards language used by going beyond the known usages and rules of grammar, syntax and vocabulary. It triggers unmotivated readers owing to being so open to explorations and different interpretations. It also evokes feelings and thoughts in heart and in mind and makes students familiar with figures of speech (i.e. simile, metaphor, irony, personification, imagery, etc. due to their being a part of daily language use.

Short fiction is a supreme resource for observing not only language but life itself. In short fiction, characters act out all the real and symbolic acts people carry out in daily lives, and so in a variety of registers and tones. The world of short fiction acts as mirrors and illuminates the human lives (Sage 1987: 43).[3] The inclusion of short fiction in the ESL/EFL curriculum offers the following educational benefits (Arıoğul 2001: 11-18).[4] It makes the students' reading task easier as it is simple and short when compared with the other literary genres. It illuminates the students to write short stories. Makes the peers analyze the theme of moral values, love, despair, friendship, etc. In brief, the use of a short story seems to be a very helpful technique in today's postmodern world of language learning.

Using drama in a language classroom is a good resource for language teaching. It is through the use of drama that learners become familiar with grammatical structures in contexts and also learn about how to use the language to express, control and inform. It raises the students' awareness towards the target language and culture. In this context, the use of drama as a tool rather than an end gains importance in teaching a foreign language. The language learning should be culture-free that is the context of the drama should fuse into a language learning process with high interest, relevance and enjoyment. Learners should make use of it to promote their comprehension of life experiences, reflect on particular circumstances and make sense of their extra linguistic world in a deeper way (Sarıçoban, 2004: 15).[5] The educational benefits of drama, according to (Lenore 1993)[6], are as follows: it stimulates the imagination and promotes creative thinking, develops critical thinking skills and promotes language development. It heightens effective listening skills, strengthens comprehension and learning retention by involving the senses as an integral part of the learning process, increases empathy and awareness of others, fosters peer respect and group cooperation and reinforces positive self-concept. It does provides teachers with a fresh perspective on teaching, transforms the classroom strict atmosphere into a humorous atmosphere, exposing the learners to the target culture as well as to the social problems a society may be undergoing. Thus, helping the learners, to improve their level of competence with respect to their receptive and productive skills.

In other words, the use of drama seems to be an effective technique in today's communication-based, student-centered English language teaching. Since it is an authentic material, it helps students to promote their comprehension of the verbal/non-verbal aspects of the target language they are trying to master. Particularly, teachers, who wish to make language learning more colourful, motivating and interesting, can make use of drama in their language classes.

We can stress on that Literature plays an important role in teaching four basic language skills (Listening, speaking, reading and writing). However, when using literature in the language classroom, skills should never be taught in isolation but in an integrated way. Teachers should try to teach basic language skills as an integrated part of oral and written languages use, as part of the means for creating both referential and interactional meaning, not merely an aspect of the oral and written production of words, phrases and sentences.

The Dramatization is the best method while using the different genres of literature that requires classroom performance of scripted materials. Students can make up their own scripts for short stories on sections of novels, adapting them as closely as possible to the real text. What a character would say and how they would say it. Script written by students is also probable with plays. Poems comprising one or more personae may also be scripted by students. Students should attentively read assigned sections of dialog in advance and be able to answer questions about character and plot. They should indicate vocabulary or idioms, or dialog they don't understand and words they cannot pronounce. Students next rehearse the scene with their partners. Although they memorize it, they learn it well enough to make eye contact and say lines with understanding and feeling. Moreover it discusses the semiotic aspects of staging the scene (i.e. facial expressions gestures, and the physical aspects). At last the dramatization is presented before the class.

Other important aspects are role playing and group activities. However, in role playing, students picture characters from the work being read and join in a speaking activity other than a dramatization, such as an interview or panel discussion. And in Group Activities we need to make each student responsible for facts and ideas to be contributed and discussed, it stimulates total participation. All students are involved and the participation is multi-directional. When teaching English through literature, some of the group activities used in language classroom are general class discussion, small-group work, panel discussions, and debates. All of these group activities both develop the speaking abilities of the students during the act of such activities so as to correct such errors (Stern 1991: 337).[7] Therefore, Literature can be useful in the languages learning process owing to the personal involvement it fosters in the readers. Once the students read a literary text, it begins to inhabit the text. He is drawn into the text. Understanding the meaning of lexical items or phrases becomes less significant than pursuing the development of the story. The student become enthusiastic to find out what happens as events unfolds via the climax; he feels close to certain character and shares their emotional responses. This can have beneficial effects upon the languages learning process. At this juncture, the prominence of the selection of a literary text in relation to the needs, expectation, and interests, languages lend of the students is evident. In this process, he can remove the identity crisis and develop into an extrovert.

While the students are exposed to different genres and application of literature they become familiar with many features of the written languages, reading a substantial and contextualized body of text. They learn about the syntax and discourse functions of sentence, the variety of possible structure, the different ways of connecting ideas, which develop and enrich their own writing skills. Students also become more productive and adventurous when they begin to perceive the richness and diversity of the languages they are trying to learn and to begin to make use of some of that potential themselves. In this way, they improve their communicative and cultural competence in the authentic richness, naturalness of the authentic texts.

Thus I would like to conclude that Literature usage brings creativity and involvement of the students and then to instruct students on language module becomes easier. The teacher just needs to have a good number of literary texts and the quintessential point is the teacher needs to know how to use these texts for language learning without making the students realize that they are studying language as it is said very truly said by Mark Twain. What work I have done I have done because it has been play. If it had been work I shouldn't have done it.[8]

Notes

1. O'Connell's Fitch (2009). "Get lit up: literature as a teacher's best friend" in *Teaching English*, British Council.
2. Saraç, S. (2003). "A Suggested Syllabus for the Teaching of Poetry Course in ELT Department of Turkey", *Storn*, 1991.

3. Sage, H. (1987). Incorporating Literature in ESL Instruction. New Jersey: Prentice Hall.
4. Arıoğul, S. (2001). "The Teaching of Reading Through Short Stories in Advanced Classes", Unpublished M.A. Thesis. Ankara: Hacettepe University.
5. Saricoban, A. (2004). "Using Drama in Teaching Turkish as a Foreign Language" in Eurasian Journal of Educational Research. No. 14: 13-32.
6. Lenore, K.L. (1993). *The Creative Classroom: A Guide for Using Creative Drama in Classroom*. U.S.A.
7. Stern, S. (1991). "An Integrated Approach to Literature in ESL/EFL" in *Teaching English as a Second or Foreign Language*. ed. Murcia, M. Boston: Heinle & Heinle Publishers.
8. Twain, Mark. www.twainquotes.com/Work.html

10

English Language Acquisition through Literature

Gandi Sobhan

Introduction

It is widely recognized that a literary text with richness and variety can be stimulating for language learners and can be used to elicit a wide range of responses from the learners which facilitate language teaching and learning. It can stimulate imagination of the learners, offer specimens of authentic use of language and provide ample opportunities for discussion. It ensures students' personal involvement in the learning process and bridges the gaps between the cultures and makes them familiar with the norms and behaviors of the people of the target language. Thus the use of literary text in language class can act as a means of cultural enrichment. It helps the learners to get familiar with the socio-political backgrounds of target language society and also makes them understand how communication takes place in a particular community. This broadens their horizon of understanding the common human nature. Moreover, the learners learn to be more tolerable and sensible when they confront the differences in other culture and their own. Additionally, literature deals with universal issues with what students can relate them with less difficulty and simultaneously feel themselves as part of the whole humanity. Learners are also exposed to the various structures and functions of language through literary text.

Objective of the Study

The objective of the study is to re-examine the benefits of using literature in language classes. This study bridges the gap between the theory of teaching language through literature and its practice by applying the technique. It also aims to explore the appropriate classroom activities which facilitate language teaching and learning.

Research Methodology

This paper projects from a thorough-review of various books and articles on the same topic, classrooms were also observed as the researchers are the teachers of the program. A pre-test was taken to learn about the proficiency of the learners and the areas in which they need special care and development. The test was of 40 marks with equal weight on grammar, need special care and development. The pre-test was conducted by giving equal weightage to grammar, reading comprehension, vocabulary and writing. To evaluate the oral proficiency of the learners, interviews were taken and their problems they faced were analyzed. The priority and the focus of the activities were determined on the basis of the average score obtained in each section of the test. The classroom activities and materials were designed accordingly.

Hypothesis

The present paper underscores the need and importance of literary texts for a comprehensive attainment of higher levels of language skills. It is based on the primary assumption that teaching literature or literary texts makes language acquisition more use-focused instead of form-focused. Learning literature creates many positive attitudes on learning and acquisition of English as a foreign or second language. This paper tries to touch the benefits of the inclusion of literary texts in EFL curriculum at all stages of language learning in general and at the primary stage in particular. Literary texts take into account the functions of language in different realistic situations outside the conditioned atmosphere of the classrooms. The employment of such literary components such as narratives, short stories, one-person acts, fables, dialogues and short social situations, will help learners to sue different forms of the language in one notion of the language. It will, more importantly, motivate and inspire the learners to know more and keep his or her interest intact.

Historical Evolution

Literature and language are closely related and this is a fact none can deny. Literature is constituted by language and it represents one of the most recurrent uses of language. Both linguistic and language analysis methods can be used to understand literature from the learner's point of view. Brumfit and Carter (1986: 1) already emphasized the role of literature as an ally of language this technique is by no means novel, since literature has been a widely used teaching tool in different language teaching methods. However, here the perspective changes giving more relevance to the literary text as a work of art. First of all, let us think over the changing role of literature in the tradition of second language teaching to end with an account of its current situation within the communicative approach.

In the grammar translation method, literature was the central component. Literary texts of the target language were read and translated. Used as examples of good writing and illustrations of the grammatical rules. The focus of this teaching method was on form, on learning the rules of grammar and the lexical items as they appeared in the text. There was no literary interest, nor interest on content. After this method fell into disuse, literary texts were forgotten by teachers of second language.

For the structural approaches to language teaching, literature was discredited as a tool, because it represented the old tradition. The functional notional method ignored literature, because in this method the importance lies on communication and they present authentic language samples. Literature was not considered either to have a communicative function or to be authentic example of language use.

Review of Literature

The discourse that whether literature can be helpful in the learning of foreign language has evoked divergent views.

It is widely believed that the study of language has to be in accordance with special reference to the needs of the language learners. There have been different points of views about the place of literature or literary texts in the foreign language or second language curriculum.

Prof. Charles Blatchford of the Department of English as a second language at the University of Hawaii (1972) opines, "The study of English literature is a luxury that cannot be indulged during the limited amount of time allocated to English."

Prof. Blatchford's expression is based on his understanding that the learners of EFL at the primarily and secondary levels are primarily concerned with the acquisition of the functional skills of the target language that would help them in dealing with everyday occurrences that can be expressed through the basic skills.

Books relating to the methodologies of language teaching have focused in detail on the attitude of individual teacher towards the changes that have taken place and his role in the spread of innovative modes of teaching. Widdowson argues that:

> Language teachers have the responsibility to mediate changes in pedagogic practice so as to increase the effectiveness of language teaching.

With so much of discussion on the importance and usefulness of the literary texts or literature as effective language teaching tools, it is imperative to frame a language course that corresponds to the social contexts of the language learners. There is a practical need to design a syllabus that suits the needs of the learners and at the same time, enables them to express themselves in social circumstances with ease and interest. Many language-training courses are useful in bringing about a change in the behavioral pattern of the learners enriching their verbal fluency.

Elsa Auerbach in her book, *Making Meaning Making Change* has attempted as impressive and convincing account of the participatory and the more traditional ends—means approach to curriculum design. She develops a practical manual for carrying out the participatory language learning curriculum.

In the participatory model, the teacher and students work together to produce a context-specific curriculum based on the needs and desires that the students themselves experience. The teacher simply becomes, therefore, a completed different kind of leader. He discovers novel and innovative ways to induce the students to identify their own needs and interests, introducing topics and activities in the class, which allow students to use language to further their needs and interest. He also plays the role of the organizer of educational resources with a view to expand the student's knowledge of the language because of their use of it.

Rather than presenting the students with synthetic materials developed outside the classroom, Auerbach advocates that teachers combine conscious listening namely a sympathetic awareness of what student's real concerns are, with catalyst activities i.e. language activities that get students to open up and express their real thoughts and feelings. Making meaning contains an impressive list of such activities, which can include what are often called icebreakers to get students talking, class newspapers, picture albums, class rituals, or student produced graphics.

Once the teacher has identified major themes in students' lives with these ways in, she can use a variety of ready to hand tools to draw students into the deliberate use of language to address the issues they see as important. These tools can include fables, proverbs, published works of fiction. Even children's books. One of the most powerful tools is what she calls codes, carefully scripted dialogues in which characters reveal very controversial attitudes towards pressing social questions, such as racism, crime, or sexual harassment. By involving students in discussion about these codes, they not only acquire the language to address these issues, but they also begin to learn how to take positions on these issues themselves.

Culture and language learning studies prove that linguistic and literary studies touch at various points. As professor Blatchford argues: The linguistic interest of culture learning is broader, its approach more scientific and pragmatic, but there is no reason why it should not include in its scope the literary uses of language.

Literary texts include cultural uses of linguistic expressions such as stylistics, pragmatics and semantics. This social communication reflects the usage of different language aspects in the literary texts. Moreover, in the study of language and culture, literary study can make a valuable contribution in tracing the development of the language in all its components and skills. What is more important is that, non-native students need to be exposed to various literary texts in order to be able to consider the other's culture in their international communication. Therefore, the non-native learner's curriculum should include teaching literary texts or literature to facilitate such international communication for the students. Furthermore, literature consists of some lexical items and expressions, which cannot be found in the linguistic texts. Literary texts and literature texts contextualized and socialized language items and lead naturally to the use of actual words and expressions in real situations.

As regards the learning of English as a Second language at the higher level, Prof. Blatchford says, "There may be more justification for literary studies where English is a second rather than a foreign language." It is an undeniable fact that the resources of language can be fully utilized by taking recourse to literature as an important aspect of language learning. For great skill and effectiveness, literature is necessary for language learning. W.R. Lee in his editorial in the *Journal English Language Teaching* says,

> Literature is rooted, so far as the foreign language learner is concerned, in the oral basis of language learning; rooted in lively and meaningful oral drills, in spoken and acted dialogues, in simple dramatization of stories; indeed in those very procedures which make for successful and interested learning of the language.

It is interesting, in the light of the above observation, to note how a child listens to the nursery rhymes and learns the vocabulary through oral drills without going through the oftentimes tedious practice of turning over the pages of a dictionary of usages.

Main Reasons for Using Literary Texts in English Language Classes

As Collie and Slater says the importance of using literary texts in English Language classes because these are valuable authentic material, cultural enrichment, language enrichment and personal involvement. In addition to these four main reasons, universality non-triviality, personal relevance, variety, interest, economy and suggestive power and ambiguity are some other factors requiring the use of literature as a powerful resource in the classroom context.

Teachers are challenged daily with students who do not fit into the curriculum. In a classroom, there are many students with special needs, language differences and with different learning styles. It is in the hands of the readers to make their sources interesting. As such, Literature is an amalgamation of prose, poetry and dramas. Prose text will be used to teach language, vocabulary, phrasal verbs, contemporary issues, theories like psychoanalytical issues, communicative skills which further facilitates to discussion among peer members and most probably reading.

Poems in English Language Teaching

The accomplishment of poetry lessons depends upon on the teacher's level of creativity, enthusiasm, reading aloud with tone variation, a lecdem or with the approaches he/she implements to generate the learner's interest in the poetry. It should be learner-centered so the teachers should make in a way so that they come to know. Poetry can pave the way for the learning and teaching of basic language skills. Most poetry consciously or unconsciously makes use of metaphor as one of its primary methods and it serves as a great source for the students to understand the author's interpretation.

Role of Short Story in Language Teaching

Short fiction is a supreme resource for observing not only language but life itself. In short fiction, characters act out all the real and symbolic acts people carry out in daily lives, and so in a variety of registers and tones. The world of short fiction acts as mirrors and illuminates the human lives.

Role of Drama in Language Teaching

Using dramas in a language classroom is a good resource for language teaching. It is through the use of drama that learners become familiar with grammatical structures in contexts and also learn about how to use the language to express, control and inform. The use of drama raises the student's awareness towards the target language and culture.

In this context, the use of drama as a tool rather than an end gains importance in teaching a foreign language. The language learning should be culture-free that is the context of the drama should fuse into a language learning process with high interest, relevance and enjoyment. Learners should make use of drama to promote their comprehension of life experience, reflect on particular circumstances and make sense of their extra linguistic world in a deeper way.

Role of Novel in Language People

The use of a novel is a beneficial technique of mastering not only linguistic system but also life in relation to the target language. In novel, characters reflect what people really perform in daily lives. Novels not only portray but also enlighten human lives. Using novel in a foreign language class offers the following educational:

- develops the advanced level readers' knowledge about different cultures and different groups of people,
- increases students motivation to read owing to being an authentic material,
- offers real life/real life like settings,
- gives students the opportunity to make use of their creativity,
- improves critical thinking skills,
- paves the way for teaching the target language culture,

- enables students to go beyond what is written and dive into what is meant.

Conclusion

Literature or literary text can bridge, to a large extent, the acute realization of the cultural differences that is eating into our understanding of normal and natural human differences. Literature opens the windows to intercultural awareness while at the same time nurturing empathy, a tolerance for diversity, and the fostering of intelligence. Poetry would go a long way in providing language learners with the expansion of their experience of larger human reality which in turn can shape his language and provide more meaning and richness to it.

It is imperative on the part of the language teacher to provide learners with interesting short stories from the finest treasures of English literature to induce in them a desire to make reading as a habit and develop text reading strategies. Foreign language learners benefit from reading target-language literature because it gives practice in the pragmatic contextualization of linguistic expression.

There is no doubt, a close relationship between educational goals and literary texts that are selected for study. The educationists, therefore, should make an appropriate selection from literature to meet the learner's needs, level, ability and interests at all stages. For example, for the primary pupils, simple verses, sayings, one-act plays and games would be fun for them. Generally, young learners acquire a useful contextualized language and keep by heart simple wisdom, songs, proverbs and short stories. Literary texts can play a vital role in developing language skills among the non-native learners of English and help them to use language for communicative purposes in the real world.

11

Teaching English Language through Literature

A. Babu Rajendra Prasad and *Archana Sharma*

Literature is the mirror of society. Literature from time immemorial has appealed to students of all ages. Literature gives permanent happiness to anyone who reads with diligence and passion. John McRae (1994) makes an earnest attempt to differentiate between classical literature and pulp fiction by using 'L' and 'l' respectively.

Colonization almost came to an end in the late 1940s and 1950s. Once colonization came to an end, Literature of different countries gained prominence. Apart from traditional literature of the U.K. and the U.S.A., literature from other parts of the world captured the imagination of readers. In the earlier times, people were really skeptical to think beyond Shakespeare and Milton. Twenty-first century reflects the changing mindset of people all over the world.

The rise of ELT led to the gradual sidelining of Literature, as focus shifted to functional use of language. The revival of literature is inevitable as students find it hard to decipher the nuances of language in the ELT classroom. Various genres of literature like short stories, poems, novels, plays etc. can be used effectively in the ELT classroom to make learning a joyful experience for students.

Nowadays, one finds the classroom atmosphere really out of sync with the ground reality. Students are crammed inside their classroom from early morning till dusk with emphasis solely on rote learning. Due to immense pressure from higher authorities and peer groups there is a mad rush to complete the syllabus in time, which enables the students to revise and perform well in the examinations. Though this method is highly productive in giving good results, the problem is students are not able to retain anything substantial once the exams get over.

Literature can be taught to students through audio-texts, music CDs, film clips etc. which will help the students to understand the beauty of language without much difficulty. ELT experts lay emphasis on four skills—Listening, Speaking, Reading and Writing. Through Literature, students can be taught all the four skills by paying attention to sentence structures and new vocabulary.

Literature starts in delight but ends in wisdom. In other words, literature not only instructs but also delights. Literature helps students appreciate diverse cultures apart from their own cultures. Certain emotions like anger, greed, love, jealousy etc. are universal. Once the students have absolute control over their emotions, it will help them in their professional lives also. In short, one can say that literature serves a dual purpose. It informs and delights at the same time.

McRae (1994) is of the opinion that literary texts are representational rather than referential. Referential language is very informational and as a result, less appealing. On the other hand, representational language appeals to one's emotions and as a result extremely interesting. Referential language appeals to the imagination of students and makes them empathetic towards the society as a whole.

Rote learning can be replaced by participative learning. Students can be encouraged to participate in skits, one act plays, presentations, etc. once they have a good command over the prescribed literary texts.

Literary texts may be selected based on interest and relevance to students. The level of students should be checked thoroughly before prescribing any literary texts. It is suggested that the texts be slightly shorter so that the students make optimum use of them before the stipulated time. Meticulous planning is necessary to ensure that the learners get literary texts that are culturally appropriate.

Duff and Maley (2007) raise a wide variety of questions to analyze the congruity of suggesting certain literary texts for students. Some of the questions are:

1. Is the material really interesting for the learners?
2. Is the literary style comprehensible?
3. Is it possible to complete the text within the schedule?

Duff and Maley (2007) also propose easy tasks to stimulate the interest of students. One should proceed gradually from easy tasks to difficult tasks. Teachers can completely exploit the material by conducting brainstorming sessions, pre-reading tasks etc. for the benefit of students.

Pulverness (2003) offers valuable advice for teachers to make learning English language a joyful journey. In order to draw the attention of students, teachers are expected to pay a lot of attention to pre-reading tasks, icebreakers etc. Students can be encouraged to modify the texts, change the ending etc. using their creativity, ingenuity etc.

Over the years, teaching language to students has undergone a sea change. Nowadays language is taught to students without the help of literature. English Language Teaching (ELT) gained prominence in India in the last two decades after the rapid mushrooming of Engineering Institutes all over India.

Language teaching is incomplete without literature. The earlier generations had solid foundation in language, because they learnt classics written by literary writers like Shakespeare, Wordsworth etc. Unfortunately, the modern generation does not have any exposure to classics. This severely hampers not only their intellectual growth but also emotional growth.

Technical education is not complete, if one does not pay any attention to values, character building, soft skills etc. All the above mentioned things can be easily and effectively inculcated in students through literature.

Professionalism without human touch is quite ominous. Just a few years back a new course titled "Human Values and

Professional Ethics" (HVPE) was introduced as per the strict instructions of the former Vice Chancellor of UPTU, Prof. Prem Vrat.

Now the question comes in everyone's mind about the outcomes of introducing a new course HVPE. Whether the new course can succeed in fulfilling its objectives is the million dollar question. In this context, literature can first play a supporting role to subjects like Professional Communication, Human Values etc. before taking a full-fledged role to create versatile engineers.

For beginners, classics from Indian Writing in English can be introduced so that they get a peek into the glorious culture and tradition of our motherland. Great writers like R.K. Narayan, Mulkraj Anand, Rabindra Nath Tagore etc. have permanent sway over the readers.

Once the students get a fair idea about the great Indian Writers, it will become easy for them to appreciate the works of literary masters like Sophocles, Euripides, and Aeschylus.

Further, the students should be exposed to literature from commonwealth countries like Canada, Australia, New Zealand etc. This will help them to appreciate the cultures of different countries. Shaping the personality of the student is the need of the hour. Literature will play a pivotal role in this direction if it is inculcated in students right from the beginning.

Berardo (2006) and Wallace (1972) highlight the importance of authenticity to make language learning a beautiful experience. In other words, students find it really fulfilling to read authentic texts instead of the artificial language used in certain sources. Certain factors should be taken into consideration while selecting authentic material in the ELT Classrooms. The factors are as follows:

1. They should have a positive impact on students.
2. They should expose students to real language (language in day-to-day conversation).
3. They should cater to the different needs of the students.

Literary texts will expose students to use the appropriate language according to the situation and condition. Cruz (2010) and Kramsch (1998) speak about the importance of fifth skill that is learning culture apart from the four skills—Listening, Speaking, Reading and Writing. Students will really enjoy learning culture which they firmly believe in and also accepted by society. Care should be taken in selecting appropriate texts which instill the right cultural values in students.

Once the students get good command over the language doing well in campus interviews, group discussions etc. will become a cakewalk. In addition, one can say that time can be saved for students if any extra lecture in the form of career development classes and personality development classes are reduced considerably. There is no doubt that literature will help the learners to get good command over the language. In other words, language is something that has to be caught and not taught. If literature is made part of the curriculum in technical education, language learning will become a really enriching experience for the students.

References

Duff, A. and Maley, A. (2007). *Literature* (Resource Books for Teachers), Oxford University Press.

Maley, A. (2001). "Literature in the language classroom" in *The Cambridge Guide to Teaching ESOL*, Cambridge University Press.

McRae, J. (1994). *Literature with a small 'I'*, Macmillan Education.

Pulverness, A. (2003). *'Literature' in English Teaching Professional*, October, Issue 29, Modern English Publishing

Berardo, S.A. (2006). *The use of authentic materials in the teaching of reading*. The reading matrix.

Wallace, C. (1992). *Reading Oxford*. New York: Oxford University Press.

Cruz, J.H.R. (2010). *The role of literature and culture in English Language Teaching*.

Kramsch, C. (1998). *Language and Culture*. Oxford: Oxford University.

12

Web 2.0: A New Wave of Innovation for Teaching and Learning in ELT

Noor Rizvi

Abstract

The rapid advances in ICT in recent years have resulted in an extensive search for possible uses of ICT in educational settings. Many educators all around the world, including English language teachers, are now taking innovative steps to integrate technology into their teaching environments. In language teaching, language teachers have a wide variety of choices for integrating technology into their classes. One of these is the use of Web 2.0 tools. Although there is no consensus on exactly what Web 2.0 is, the term refers to a second generation of World Wide Web, making it available for people to collaborate and share information online easier. There are hundreds of these tools on the Internet, making it difficult for language teachers to determine the useful ones for language education. The aim of this study was to explore ELT (English Language Teaching) student teachers' perspectives on the use of web 2.0 technologies in language learning contexts. This study is to introduce some of the most useful Web 2.0 tools for teaching English as a foreign language.

Introduction

In recent years, we have witnessed unprecedented advances in ICT. Naturally, these advances have also affected the world of education and the field of language education is no exception. The use of technologies in educational settings has gained popularity. In fact, in comparison with other disciplines in social sciences, language teaching requires the use of technology more. The use of technology in educational settings has certain benefits. It "can increase motivation, decrease anxiety, foster more student-centered activities, provide students with authentic materials and audiences". In other words, educational technology can enrich learning in teaching environments. When considered the field of language education, the potential of new technologies is limitless. In line with the limitless potential of technology for language education, it is generally accepted that the use of technology becoming widespread all over the world has also brought about considerable changes on the part of both students and teachers. It is suggested that "the advancement in technology has been revolutionizing the way educators teach and students".

English language teachers are now taking innovative steps to integrate technology into their teaching environments. Teachers have a wide variety of choices for integrating technology into their classes. One of these choices is the use of Web 2.0 tools. With these tools, if integrated properly into language lessons, teachers can create a more engaging, interactive and motivating learning environment in their lessons.

WEB 2.0

Millions of people have been using the tools that are called Web 2.0. Although there is no consensus on exactly Web 2.0 is, the term refers to a second generation of World Wide Web, making it available for people to collaborate and share information online easier. Actually there are many definitions in the literature defining what Web 2.0 is. However, the definitions can display an extensive variety depending on how you approach Web 2.0. Web 2.0 is "a Web technology that aims to enhance creativity, information sharing and collaboration among users". The key words in this definition creativity, information sharing and collaboration actually represent how they can be used in education, in this case, English language teaching.

Web 2.0 Tools

Materials used in traditional classrooms are mostly static text-based materials. These include main course books, workbooks, lecture notes and handouts. All these materials are to a great extent static in essence and language teachers have the responsibility of bringing interactivity and dynamism into their teaching environments. However, the use of Web 2.0 tools can add interactivity to language teaching and learning environments and materials used in these environments. There have been many studies conducted to explore the use of Web 2.0 tools in language teaching settings. The number of these studies are continuously increasing since educators and scholars have been seeking to investigate different aspects of Web 2.0 tools. However, there is absolutely a need for experimental studies to investigate the use of Web 2.0 tools in language teaching in terms of many aspects. When considered the variety of Web 2.0 tools, the use of these tools mostly depends on the teachers' enthusiasm in integrating technology into their lessons. We believe that, if used appropriately, these tools will have a positive effect on the teaching and learning process.

On the Internet, language teachers can find a great many Web 2.0 tools that can be used in language teaching. These tools as aforementioned can bring dynamism and interactivity to the language teaching and learning environments. If Web 2.0 tools used properly by the teacher in line with the objectives of the language lesson, after a careful planning, it may support the language learning process of the students. The following list includes some of the Web 2.0 tools that can be used in language teaching for various purposes. The tools introduced briefly in this list are based on practical experiment and experience. However, any possible readers of this paper can visit the web page developed in relation with the tools introduced in this paper for practical ideas about using these tools in language learning.

List of Web 2.0 Tools for Language Teaching

www.blendspace.com: Blendspace is a kind of a content curation tool. It is an easy-to-use tools for creating lessons including multimedia elements in a few minutes. It allows teachers to create a lesson by combining a great variety of resources.

www.padlet.com: Padlet, a virtual notice board, can be used in a variety of ways depending on the creativity of the language teacher. Unlike real notice-boards, padlet allows students to post stickies with multimedia elements. Teachers and students can also export "the digital wall" they created in a variety of formats including pdf, image, csv., etc. and share it via social media sites.

scoop.it: Scoop.it is a content curation tool by which you can publish online publications like an online magazine. Language teachers can use this tool in a variety of ways including classroom projects. It is so simple to create a professional-look online magazine.

www.livebinders.com: Livebinders is a tool that is used for compiling internet resources. You can organize them in a variety of formats. Language teachers can determine different web pages and their content in multiple formats in line with the objectives of the lesson. In other words, teachers can prepare a guided tour on the internet related to the subject of the lesson.

google drive (forms, documents): Google drive is a cloud-based storage service for storing all kinds of documents. Teachers can use form and document sections of google drive in a variety of ways. They can create quizzes and lessons including multimedia elements by using google forms. They can also use document section of google drive for collaborative projects.

vialogues.com: Vialogues is a tool for creating a video-based discussion. Language teachers can use this tool to create lessons around video. Teachers can also add polls and quizzes and comment on the video lesson. Students can post comments related with the video.

Voxopop: Voxopop is a web based audio tool that allows users to record their speaking on a given topic. Teachers can use this tool especially for discussions. It is an engaging tool for developing speaking skills of the students using voice recorded answers of them on a given discussion topic. Other students can also listen to the these voice recorded answers of their classmates. It can also contribute to participation of those students who are shy or unwilling to participate in the class discussions.

Lessonwriter: Lessonwriter is a website for creating reading lessons. English language teachers can paste a text that they determine for use in class. This tool automatically generates vocabulary, pronunciation, word roots and grammar support to help students. Exercises and questions related with the given text can also be added. Teachers can also have full control in creating the reading lesson from scratch. Lesson writes also provides a lesson plan to the teacher.

Conclusion

Teachers, especially language teachers, are becoming more and more interested in and enthusiastic about integrating ICT into their teaching environments. Web 2.0 tools can create a more student-centered language learning environment since they allow students to become creators of their own knowledge rather than passive recipients. Language teachers have started to realize that Web 2.0 tools are providing opportunities to enrich and support their students' learning. However, they have to choose the most appropriate ones of these tools, most of which are freely available on the Internet. The tools may become beneficial for teaching a foreign language in the hands of creative and knowledgeable language teachers. It is therefore crucial to raise awareness of language teachers about choosing appropriate Web 2.0 tools and to guide them how to integrate these tools into their own language teaching environments.

Technology does not guarantee success in language learning. We have seen many unsuccessful results in the history of language teaching despite investing so much on equipping language learning environments with highly advanced technological devices in the expectation of success. Again, Web 2.0 tools can not be seen as a magic solution to the challenges encountered by language learners in the process of learning a foreign language. It is clear that, "...the key to successful use of technology in language teaching lies not in hardware or software but in "humanware"—our human capacity as teachers to plan, design and implement effective educational activity". Technology can only become effective and useful in language teaching and learning environments in hands of competent teachers. When it comes considering the use of Web 2.0 in language education, teachers should first decide whether these tools serves to achieve objectives of the language lesson and whether they meet the pedagogical needs of teaching situation. If these two criteria are taken seriously into consideration, Web 2.0 tools can aid to create a more communicative and collaborative language teaching and learning environment.

References

Abdous, M., Camarena, M.M., and Facer, B.R. (2009). MALL technology: Use of academic podcasting in the foreign language classroom. *ReCALL*, 21(1): 76-95. doi:http://dx.doi.org/10.1017/S0958344009000020

Başal, A. (2011). Web Tabanlı Yabancı Dil Oğretiminde Oğrenme Nesneleri: erişi, kalıcılık ve tutumlara etkisi. Unpublished Doctorate Thesis. Elazığ: Fırat Universitesi. Eğitim Bilimleri Enstitüsü.

Chun, D.M., & Plass, J.L. (2000). Networked multimedia environments for second language acquisition. In M. Warshauer and R. Kern (Eds.), *Network-based language teaching: Concepts and practice* (151-70). New York: Cambridge University Press.

Cruz, Y., Boughzala, I., and Assar, S. (2012). Opportunities and obstacles for mobile learning in a business school. International Conference on Communications and Information Technology (ICCIT). doi: 10.1109/ICCITechnol.2012.6285824

Ducate, C.L., and Lomicka, L.L. (2008). Adventures in the blogosphere: From blog readers to blog writers. *Computer Assisted Language Learning*, 21(1): 9-28.

Erben, T. (2013). *Calling All Foreign Language Teachers*. Hoboken: Taylor and Francis.

Jonassen, D. and Reeves, T. (1996). Learning with technology: Using computers as cognitive tools. In D.H. Jonassen (Ed.), *Handbook of research on educational communications and technology* (693-719). New York: Macmillan.

Kartal, E. (2005). Bilişim-İletişim Teknolojileri ve Dil Öğretim Endüstrisi. The Turkish Online Journal of Educational Technology—*TOJET*, 4(4), 82-87.

Kessler, G. (2009). Student-initiated attention to form in wiki-based collaborative writing. *Language Learning and Technology*, 13(1): 79-95.

Means, B. (1994). Using technology to advance educational goals. In B. Means (Ed.), *Technology and education reform: The reality behind the promise* (1-22). San Fransisco: Jossey-Bass Publishers.

O'Bryan, A., and Hegelheimer, V. (2007). Integrating CALL into the classroom: The role of podcasting in an ESL listening strategies course. *ReCALL*, 19(2): 162-80. doi: 10.1017/S0958344007000523

Pinkman, K. (2005). Using blogs in the foreign language classroom: Encouraging learner independence. *The JALT CALL Journal*, 1(1): 12-24.

Seljan, S., Banek, M., Špiranec, S. and Lasić-Lazić, J. (2006). CALL (Computer-Assisted Language Learning) and Distance Learning. Proceedings of the 29th International convention MIPRO 2006. Rijeka, 2006: 145-50.

Travis, P., and Joseph, F. (2009). Improving learners' speaking skills with podcasts. In M. Thomas (Ed.), *Handbook of research on Web 2.0 and second language learning* (313-30). Hershey, PA: Information Science Reference.

Tu, C., Blocher, M. and Ntoruru, J. (2008). Integrate Web 2.0 technology to facilitate online professional community: EMI special editing experiences. Educational Media International, 45(4): 335-41.

Warner, C.N. (2004). It's just a game, right?: Types of play in foreign language CMC. *Language Learning & Technology*, 8(2): 69–67.

Warschauer, M., and Meskill, C. (2000). Technology and second language learning. In J. Rosenthal (Ed.), *Handbook of undergraduate second language education* (303-18). Mahwah, New Jersey:sss

Wells, P., de Lange, P.A., and Fieger, P. (2008). Integrating a virtual learning environment into a second-year accounting course: determinants of overall student perception. *Accounting & Finance*, 48(3): 503-18.

13

Literature: The Indispensable Medium in English Language Teaching

Koel Hazra

Introduction

Language teaching is a process whose aim changes not only from country to country but from individual to individual. The problems faced in teaching foreign languages forced the teachers to find out and develop some new methods and techniques. The use of literature in the ELT classroom is enjoying a revival for a number of reasons. Having formed part of traditional language teaching approaches, literature became less popular when language teaching and learning started to focus on the functional use of language. However, the role of literature in the ELT classroom has been re-assessed and many now view literary texts as providing rich linguistic input, effective stimuli for students to express themselves in other languages and a potential source of learner motivation. In recent years, the role of literature as a basic component and source of authentic texts of the language curriculum rather than an ultimate aim of English instruction has been gaining momentum. Among language educators, there has been a hot debate as to how, when, where, and why literature should be incorporated in ESL/EFL curriculum. Vigorous discussion of how literature and ESL/EFL instruction can work together and interact for the benefit of students and teachers has lead to the flourishment of interesting ideas, learning, and improved instruction for all. Many teachers consider the use of literature in language teaching as an interesting and worthy concern (Sage 1987: 1). In this paper, why a language teacher should use literary texts in the language classroom, what sort of literature language teachers should use with language learners, literature and the teaching of language skills, and benefits of different genres of literature to language teaching will be taken into account. Thus, the place of literature as a tool rather than an end in teaching English as a second or foreign language will be unearthed.

Literature plays an important role in teaching four basic language skills like reading, writing, listening and speaking. However, when using literature in the language classroom, skills should never be taught in isolation but in an integrated way. Teachers should try to teach basic language skills as an integral part of oral and written language use, as part of the means for creating both referential and interactional meaning, not merely as an aspect of the oral and written production of words, phrases and sentences.

Literature and language are closely related and this is a fact none can deny. Literature is constituted by language and it represents one of the most recurrent uses of language. Language and linguistic analysis can also be employed to access literature from the learner's point of view. Brumfit and Carter (1986: 1) already emphasized the role of literature as "an ally of language". This technique is by no means novel, since literature has been a widely used teaching tool in different language teaching methods. However, here the perspective changes giving more relevance to the literary text as a work of art. First of all, let us go over the changing role of literature in the tradition of second language teaching to end with an account of its current situation within the communicative approach. In the grammar translation method, literature was the central component. Literary texts of the target language were read and translated, used as examples of good writing and "illustrations of the grammatical rules" (Duff and Maley 1990: 3). The focus of this teaching method was on form, on learning the rules of grammar and the lexical items as they appeared in the text. There was no literary interest, nor interest on content. After this method fell in disuse, literary texts also went forgotten for teachers of second languages.

For the structural approaches to language teaching, literature was discredited as a tool, because it represented the old tradition. The functional-notional method ignored literature, because in this method the importance lies on communication and they present authentic language samples. Literature was not considered either to have a communicative function or to be authentic example of language use. Nonetheless, in the last decade or so the interest in literature as one of the most valuable language teaching resources available has revived remarkably (Duff and Maley 1990: 3). This is in consonance with the new currents within the communicative approach that see in reading literature the perfect realization of their principles, namely developing communicative competence, that is teaching learners to communicate in the second language and accounting for real, authentic communicative situations (Sanz and Fernández 1997). Literature reading is, no doubt, a communicative activity and literary texts are, who could nowadays deny such thing, authentic examples of language use. Many authors, among them Brumfit and Carter (1986) and Lazar (1993), reject the idea of the existence of a specific literary language and claim that the language used in literary texts is common language with a high concentration of linguistic features like metaphors, similes, poetic lexis, unusual syntactic patterns, etc. (see Lazar 1993: 7 for a more detailed account of the characteristics of the literary use of language). These are not literature specific since these features also appear in ordinary language use and also in nursery rhymes, proverbs or publicity slogans, just to cite a few examples, however, in literature these show a higher incidence. We talk therefore, of a literary use of language.

Literature plays an important role in the English programs of many non-English speaking countries. However, there are some problems encountered by language teachers within the area of teaching English through literature. First, there are very few pedagogically-designed appropriate materials that can be used by language teachers in a language classroom. Second, there is a lack of preparation in the area of literature teaching in TESL/TEFL programs. Third, there is the absence of clear-cut objectives defining the role of literature in ESL/EFL. Many instructors try to include literature in their classroom, but lack the background and training in that field.

The teacher has an important role in teaching English through literature. First, he should determine the aim of language teaching in relation to the needs and expectations of the students. Giving a questionnaire or interviewing with the students orally, the teacher can set up the aim and the objectives of the language teaching. Second, he should select the appropriate language teaching method, teaching techniques, and classroom activities. Then, the teacher should select the literary texts relevant to the aim and the objectives of his teaching. While selecting literary texts to be used in language classroom, the students' language proficiency, interests, age, sex, etc. should be taken into account in order not to bore students with inappropriate materials. At elementary levels, for example, students should be given simplified or specially written stories. At advanced levels, however, students are given literature in its original form so that they can develop their literary competence in the target language. To put it another way, students learn practically the figurative and daily use of the target language in the literary texts and encounter different genres of literature (i.e. poems, short stories, plays, etc.) at advanced levels. Observing how characters in a play or a short story use figures of speech, such as simile, metaphor, metonymy, etc. so as to express their communicative intention, students learn how to write English more clearly, creatively, and powerfully.

References

Brumfit, C.J. and A.C. Ronald. eds. *Literature and Language Teaching*. Oxford: Oxford University Press, 1986.

Carter, R. and M. Long, eds. *Teaching Literature*. London: Longman, 1991.

Duff, A. and A. Maley. *Literature*. Oxford: Oxford University Press, 1990.

Lazar, G. *Literature and Language Teaching*. Cambridge: Cambridge University Press. 1993.

Sage, H. *Incorporating Literature in ESL Instruction*. New Jersey: Prentice-Hall, Inc. 1987.

Sanz, M., and C. Fernandez. *Principios Metodológicos de los Enfoques Comunicativos*. Madrid: Fundación Antonio Nebrija, 1997.

14

'Teaching Unplugged': Learning 'their' Way and Setting Standards

Yogita Bhamare

Abstract

Using a language is the best method of learning it. However, the real challenge for educators today is getting learners to carry over their classroom learning from controlled practice to spontaneous real-life use of it. The traditional way of teaching may fall short in attaining this aim. However, combined with Dogme ELT, this aim could be achieved. This paper is based on the presenter's 10 years of experience in teaching international students from 25 different countries at ELTIS, Pune, using various pedagogical methodologies. The presenter intends to throw some light on her use of the Dogme ELT approach in language teaching at ELTIS. The presenter will also share her original, collaborative tasks that involve learners in using and enhancing both, their linguistic and technological quotient. The paper focuses on how Dogme ELT puts the learner back at the centre of the language learning process in the real sense.

Keywords: Traditional Teaching, Trends, Dogme ELT, Technology in Classrooms, Collaborative Tasks, Learner-centric Approach.

New Teaching Trends

Teaching English as a foreign language can no more be accomplished by a typical chalk and talk method. In the age of digital technology, language teaching has also adopted new trends and pedagogies. Every now and then there have been additions to language teaching resources both, through printed references books or in the form of ICT. Online learning resources open a brand new chapter in what is referred to as "edutainment".

To explain this further I would like to cite examples of new mobile apps.

The idea of spaced repetition is a catchphrase at the moment. In 1885 Hermann Ebbinghaus carried out an experiment to measure how quickly we forget. He discovered that, unless new information is reinforced, we quickly forget what we have learned. Based on his findings, there are many language learning apps such as Lingopolis which uses the principles of spaced repetition. It is a ground-breaking combination of a computer game and an English learning application. It is a kind of learning process that takes you from the basic up to the proficiency level, without making you yawn once.

The real challenge for educators today is getting learners to carry over their classroom learning from controlled practice to spontaneous real-life use of it. Digitalisation has made it possible as it is connecting learners with the outside world.

Students these days are more tech savvy and have access to an incredible amount of English-language material online. Although it is beneficial for them, it can be a bit overpowering. Students do not always know where to get access for the most appropriate material and what to choose to suit their needs of language learning.

On the other hand, teachers need to put in extra time to find, select and prepare materials themselves which can be off-putting.

To solve such problems, sites like Easier English Wiki and Newsmart have found out a golden mean which provides teachers as well as students with free materials based on articles from New International magazines. At the moment, there are users from more than 96 countries improving their English Grammar and language skills using these apps.

Web tools and unprecedented access to authentic materials online mean teachers can create courses tailored to the specific needs and interests of their students.

But not all the latest trends rely on technology. A very noticeable trend is towards more creativity in the classroom. This probably started with Ken Robinson's talk, 'How Schools Kill Creativity'. After viewing and inspired by it, educators have definitely brought creativity back to the forefront of teaching and materials design.

21st Century Skills and Best Teaching Practices

What students need to be taught today is 21st century skills. Students, along with Grammar and the Language Skills, should be equipped with 21st century skills. These are the skills that are thought to be of particular importance in today's world, for example, critical thinking, problem-solving and collaboration.

These 21st century skills are useful but less often they are taught in the classroom. In a world where people are unlikely to stay in the same job for life, and interpreting and using information is becoming more important than memorising it, the emphasis on such skills needs to be greater. The greatest challenge for the educators today is retaining the interest of the students in the classroom, making the classes more and more interactive brining in various language techniques and methodologies and yet to complete the syllabus. No wonder then, the 21st century (essential) skills get a back-seat in many schools and educational Institutes.

At ELTIS (English Language Teaching Institute of Symbiosis), Pune, we have successfully integrated these 21st century (essential) skills with the teaching of Grammar and other Language Skills by adopting Dogme ELT approach. Teaching style at ELTIS has always been quite 'Dogme-esque' and eclectic.

What is Dogme ELT?

Dogme ELT is (in the 'post-method' era) not so much a methodology, but rather it is seen as an approach or a movement. Fundamentally, it is an authentic approach which encourages conversational communication between learners and teacher, without the use of published materials and other teaching aids. In other words, Dogme puts the learner back at the centre of the language learning process.

Dogme ELT has its roots in Communicative Language Learning, but can also be compared with TBL i.e. Task-Based Learning (Meddings and Thornbury, 2009).

Dogme ELT has taken its name from Dogme 95, a Danish film movement associated with Lars von Trier. The intention of the movement was to do away with cinema of an obsession with technique and enslavement to technology. They wanted to create films using minimal means but for maximum effect (Thornbury 2006).

The Dogme ELT movement was born out of an article and subsequent online discussion group, initiated by an internationally recognized academic, teacher trainer and author Scott Thornbury. The Dogme ELT movement provided a forum where teachers who wished to liberate themselves from an overdependency on materials and technology could ponder upon their beliefs (Meddings and Thornbury 2009).

How Dogme ELT Functions

During their initial debate, ten key principles come forward, each with a key word.

These principles, laid out by Meddings and Thornbury (2009) exemplify a Dogme approach, which later on, were formed into '*vows of chastity*':

1. Teaching should be done using only the resources the teachers and the students bring to the classroom—i.e. themselves—and whatever happens to be in the classroom.
2. No recorded listening material should be introduced into the classroom: the source of all listening activities should be the students and the teacher themselves.
3. The teacher must sit down at all times that the students are seated.
4. All the teacher's questions must be real questions not display questions; such as 'What's the past of the verb to go?'
5. Slavish adherence to a method is unacceptable.

6. A pre-planned syllabus of pre-selected and graded grammar items is forbidden. Any grammar that is the focus of instruction should emerge from the lesson context, not dictate it.
7. Topics that are generated by the students themselves must be given priority over any other input.
8. Grading of students into different levels is disallowed: students should be free to join the class they feel most comfortable in.
9. The criteria and administration of any testing procedures must be negotiated with the learners.
10. Teachers themselves will be evaluated according to only one criterion: that they are not boring.

Dogme ELT and Its Core Concepts

These vows of chastity can be further thought of in terms of three core precepts:

Dogme is about teaching that is:

- Conversation-driven: students' language needs and their interests take the place of materials containing prescribed language points which are delivered by the teacher.
- Focuses on emergent language: grammar and vocabulary work arise naturally during the lesson, but do not drive the lesson.
- Materials-light: classroom becomes a no-go zone for the English language textbook.

Meddings and Thornbury (2009) go on to describe these stand-out precepts for teaching 'unplugged' in more detail:

1. Conversation driven. Conversation is the fundamental form of a language. However, many a time it is viewed as a product of learning which is often left for the end—after the teaching of grammar or sometimes it is even neglected. What happens generally in the classroom is communication, which focuses on transactional tasks whilst conversation focuses on interactional tasks i.e. discourse.

Discourse is the use of language to fulfill the specific needs of its users in specific contexts. Real-life language use happens as discourses that apply larger parts of language. Dogme takes such an approach.

Classroom talk that replicates natural conversation is more effective than traditional classroom talk which is teacher initiated. This concept is central to the Dogme approach.

Conversation promotes socialization. A conversational mode of classroom talk would better establish a 'discourse community', and that is why Dogme views conversation as a means of language learning, not just an end.

2. Materials light. Many educationalists do not support Dogme ELT because of its "no go zone" rule for course-books in the classroom. However, the Dogme approach is not anti-materials or anti-technology as such, but it rather rejects the kind of materials that do not conform to the ideas mentioned in the vows of chastity. Traditional course-books serve up what Thornbury calls 'Grammar Mcnuggets', i.e. pre-graded and pre-selected items, with no concern for learner needs or relevance. However, the use of authentic materials in the language teaching is what the real Dogme ELT would mean.

3. Focus on emergent language. Dogme-skeptics mentioned that the approach lacks structure, and is unable to cover items on a syllabus, and are concerned that students will not learn anything. However, advocates of Dogme argue that language is not fixed, but is dynamic; it evolves and changes. They also affirm that learning is an emergent process, driven by exposure and use. They assert that if learners are given opportunities to use language, their inherent learning abilities will be activated, and language will emerge rather than be acquired. This principle is echoed by the work of Steve Krashen's comprehensible input model, where learning "takes care of itself" (Krashen 1985). The Dogme view is that grammar and lexis syllabi should emerge, and not predict learner needs, but to respond to them (Ryan Smith, Delta Module 2 Essay).

How ELTIS Makes use of Dogme ELT

Teacher creativity is nothing new. Good teachers have always found inventive ways to make learning come alive and open opportunities for their students.

ELTIS has been into the field of teaching languages for 42 years and we have been following a balanced approach to language teaching which is greatly inspired by Dogme ELT.

At ELTIS, it has been possible to adapt such an approach because ELTIS is a language institute and here the main objective is to prepare the learner to be able to use languages effectively in the real world. We have mixed ability classes consisting of students from more than 25 different countries.

Core Concepts of Dogme ELT and Teaching at ELTIS

ELTIS aims more on producing a fair user of language than covering the syllabi.

In a way, as an ELTIS teacher, I am fortunate to be able to use a blended and at times eclectic approach in language teaching. Students coming from different parts of the world have different learning habits. To suit their language needs and to fulfill the requirements of mixed ability classes, we need to blend various language teaching approaches. Taking Dogme ELT as the base, it is easier to adapt and blend various language pedagogies.

At ELTIS, we do have prescribed course-books for different courses. However, theme based teaching is the main focus. We do not aim to complete the course-books but to fulfill the set level-wise learning objectives. Mostly the course books act as reference books for the teachers and/or workbooks for the students.

Activity-based teaching is the USP of ELTIS where there is very little room for chalk and talk method. The language activities used in classrooms are mostly produced and developed by the teachers. We make an extensive use of audio-visual aids and the internet and computer technology (ICT) in our regular classroom teaching.

Teaching plan at ELTIS focuses on conversation between the teacher and the students and between students and students rather than communication between the teacher and the students.

For example: Simple Present Tense is taught by striking up a conversation between the teacher and the students and later between students and students. The teacher may start talking about her daily routine stressing the verbs and ask students to talk about theirs. She may further ask the students to talk about the daily routine of their parents, best friend, school bus driver, etc. She does not correct the students but asks other students to correct if there is any mistake in verbs.

To add more fun to it, the teacher can make 4 groups, assigning each one profession, such as, doctors, traffic police, sports persons and actors and ask them to imagine and speak about their daily routine.

Students may come up with role plays as to whose life is more interesting/more tiring as an additional activity to daily routine.

Here, conversation takes place first and then the structure is taught to the students. In fact, students themselves learn the structure of Simple Present Tense.

Another effective way to teach language is movie or film segments. Everyone likes to watch movie, then why not exploit it as a language teaching aid? Careful selection of movies and segmenting them as per the (language teaching) needs works wonders in the classroom.

I have used the movie "The Pursuit of Happyness" in my language classroom at different levels. This movie can be used to teach almost all grammatical aspects.

I segmented the movie in 7 to 8 parts. After teaching the students Simple Past and Past Continuous, I use one of these segments, as a reinforcement activity (where the protagonist, Chris Gardener, has to take care of his son when his wife leaves him). Students understand and memorise the structure of Simple Past Continuous. However, after watching this segment they definitely understand how to use the tenses in language and it happens effortlessly as movies are close to their hearts.

Similarly to develop the listening ability, they need a great deal of exposure to spoken language and ample practice in various listening situations. However, in addition to exposure and practice, it is vitally important for the listener to become engaged in the process of listening and develop a desire to comprehend. And what could be the best way to engage the students in this process but music and songs in particular?

While teaching them Parts of Speech, I used a beautiful song by Pixar, "Remember When". Without telling the students the teaching plan, I just made them listen to the audio of the song. Then I played the video of it where the lyrics of the songs were shown.

As a post listening activity, I distributed a worksheet of the printed lyrics of the song. The students were asked to fill in the missing words. In each stanza I had intentionally omitted words like nouns, adjectives, adverbs etc.

After they filled in the missing words we had a discussion on the words and their relation with the particular line. This way they learnt nouns, adjectives and other parts of speech with the help of the song.

Later on, I explained the parts in more details. I could sustain students' interest and attention successfully by using song to teach a grammar unit which otherwise students find boring.

I do not need to bring in any pre-recorded material to my class where an authentic material like a song serves my purpose.

Teaching adult learners is a challenging, demanding job, and we need to find pleasure in our work to be at our best in the classroom. Movement, songs, and stories can really help our students learn, and what's even better, we can all have fun along the way. These activities create situations where learners are completely focused and well-behaved, work with purpose, and learn enthusiastically.

We are currently experiencing a renaissance of digital technology. Thanks to the ubiquity of smart phones, we now actually can bring people closer, message and chat with them from anywhere, anytime. And resourceful educators are finding ways to use this device (which is otherwise used as a phone) in the classroom to engage their students.

On an average, every second student possesses a smart phone at ELTIS. Their life seems to be in their palm. They have everything in it they could have had on computer. I do not need to say much about students and smart phone addiction. Why not make a smart use of their smart phones to teach language?

With the changing trends, ELTIS is now helping the developers of a Mobile App which will help students chat with their tutors from wherever they are. This app is basically designed to help students with their speaking deficiencies which would be helpful to them at an individual level.

Conclusion

It is interesting to see how these kinds of lessons are accepted with different group dynamics, different learning styles and even one to one teaching. However, it might not be very practical and in some cases it might be unsuitable to abandon materials and other aids entirely. In fact, it would be difficult to do so in certain situations, e.g., examination courses or other ESP groups.

Additionally, at ELTIS, we try and use interesting and authentic texts in the classroom. ELTIS teaching style has always been quite 'Dogme-esque' and eclectic. Hence we, as innovative teachers pick and choose the best and most interesting aspects of the approach and add it to our own teaching repertoire, such as the strong focus on emergent language.

Here are just a few points which we need to take care of. These points are known, and used, by many educators:

- Check for understanding often and in a variety of ways.
- If you do not have a well-thought-out plan for your students, they will have one for you.
- Set up the next activity while students are completing the current one—this makes for a smooth and speedy transition with little to no downtime.

- Design the end goals and end product first (also known as backward planning).
- Share models with students of the product or outcome you want them to create or design—and also continually model in your own behaviour how you want them to act and treat each other.

At ELTIS every student is different with varied needs and learning styles and backgrounds and ELTIS teaching philosophy sits well with the key principles of Dogme, i.e. student-centered, authentic and conversation-driven.

As for the 'vows of chastity', we select what suits best for us. As Vow number 5 clearly states:

"Slavish adherence to a method…is unacceptable!"

References

Thornbury, S., and Meddings, L. (2009). "Teaching Unplugged: Dogme in English Language Teaching", DELTA Publishing.

Thornbury, S. (2010). *Doing a Dogme Lesson*. http://www.youtube.com/watch?v=C5ZPlrMajDA.

Thornbury, S. (Feb/March 2000). *A Dogma for ELF, IATEFL*, Issues 153.

Webliography

https://playlingo.co/games/lingopolis/

https://olivegreenthemovie.com/about/en/

https://www.getnewsmart.com/

http://eewiki.newint.org/index.php/Main_Page

http://product.pearsonelt.com/speakout/

15

Bilingual Approach in Teaching English to Students of Hindi Medium Background: An Analysis

Gopal Krishna Dwivedi

Abstract

Students of 'Hindi medium background' denotes many things. It denotes that their family members and they themselves might not have been comfortable with English since childhood. It denotes that they did not get that exposure to English which the students of English medium or convent schools provide to their students. And when any such student of Hindi medium or any other regional language background becomes adult and looks for job options, he immediately realizes that his poor command over English is the biggest barrier between him and the good job, good salary, good life and good future. It saying "English is a funny language" is an outdated joke now because practically everybody knows that English may open the doors to the treasures of the world. Most of the corporate jobs and urban lifestyle demand good command over English communication, written and oral both. Every year thousands of students from rural or semi-rural areas move towards cities and get admission in various professional courses on the basis of their academic performance but at the same time many of them are not comfortable with English, neither in understanding nor in speaking nor in writing. They still do well in academics but their poor English communication hinders their placement and progress after the completion of the course. This paper discusses and analyzes the practical measures that could help the students of Hindi medium background improve their English communication, written and oral both.

Keywords: Spoken English, Easy English, English Conversation, Conversational English, Communication Skills, Effective Communication, English Language, English for Hindi Medium Students.

Introduction

Over a period of time English has evolved as the means to a good career, global exposure and prosperity. Be it operating a cell phone, computer and video games or be it reading the user's manual of various products, understanding the instructions and the content given in English becomes essential. Most of the people we meet everyday are either already good at English Conversation or have a deep desire to be so. During my 12 years' career as English teacher, I have across with many students of Hindi medium background who have the similar wish and through my interrogation and observation, I realized that many of them were living with myths or fantasies which did not let their dream of speaking English fluently come true. In this article, I have made some very original and effective suggestions on the basis of my experience, observation and learning.

Bilingual Approach in Teaching English

English can be learnt through three methods in my opinion. The first method is exposure to English speaking environment. If most of the teachers, classmates, neighbours or parents speak English most of the time, the learner picks it up very quickly and through his/her observation like a child, he/she develops a good learning.

The second method is self-learning which requires high self-motivation and dedication. When somebody decides to learn English at any cost, he devotes himself completely to the task and explores various resources like internet, books, CDs, Newspaper etc. This also helps to some extent although the number of such successful learners remains very small.

The third and the most common method of learning English is through coaching and classroom teaching. This is a measurable and effective method which could bring desired results in the given time frames provided the student also has the real interest and desire. Since this method is the most effective and the most common method, the instructor should ensure that the instructions and examples given are very well understood by the students. If the student does not understand English at all, the teacher must get bilingual. The instructions and suggestions must be made in English and in the language of the student also. If the instructions are made only in English which he/she does not understand, it'll not bring the desired learning and result. The briefings should always be followed by detailed activities in which the students get enough chance for practicing spoken and written English.

Bilingual Approach in Learning English

We have seen that a broken down vehicle is first pushed by someone and then it starts and runs on its own. We have seen the process of kite flying also in which initially a partner holds the kite, pulls and throws it up towards the sky and soon the flyer manages the kite well flying it higher and higher. Similarly, there will be some situations where a beginner gets stuck and does not find an appropriate substitute of the word of his mother tongue. In such cases, one should not remain stuck in recalling the right word rather he should go ahead by using the word of his mother tongue in-between. Supposing Hindi is the mother tongue and one forgets the English of 'Aakaash'. He should continue speaking saying "I was looking towards 'aakaash' and a drop of water fell on my face." This way he can maintain the flow of his expression and save himself from the embarrassment of getting stuck. Later he can consult a friend or a dictionary to find out the right words.

Excuses Never Help

I have come across hundreds of such students who waste their precious years with the excuse or confusion, saying that— "I shall start speaking English once I know a little bit of it. Speaking wrong English will make me a butt of ridicule". This is similar to a scene where a beginner stands at the swimming pool and says "I shall go into the swimming pool once I know a bit of swimming because otherwise it may be risky." Isn't it funny? How will he learn a bit or more of swimming without going into the swimming pool? Similarly, how will and how can one learn English speaking without making a start.

Mirror-Practice Does Not Help

One hour daily practice is a must and that also with someone else, not with the self. Practicing with the other helps psychologically too. Many beginners experience that they are more fluent when they speak to themselves but they get stuck or start stammering as they start talking to others. Some students report that they are more fluent in talking to another beginner but they are less fluent while talking to someone who has very good command over English. Therefore, one hour daily practice means one hour daily conversation with someone else, not with the self. Practicing before the mirror is equal to practicing with the self.

Traditional Approaches Do Not Help Much

No matter how many CDs or books of standard English Course one has, no matter how famous coaching classes one joins, still he cannot fulfill his desire of speaking English fluently until he has a routine of practicing for at least one hour daily. CDs, Books and Coaching may give knowledge but they fail to give the practical exposure and confidence required for speaking English fluently. Therefore, practicing for at least one hour daily has no substitute.

It Can Start Even with Wrong English

Initially a beginner or learner should not bother if he is speaking right English or wrong English. He should just start. By and by he will get aware and familiar with the correct words and the rules of correct English which will automatically improve and purify his language. Initial focus on correct grammar often results in discouragement and disinterest. This is similar to an example where a lady working in the kitchen initially takes 'daal' (pulse) in a plate. Later she keeps on finding the impurities into it and finally pure 'daal' is left at the end. Similarly, a learner may start with wrong English even, later he will reach the desired destination of speaking correct English.

Comics and Children's Story Books Give A Good Start

Let's have an example of a doctor and a patient. Initially the doctor advises a patient to take only the upper layer of a *Chapati*. Later he allows the whole *Chapati*, followed by curry and *Chapati* and finally *Parantha, Puri* or other oily stuff. If the patient ignores the advice and takes *Puri* or oily stuff as his first diet, he is not able to digest it properly and becomes sick again. Similarly, those who are struggling with English communication should make a fresh start with the English comics and the English storybooks meant for children. Since they are prepared for children, they consist of beautiful pictures or cartoons. These pictures and cartoons facilitate easy comprehension and help the learners a lot. Since these books are written for children, most of the words used are carefully chosen and simple ones. Therefore, the learners of English not only enjoy these stories but also improve their vocabulary and confidence. No matter how learned we are, whenever we pick any children's book either a course book or a storybook, we always find some new words not known to us earlier.

Initial Focus Should Not be on Grammar

Initially a beginner should focus only on what he wishes to speak or share. He should not bother about the rules of correct grammar. For example when a learner of English is telling his friend how he reached the college, he should only think about how he had his breakfast, bid goodbye to his parents, caught a bus and reached the college. He should not think if he should use the first form of the verb or the third, whether he should use did will come or done. While speaking one should avoid thinking of grammar. Later he can make a replay of the conversation and make corrections in mind that will help him speak more correct English next time.

School Level Grammar Books Are of Great Help

Many beginners carry a myth in their minds that most of the fluent speakers of English speak grammatically wrong English, they just have flow, style and confidence. But the reality is—most of the good speakers of English, politicians or professionals, mostly speak correct English. But no one learns the rules of correct grammar overnight. This comes by and by and may take years. For understanding the rules of grammar, grammar books of class 10th and 12th are highly useful as they are written for young students so they are simple and carry enough examples and exercises. For non-English medium students, State Board's English grammar books of 10th and 12th class are most suitable and really paying. Later they can switch to more standard grammar books.

Sentence Can Work Like a Formula

A beginner who does not know enough grammar should consider each correct sentence as a formula for constructing many other similar sentences. For example—a student listens to his English teacher saying 'nothing can be done' (meaning: *kuchh nahi kiya ja sakta*). He can use this sentence as a formula (nothing + can + be + verb III) for constructing many other similar sentences like—nothing can be told, nothing can be seen, nothing can be calculated, nothing can be asked, nothing can be guessed, etc.

Sugar-coat Grammar

Whoever teaches or trains people struggling with English, should not start with the difficult usage and structures of grammar. Rather he/she should start with simple usage and words of English like It, There, May, Might, Can, Could, Should, Would giving examples from day-to-day usage. Teaching grammar without calling it grammar does not scare the learners and maintains their confidence and interest.

Reading Newspaper Differently

Over-excited or over-confident candidates subscribe to the English newspaper with the notion and expectation that it'll improve both their vocabulary and communication that too in a very short span of time. But on the contrary, most of them feel extremely low and discouraged after the first few days of the subscription. The news items and articles in such newspapers are mostly written by the editors and the authors who have been working with English for years. In the course of time, many difficult and standard words just creep in as a regular part of their expression. Beginners from rural background are unfamiliar with many such words. Hence, they get stuck even in the first few pages of the same issue of the English newspaper. They consult the dictionary repeatedly and after spending hours on the venture, they find that 20-30 pages are still left unread and the next day another issue of the newspaper pops into their shivering hands.

Subscribing English newspaper is ok but the reading style has to be different. I would suggest the beginners two simple steps for reading English newspaper. The first step is to consult the dictionary only for the difficult words appearing on the front page of the newspaper. Rest all difficult words of the same issue should be ignored as the mind too has a limit to retain. Cramming of words does not help as we start forgetting them soon.

The second step is to read the headlines only. Reading full body of each and every news item should be avoided. If required, punch-lines or additional bullets can be read. Thus, the reading of newspaper becomes speedy resulting in improved interest and enthusiasm. If some news item is really important or interesting, the reader will automatically feel compelled to read it full because of his interest in the story.

What Else Helps

Short speeches on simple topics like My Mother, My Father, My Best Friend, My Daily Routine, My School Days and My Favourite Movie help a lot. Such speech competitions can be organized in the hostels, clubs or the neighbourhood. They help a lot in various ways. Besides, watching Hindi news bulletin on TV followed by English news bulletin improves our vocabulary and grammar both. Global updates are an additional benefit. Watching English movies with subtitles in the mother tongue is also helps a lot. Keep a good full size dictionary at hand so that you can consult it more often. Verifying meanings of the unfamiliar and not so familiar words in the dictionary makes us exact and confident.

Conclusion

Thus a bilingual approach blended with affection, hard work and sincerity definitely brings the desired learning and the students of Hindi medium background or of any other regional language background start gaining the confidence and the skill of communication in English effectively. The prerequisites for the purpose include—will power, a good companion and a practice of one hour daily. Out of my twelve years experience of teaching and training, I can assure that if the aforementioned suggestions are properly followed, we start noticing the difference in just one month. After three months, the candidate starts feeling really confident and after six months of regular practice, he becomes a comfortable communicator in English.

References

Dhanavel, S.P. (2012). *English Language Teaching: India The Shifting Paradigms,* New Delhi: Tata McGraw Hill Education Private Limited.

Cook, Vivian, *Second Language Learning and Language Teaching.* London: Arnold.

16

The Status of Implementation and Use of Lesson Plan in English Language Teaching in Schools

Purnima Tiwari

Abstract

English as a language has great reach and influence; it is taught all over the world. But English teaching in India still remains a challenge. English is taught just to secure marks or to pass out. So the language ability of the students is something one needs to focus on and improve. At this stage, proper planning of lessons to be taught is essential, because every time a lesson is planned and taught, teachers can evaluate the plan, identify the parts that went well and those which were less effective and thereby improve upon the plan. A well developed lesson plan reflects the interests and needs of student. The present study attempts to identify the different factors that cause problem in the implementation of lesson plan and it also tries to know the strategies being used by English Teachers in classroom teaching.

Introduction

Background and Rationale of the Study

In a multilingual, multicultural country like India English Education assumes a unique place. In fact all education begins with language and English language is central to the whole process of education. It is therefore, essential that language teaching should be done systematically so that learners understand and grasp properly whatever is taught to them in class. But there are several problems with teaching English at the school level. Besides the problems inherent in foreign language learning there are certain unfavorable conditions which prevent effective teaching and learning in Indian schools.

Need and Significance of the Study

In our country English is important for a number of reasons. India is a land of diversity. Different people speak different languages but they can communicate with one another with the help of English. Secondly, all advanced knowledge in science, technology and medicine is available in English. The results of the latest researches come to India through the medium of English. Today the world has become one family. It is all due to English. English is an international language. English is the language of the Constitution, the Supreme Court, the High Courts and official departments. English is now firmly rooted in the soil of India. It has become a part of Indian life. Thus English has great importance for the integrity of India and for the better development of the country.

Therefore teaching of English has become compulsory. The current status of English has turned a significant percentage of the world's population into part-time users or learners of English.

Now-a-days the students face a lot of difficulties in learning English, so there should be a pilot study to assess the feasibility of implementing remedial measures and the problems in implementation, only then would it be possible to implement these measures. There is an urgent need to study the status of implementation and the use of lesson plan in regular English language teaching in schools, so as to identify the lacunas in English language teaching to a certain extent.

What Should go into an English Language Lesson?

Every lesson and class is different. The content depends on what the teacher wants to achieve in the lesson. However it is possible to make some generalizations. Students who are interested in, involved in and enjoy what they are studying tend to make better progress and learn faster.

When thinking about an English lesson it is useful therefore to keep the following three elements in mind—Engage-Study-Activate.

Engage: This means getting the students interested in the class. Engaging students is important for the learning process.

Study: Every lesson usually needs to have some kind of language focus. The study element of a lesson could be a focus on any aspect of the language, such as grammar or vocabulary and pronunciation. A study stage could also cover revision and extension of previously taught material.

Activate: Telling students about the language is not really enough to help them learn it. For students to develop their use of English they need to have a chance to produce it. In an activate stage the students are given tasks which require them to use not only the language they are studying that day, but also other language that they have learnt.

What is a Lesson Plan?

A lesson plan is a teacher's detailed description of the course of instruction for one class. It can be said that a lesson plan is a framework for a lesson. If you imagine a lesson is like a journey, then the lesson plan is the map. It shows you where you start, where you finish and the route to take to get there. A daily lesson plan is developed by a teacher to guide class instruction. Essentially the lesson plan sets out what the teacher hopes to achieve over the course of the lesson and how he or she hopes to achieve it. New or inexperienced teachers may want to or be required to produce very detailed plans—showing clearly what is happening at any particular time in the lesson. As teachers gain experience and confidence planning is just as important but teachers develop the ability to plan more quickly and very experienced teachers may be able to go into class with just a short-list of notes or even with the plan in their heads.

Whatever the level of experience, it is important that all teachers take time to think through their lessons before they enter the classroom.

Why is Planning Important?

One of the most important reasons to plan is that the teacher needs to identify his or her aims for the lesson. One major explanation is that when a plan is ready, teachers can focus on its implementation. When teachers do not have to think so much about what they need to do next, they are able to focus on other parts of the lesson. Here are some more reasons which indicate why planning is important:

Clarity. Lesson plans help to be clear about what you want to teach. Teachers need to make wise decisions about the strategies and methods they will employ to help students move systematically toward learner goals.

Unpredictable Events. Lesson plans may also include a room for unpredictable events. This helps teachers to be ready to cope with whatever happens.

Framework. Lesson plans give your teaching a framework, an overall shape.

Reminder. Lesson plans may also play the role of a reminder for teachers when they get distracted.

Commitment. It suggests a level of professionalism and real commitment.

What are the Principles of Planning?

Aims—considering realistic goals for the lesson, not too easy but not too difficult. You may find the following checklist useful:

(a) What do the students know already?

(b) What do the students need to know?

(c) What did you do with the students in the previous class?

(d) How well do the class work together?

(e) How motivated are the students?

Variety—an important way of getting and keeping the students engaged and interested.

Flexibility—expect the unexpected! Things don't always go according to plan in most lessons. Experienced teachers have the ability to cope when things go wrong. It's useful when planning to build in some extra and alternative tasks and exercises. Also teachers need to be aware of what is happening in the classroom. Students may raise an interesting point and discussions could provide unexpected opportunities for language work and practice. In these cases it can be appropriate to branch away from the plan.

In addition to the above reasons, it is worthwhile mentioning that lesson plans will have positive impact on both the teacher and the learner.

For the teacher—

(a) They don't have to think on their feet. They don't lose face in front of their learners.

(b) They are clear on the procedure to follow.

(c) They build on previous teaching and prepare for coming lessons.

For the learner—

(a) They realize that the teacher cares for their learning.

(b) They attend a structured lesson: easier to assimilate.

(c) They appreciate their teacher's work as a model of well-organized work to imitate.

Implementing the Plan

Implementing the lesson plan is the most important (and difficult) phase of the daily lesson planning cycle. In this phase, the lesson plan itself will retreat into the background as the reality of the class takes over. As many experienced teachers know, it is easy to get sidetracked by the unplanned events. However, teachers should remember that the original plan was designed with specific intentions and the plan was based on the teacher's diagnosis of the learning competence of the student. Nonetheless, teachers may need to make certain adjustments to the lesson at the implementation phase. I would suggest two broad reasons for teachers to deviate from their original lesson plan: first when the lesson is obviously going badly and the plan is not helping to produce the desired outcome; second, when something happens during an early part of the lesson that necessitates improvisation.

When the lesson is not succeeding, teachers should make immediate adjustments to the original lesson plan.

Evaluating the Plan

The final part of the daily lesson planning happens after the lesson has ended, when the teacher must evaluate the success (or failure) of the lesson. It is important to think after teaching the lesson and ask "whether it was good one or not, and why". This form of reflection is for self-development.

When evaluating a lesson, the first and the most important criterion is a student learning because that is why we have lesson in the first place. Even though it may be difficult to judge how much has been learned in a lesson, but we can still make a good guess. This guess can be based "on our knowledge of the class, the type of activity they were engaged in, and some informal test activities that give feedback on learning". We can use following criteria for evaluating lesson effectiveness:

(a) The class seemed to be learning the material well;
(b) The learners were engaged in the English language throughout;
(c) The learners were attentive all the time;
(d) The learners enjoyed the lesson and well motivated;
(e) The learners were active all the time;
(f) The lesson went according to the plan;
(g) The language used communicatively throughout.

The following question may also be useful for the teachers to reflect on after conducting a lesson (answers can be used as a basis for future lesson planning):

(a) What do you think today's lesson was about?
(b) What tasks were most successful? Least successful? Why?
(c) Did you finish the lesson on time?
(d) What changes (if any) will you make in your teaching and why?

Additionally, for further clarification of the success of the lesson, teachers can ask their students the following four questions at the end of each class; the answers can assist teacher for the future lesson planning:

(a) What do you think today's lesson was about?

(b) What part was easy?

(c) What part was difficult?

(d) What changes would you suggest the teacher make?

Conclusion

A good lesson plan helps teaching to be effective and thereby gives satisfaction to the teacher. Teaching learning material is prepared according to the lesson plan and that makes it easy to elicit whatever is planned. Students do not get distracted when a lesson plan is followed. Lesson plan helps the teacher to finish the syllabus faster, and is not time consuming or burdensome to the teacher. Following the lesson plan everyday is possible and in fact helps the teacher for self-improvement. The purpose of teaching English is met with the help of a lesson plan.

The teachers follow a specific lesson plan with definite objectives in mind while planning a lesson. It is good to make alternative lesson plans. Teachers like to plan their lesson before every class. A clear plan will also maximize the time and minimize the confusion of what is expected of students, thus making classroom management easier. English is not taught only for the sake of examination and therefore efforts are being made to improve the language skills among the students and accordingly care is taken to give weightage to all the four language skills while preparing a lesson plan. The number of periods allotted to teach English in school is adequate and the time given in the time-table is sufficient. Teaching learning material (TLM) should be used in every class and the students should be given a chance to partake in preparing the TLM. Language being a skill subject needs careful handling, as it is different from content of subject. English teachers need to make a deliberate effort to assimilate new strategies, techniques, innovations and nuances of language teaching, hone their teaching skills and equip themselves further and cater to the upcoming requirements in the field of teaching English.

References

Annie Vijaya Kumari, Ch. (2006). *Methods of Teaching English*. New Era Publications, Guntur.

Arun K. Gupta (1984). Teacher Education: current and prospects. Sterling Publishers Pvt. Ltd., New Delhi.

Caine, R.N. and G. Caine (1990). "Understanding a Brain-Based Approach to Learning and Teaching." *Educational Leadership* (October).

Curtis and Boutwood (1960). *An Introductory History of English Education since 1800*. University Tutorial Press Ltd., London.

Dewey, John and Evelyn (1962). *Schools of Tomorrow*. New York, NY: E.P. Dutton and Company, Inc.

Hesse, M.G. (1975). *Approaches to teaching foreign languages*. North-Holland Publishing Company, Amsterdam, Oxford.

Johnson and Michael (1958). *Principles of Teaching*. Allyn and Bacon, INC, Massachusetts.

Kohli, A.L. (1997). *Techniques of Teaching English*, Dhanpet Rai and Sons, Delhi.

Krisnaswamy, N., Krisnaswamy, Lalitha (2003). *Teaching English: Approaches, Methods and Techniques*. Macmillan India Ltd., New Delhi.

Bailey, K.M. (1986). *The best laid plans*. New York: Cambridge University Press.

Hunter M., and Rusell, D. (1977). *How can I plan more effective lesson?*

17

Teaching English in Govt. High Schools of Bongaigaon District, Assam: An Analysis of Quality Evaluation

Ripunjoy Bezbaruah

Objectives

1. To acknowledge the status of English learning and teaching in Bongaigaon.
2. To assess the quality of English teaching in the light of teachers' qualification, eligibility, and skills.
3. To know the prospect of English in Government schools of Bongaigaon.

Research Problems

1. Teaching English is less prominent in Government vernacular medium schools as compared to private schools.
2. There is a lack of adequate numbers of skilled teachers.
3. Strong lack of motivational forces.

Fieldwork

Field Survey and Case Study in different Government High Schools of Bongaigaon district, Assam. There are 56 govt. high schools in Bongaigaon district according to Secondary Education Management Information System, Assam.

Tools and Data Collection

In this study, questionnaire is used and given to the students, teachers and stakeholders. We randomly selected 100 students from different schools out of which 80 students responded to our queries. On the other hand, we gave our questions to 60 teachers out of which 50 responded to those queries. Moreover some academicians are also interviewed.

Introduction

The capital of human world is totally influenced by the two strong waves of the present era—globalization and modern technology. Traditional structures of education would not enable educational institutions to meet the expansion of student numbers envisaged in this scenario, while at the same time maintaining academic standards and the quality of provision. In a paper titled "Defining Quality Education", UNICEF comments that quality education includes:

1. Learners who are healthy, well-nourished and ready to participate and learn and supported in learning by their families and communities;
2. Environments that are healthy, safe, protective and gender-sensitive and provide adequate resources; and
3. Content that is reflected in relevant curricula and materials for the acquisition of basic skills, especially in the areas of literacy, numeracy and skills for life, and knowledge in such areas as gender, health, nutrition, HIV/AIDS prevention and peace;
4. Processes through which trained teachers use child-centered teaching approaches in well-managed classrooms and schools and skillful assessment to facilitate learning and reduce disparities;
5. Outcomes that encompass knowledge, skills and attitudes, and are linked to national goals for education and positive participation in society.

So, without proper step from all sides of the knowledge world, quality education will remain a 'costly dream'. Different states have their own policy of education pattern; hence it is very significant to find out the ways in which English is being taught in the Government High Schools of Assam. Many academicians opine that the teaching methods to teach English are totally inappropriate as there is also the lack of proper English teachers.

Findings of the Study

In this study, out of 100 students, 70 students said that the quality of teaching English is not attractive in the classrooms. The old theatrical method of translation is used. Teachers just read the English sentences and translate into Assamese. In some schools situations exist which makes translation a nightmare since teachers have to translate the English text into multiple languagees like Bodo, Bengali, Hindi, etc. and the student has little or no part to play in the classroom.

Overall stress is given to the listening skill of the students. Grammar lessons are taught and they are forced to correct themselves as far as their grammatical use of language is concerned before they could speak even a small sentence. Grammar is essential but the method it is taught is very insignificant. It is a common belief in Assam that English is the most difficult subject and if anyone would like to learn the subject, must know the grammatical elements of English. Students are afraid of the English language as they are overburdened only with the grammar of the language. In fact a large number of students have failed in English in their HSLC examination mainly due to the fear of reading and writing it. It is also observed that writing and listening skills are praised but speaking and reading skills are neglected.

It is surprising that even after 67 years of our Independence; the condition of schools is astonishingly poor. In almost all the schools, classes are segmented into sections by the sole help of wooden or cloth partitions and it is not scientific. In school hours, it becomes Oliver Goldsmith's *noisy mansion* of his famous poem "The Village Schoolmaster". The worst thing is that the teachers are teaching English without lesson plans when educational research pays utmost effort to prepare lesson plans for teachers.

The most unenviable situation is that there is a lack properly trained English teachers in many schools. General graduate teachers are teaching the L2 without any effort for the right effective input of the language. Only a few teachers have proper teachers' training to teach English. It indicates that teachers are not qualified to handle the subject in a systematic manner.

Even the English teachers are not trained for CALL (Computer Assisted Language Learning). It shows clearly that the teachers are devoid of motivating their learners and strikingly enough, 100% teachers agree that they have to play the most pivotal role to motivate learners to learn English as it is not their mother tongue. But paradoxically, they absolutely have no idea how to achieve this or what to do to motivate their students...But all students said that their teachers never used any kind of modern tools either to motivate them or teach them.

English being a foreign language required some modern hi-tech educational tools to attract learners to the classrooms of English language. But all students said that their teachers never used any kind of such modern tools to teach them and even the teachers also said that they do not know how to make use of these audio-visual teaching aids for effective teaching of language.

It is found that though the evaluation system good comprises of Class Test, Unit Test, Half-Yearly and Annual Examinations; there is no scope for the students to evaluate their spoken skill. On the other hand, library facility, electricity facility, power back-up facility are hardly found in this study. All teachers use mother tongue in the class as the vehicle to give the meaning of the context to the students but recent research has identified that this translation method does never work in this present global situation of job market.

It is also observed that teaching English is less prominent in government vernacular medium schools as compared to the private schools. While studying the policies of private schools, it is clearly found that they are trying to meet the need of the students and their parents. Proper English language educators, proper library facility and rich motivation are provided in these institutions. Teachers always encourage students to cultivate their proficiency in speaking skill as well. Almost 98% of teachers have their lesson plans for effective teaching and they regularly do their own home works for enriching their teaching.

A Critical Corpus on the Findings

There is a general agreement that teaching English to its non-native speakers is always very challenging. This task requires overall involvement from the sides of teachers largely. What is significant in this study is that in this age of rapid growth of technological advancement and global impact, we teach our learners not with the help of modern educational tools but with the help of translation method. Studies show that this method may be useful with the brilliant students who have intellectual bent of mind but in maximum number of govt. schools only average learners are found; so this method is not acceptable considering the future of these learners. It cannot raise their standard of language and put them on par with the world. In fact, the students are paralyzed by the very thought of analysis of the structures in English.

For the all sides' development of the students, it is need of the hour for the states like Assam to strictly adhere to the rules of language learning. Language learning and its effectiveness is depended upon four distinct elements to be tested in a classroom- i.e., listening, speaking, writing and reading skills. Without the good cultivation of these four skills, no one can be an effective language learner. In this world, it becomes easier to help students to practice these four skills. Thomas L. Friedman in his famous book "The World is Flat" opines "....on the explosion of technologies including blogging, online encyclopedias and podcasting, to show how knowledge and resources are connecting all over the planet as never before".

Excluding listening and writing skills, the other two skills are totally neglected and as a result, the fear of learning English is increased. In all the schools, ultimate stress is given to the practice of grammar. The condition of schools is poor and even becomes worst as in many schools there is no link between the sitting arrangement of the classroom and the number of enrolled students. Classes are segmented temporally and partitioned either by woods or by cloths. The flow of disturbance is beyond imagination. The teachers are not encouraged to handle the modern technological tools which are considered the best ways to teach L2. Infrastructure is pathetic here. There is total lack of facilities like electricity, power back up, library, modern sitting arrangements and even the facility of good drinking water.

We are surprised when we find that less than 1% teachers know what a lesson plan is and they enter into the classes without a proper lesson plan but academicians say that one of the most important parts of teaching a language is the scientific lesson plan. It is the time when we are shouting the 'slogans' like 'Education for All'. It is a great concern whether quality education is imparted under these slogans or whether quality education is still a 'dream' to us.

Teachers are not well-trained to handle the class of English language. A mere degree or diploma can never be the required qualification to a language teacher. Proper research oriented language teachers' training program should be given to the teachers. Soon after the appointment such teachers must be sent for undergoing such strict methodical training program so that they can contribute to the need of the learners. It is even said by the ELT experts that without proper training no teacher is in its real sense is able to teach English to his students as it is directly connected to the motivation of the students. Training for handling modern teaching tools can surely help teachers to motivate their students. But the present set up of education does not have this idea and the result is that a huge number of students fail in the HSLC Examination.

Evaluation system plays a very significant role in the teaching-learning process. "Evaluation, as the term indicates is the assigning of value to the results obtained. We may define evaluation as the entire process of gathering information and making conclusive inferences from it. It covers testing, measurement and assessment." Evaluation is important as it is the mean through which one can evaluate student performance, teacher activities, and the program or curriculum. In the schools of the said area, as modeled by SEBA, the evaluation system is good but it is a great matter of concern that no importance is given to assess the efficiency of the students in the spoken skill. So, evaluation thus, needs to be more systematic, up-to-date and deliberate; otherwise the complete student community will suffer.

Suggestions/Recommendations

This study strongly recommends the following measures to develop the quality of English teaching-learning environment:

1. The school authority should give priority to classroom management and to the teacher student ratio.
2. Proper teacher training course should be developed and teacher educators must be recruited differently for different subjects. At the same time, teachers should be taught the handling of modern teaching aids.
3. New methods of language teaching can be developed for the maximum benefit of the learners.
4. At least, exposure to English may be made compulsory in English classrooms.
5. Lesson planning must be the compulsory component for the teachers. Teachers should motivate students and there should always be group activities for the students.
6. Provision for tutorials.
7. Implementation of new evaluation pattern.
8. Government grants should be increased and there should be a committee of experts or academicians to adjudge the utilization of grants.
9. Provision for library and reading room, internet facility, electricity facility with power back up system.
10. Revision of syllabus.
11. Government initiatives for good number of trained teachers and there should be one scrutiny committee to mark their continuous improvement and on the basis of their improvements, they should be promoted.

Conclusion

No one can deny the fact that the condition of English teaching-learning is not scientific to meet the global challenge of this age of globalization; and this is the main cause why the youngsters of Assam fail to contribute to the job market in the international scenario. Students regard the classrooms as "Absolute Hell". Mere slogans cannot change the situations hence; implementation of research oriented approaches to enlighten this present situation becomes the demand of the society. This is the time we must take the right endeavor to provide our children quality education so that they could learn the significance and consequences to rise up for their future world. Education should not be the dream; instead teachers, students, government and stakeholders—all should think of the originality of teaching and learning English comparing themselves to the global phenomena of its importance and what we have done to make our own manpower efficient in English for occupying the place of their future. If we fail, the future of a large number of young boys and girls would be destroyed by us only. The future of English is bright indeed so, by making good policies we can overcome the obstacles of teaching-learning environment of English. We may conclude by the words of R.K. Rao, "Continued stress is being placed on restructuring of curricula, teaching technologies, planning, management mechanisms, and procedures for generating resources. Paradigm Shifts are apparent, and the situation demands a relook at the higher education system and its management."

References

Assam Human Development Report 2003, Govt. of Assam, accessed on 28/5/15.

Defining Quality in Education, a paper by UNICEF, The International Working Group on Education. Italy, June 2000, accessed on 29/5/15.

Friedman, Thomas L. *The World is Flat*. Penguin Books, England, 2005.

Kudchedkar, S. (ed). *English Language Teaching in India*. Orient Longman Pvt. Ltd., Chennai, 2002.

Menon, Mohan et al. *Quality Indicators for Teacher Educators*. NAAC, Bangalore, 2007.

Rao, R.K. (ed). *Education in India*. Kalpaz Publications, Delhi, 2006.

Rao, S. Prakash. *Currents Trends in English Language Teaching*. Creative Publisher, New Delhi, 1991.

Rao, Usha. *Educational Technology*. Himalaya Publishing House, Mumbai, 1991.

Ringuet Leprince and Henard Fabrice. *The Path to Quality Teaching in Higher Education*. Accessed on 15/5/15.

18

Role of Teaching a Play/Drama in ELT Classroom

M. Vanisree

"All the world's a stage,
And all the men and women merely players;
They have their exits and their entrances,
And one man in his time plays many parts,
His acts being seven ages."

—William Shakespeare
(*As You Like It*—Act 2, Scene 7, 139-43)

Introduction

English is a global language. It acts as a link between different countries and different language groups. In today's world English acts as a window to the world of several branches of knowledge including its rich literature, arts and music. The main aim of teaching and learning English was to enable the students to appreciate and enjoy literature, especially in the professional colleges. Now-a-days English is taught as a subject with the specific purpose of developing communication skills rather than giving importance to the study of literature. In this context, a teacher also should change according to the contexts of the learners and at the same time a teacher should keep in mind that literature is a tool which not only amplifies the LSRW skills for the learners but also develops the cultural competencies.

Role of a Play/Drama

Literature acts as a motivating source of LSRW skills. Many literary texts like novels, plays, biographies, short stories, poetry, etc., can be studied in the language classroom. A Play/ One-Act Play is an organization with the intent of nurturing the appreciation of theater arts by encouraging the learners to take on different roles. Drama provides an excellent platform for exploring theoretical and practical aspects of the English language (*Whiteson,* 1996). A Playnot only help the students to build uptheir phonetics, vocabulary and grammatical structures but also helps the learners to know about different cultural, political and historical traditions elements so that the learners can develop their strengths and attributes. It also developsthe learner's imagination, critical thinking and creative use of language. This exposure is a benefit to the learners for developing themselves in academic, communicative and social skills and also provides an affluent linguistic input and effective incite for the learners to impart themselves.

A One-Act Play is different from other plays that occur over several acts. It consist only one act with one or more scenes. In recent years, the 10 minute plays known as "flash drama" that has emerged as a popular subgenre of the one-act play. A Play will provide a unique opportunity for the learners to develop their dexterity. It showcases the learner works in a wide variety of creative fields. As the learners will have an opportunity to showcase their talent the learner will develop their verbal and non-verbal skills like vocabulary, grammar, syntaxes, strong leadership skills as well as critical thinking, explore imagination, responsibility, flexibility, problem-solving and promote team work. (*One-act play* 1)

Role of a Teacher

A teacher plays an important role in teaching English language through a play. The aim of teaching play in English language classroom is different. A Play develops the learner's power of imagination, aesthetic sensibilities and literary taste. It also develops the learners favorable attitude towards the language which is essential for learning any language and in the context of the present position of the language in our country, the lack of this attitude seems to be the major problem. Through a Play the learner will not only learn the LSRW (Listening,

Speaking, Reading and Writing) skills but also the other language areas like vocabulary, grammar and pronunciation. At the same time it is very important for a teacher to update himself/herself about the latest developments, changes and trends in language teaching and also adapt in his/her teaching methods to suit and fulfill the learners' needs. The present day requirement and trend suggests that there is a need for more creativity and innovation with regards to the teaching procedures. Only then, language learning can become a fruitful and meaningful exercise. The method, approach or technique used in the classroom should invoke the active participation by the learners in the teaching-learning process.

Techniques

Teaching a Play has a different set of aims and objectives. The teacher will inspire and excite a sense of loveliness and wonder in the learners. She/he will convey the reason why the playwright wrote a particular play and at the same time the learners will feel to the playwright's thoughts. The teacher will introduce the content and difficult language items such as vocabulary and so on which are unfamiliar and complex with respect to the cultural, linguistic and intellectual elements, so that the learner does not miss the lively experience of the play. The best way of announcing the play in the class is "Today we're going to do a play" instead of saying "I am going to teach you a lesson/play today" so that, it generates an interest and make the learners to put his/her effort to involve themselves to enact the play so that the other learners can also involve and try to learn the meaning/essence by themselves. The teacher should encourage the learners who want to enact the different roles of the play. As the visual impact makes the learners to learn and remember more effectively the teacher should encourage the learners in such a way that the learners who are enacting different roles of the play must involve themselves in such a way that they should forget their originality and at the same time the other learners should feel that they are sitting in a theatre but not in the classroom. At first the teacher should give a brief introduction of the play and at the same time the teacher can also create suspense in the play to make the learner to listen and see the play more interesting asking the learners "What happens next? Can you guess the rest of the play?"

The stress and intonation pattern plays a vital role in the effectiveness of the play which makes the learners to be familiar with the sound systems of spoken English and also with variations from the normal speech patterns i.e., direct and simple language. At the same time the learner focuses on vocabulary, structures, phrases, sentences, meaning, etc. The teacher should also make the learners to enact the play with little physical action where the interest of the play is maintained by its sharp dialogue, conveying the ideological conflict of the characters. Each character/learner should maintain its own individual manner and style of speech by showing the morale of the play and giving a message. Even though a teacher divides the learners into pairs for a play a teacher should keep at least one learner aside to play as a shadow of the character/characters so that of the characters can be accompanied by their shadows when they speak their inner thoughts of the character. This technique will give an effect to the play for potential understanding and also to show a conflict between an outward appearance and inner thoughts. As the learner do the role with mime which is a good technique to get impressive results without the pressure of dialogue. This makes the learner to develop their non-verbal communication like body language, gestures, etc.

> For instance, if we take a one-act play of St. John Greer Ervine's "Progress".
>
> "Corrie: Ah, at last, at last! By Heaven, I've done it at last. Eh? Oh, oh! Come in! Come in!
>
> Servant: Mrs. Meldon.....
>
> Corrie: Yes, yes, Hannah, what is it! Has she got back?
>
> Hannah: Yes, sir. She expected you to meet her at the station, sir. She waited a long time in the cold, and then got Marshall to drive her up...." (*Using English* 107)

After learning/seeing the play, the learner learns the essential parts of the play such as about the writer and also the background and need of writing this play. Like, here the Irish Play Wright, novelist and critic St. John Greer Ervine reflects an autobiographical element, as the dramatist too had to go to war and face its horrors and atrocities. In fact he was severely wounded in France and eventually lost his leg. In his play he depicts his concept of social thinking with regard to tranquility and peace. The play represents three unities i.e., time, place and action is meticulously maintained. The main aim of this play is 'Abolition of war". It is written against the background of the First World War in which thousands were butchered and many more became disabled for life. It left many mothers as childless and incredible number of widows and orphans. This insensible devastation has created diverse reactions in social thinking. Ervine gave importance to the sentiments, namely the anti-war feeling. The learners also main moral i.e, the "Value of life is much important then the value of progress." The play will give "awareness of the destructions of the First World War".

"The play is laid in the study of Professor Henry Coorie in a remote village in the year 1919. Prof Corrie invents a bomb formula. Mrs. Meldon Charlotte, a widowed sister of Prof. Corrie is in mourning on the third death anniversary of her son Eddie, an army captain dies in the First World War. Prof. Corrie pays negligence to her bereavement and breaks the news of his invention with happy and proud. On the other hand, Mrs. Meldon is in grief and she is stricken as she has lost her only son Eddie who is of 19 years lad in the First World War. Due to this, she lost her husband who died in the grief of his son. Mrs. Meldon gently reminds him that his invention will lead to the death of hundreds of young men like her son. But Prof. Corrie ignores her words. Mrs. Meldon pleads with Prof. Corrie to destroy the bomb as Eddie's memorial. But Prof. Corrie stays indifferent to her pleading. She destroys the sheets of paper. But Corrie is not upset and says that he can reproduce them easily. Mrs. Meldon cannot tolerate his inhumanity and finally she stabs him on the back with a bayonet and kills him. She feels that this is justifiable revenge against the murderer of her son on the occasion of his death anniversary."

After the play, the learners will know how the play has sufficiently exposed the motive behind wars which is to perpetuate and extend the class interest of the war mongering imperialists and exploiters, who sit safe and secure. But far behind the fighting lines, the poor sacrifice their lives in the trenches. Above all, the learners must feel of the story by adding their expressions and thoughts. The learner can identifies and can list the words which are associated with Progress. The learners also pick out the adjectival phrases in the play. The learners also learn the frequency of use of words, its usefulness, its structural value, productivity of the words such as prefixes, suffixes, etc., universality of the words and regional value of the words, range of applicability of the words, simplicity and its meaning, grading of words in the poem. They also learn the classification of vocabulary such as active and passive vocabulary. The learner knows the correct vocabulary intimately and can use correctly and effectively in speech and writing. The learner also understands and make out the meanings of different words from its context and finally Ad-hoc vocabulary or stranger words comprise the vast number of words. The learners also learn new a word implies pronunciation, meaning, spelling and usage of the word which improves the confidence levels and also shares their ideas in writing.

The learner also learns how to expand the vocabulary such as learning:

- Associated Words—E.g: Progress: development, evolution, discovery, make progress, move forward
- Formation of words—E.g: press – impress, consequent – inconsequent
- Formation of compound words—E.g: under + Neath = Underneath
- Synonyms—E.g: Snarl – growling and threatening sound usually produced by dogs or wolves, roar, grimace, sneer, scowl, etc.
- Antonyms—E.g: Absorb – Exude, Utter – Partial
- Families of words – E.g: Absorb – Absorbed, Absorbing, Unabsorbed
- Idioms—Come Down – Go to down
- Formation of Linkers – See, Saw, Seen

- Formation of words by adding preposition to verbs and adverbs—E.g: have it up – to have something
- Building compound words—E.g: humourless + eyes = humourless eyes
- Collocation of words – E.g: inconsequent person
- Words of size—E.g: large – big, great, huge, bulky, hefty, outsized
- Learning Technical Vocabulary—E.g: Apparatus – Equipment, Machinery, etc.
- Word Origin—E.g: Snarl – Originated from German "schnarren" which means "rattle, snarl". Later transferred to English as "Snar" which in turn changes to Snarl means "make an aggressive growl with bared teeth".
- Word games—Like Learning Prefixes and Suffixes through word strips and Preparation of own dictionary so that the learner can enter the lists of new words with their meanings. E.g: force – forcing
- Learning Articles—E.g: at the station, in a large retort, etc.

Conclusion

Teaching a play in ESL Classroom is not an easy task. It requires meticulous planning with number of techniques for the presentation. A teacher uses various techniques like by using objects, symbols, gestures and insisting the learners for using/presenting new words and building the confidence of the learners so as to develop not only their verbal and non-verbal skills but also make them to analyze to carry these skills to their real life. Thus, several techniques were adopted in teaching grammar, phonetics, vocabulary, etc. in ELT classroom using a play is adopted to improve or to strengthen and empowers communicative approach of the learners and gives them many opportunities to have indulgence in their work which leads to successful and meaningful language learning.

References

Chris, Boudreault (January, 2010). *The Benefits of Using Drama in the ESL/EFL Classroom*, The Internet TESL Journal, Vol. XVI, No. 1. *http://iteslj.org/Articles/Boudreault-Drama.html.* Web

Naik, N. Shantha (2011). *Teaching English Language Through Literature.* Sarup Book Publishers Pvt. Ltd., New Delhi, Print

Using English—*A Course Book for Undergraduate Learners* (106-21), Orient Blackswan Pvt. Ltd., Hyderabad, 2013. Print

Whiteson, Valerie (1996). *New Ways of Using Drama and Literature in Language Teaching.* Alexandria, VA, TESOL. Print

http://www.oxforddictionaries.com/definition/english. Web

http://idioms.thefreedictionary.com. Web

http://www.oxforddictionaries.com/words/phrasal-verbs. Web

http://dictionary.cambridge.org/dictionary/british/phrasal-verb. Web

http://en.wikipedia.org/wiki/One-act_play. Web

http://eric.ed.gov/?id=ED420999. Web

19

Challenges of Teaching English in the Classrooms of Rural Degree Colleges in Assam

Sahab Uddin

Abstract

Education has been the primary factor in the more ceremonial communication of English around the world and hence English is said to be the world's most important language having communicative and educative value. But teaching English to the grown up students without having the very basic knowledge of the language is a kind of challenge faced by the English teachers in a rural perspective. The main purpose of this study is to find out the challenges of teaching English curriculum at Degree level in rural colleges of Assam within certain specific semester period. The current study is a mixed method observation by nature and interactions with students and teachers of rural areas to understand the views and situation of the English Language teaching and learning. Besides, interviews of English teachers are taken and English teaching classrooms are observed using a checklist in order to find out the present situation of Degree level English Curriculum and its viability in learning the language. The study indicates that most of the rural college students are poor in English language due to lack of skilled teachers, proper teacher training, using proper teaching methods and materials, physical facilities on the one hand and the poor Language foundation of the learners during primary education on the other. As a result, teaching English curriculum at Degree level in Assam is becoming a threat to the students as well as English teachers.

Keywords: English Curriculum, Language Competencies, Language Practices, Teachers' Training.

Introduction

It's a well-known fact that English is the *'Lingua Franca'* of the world and a new value for written and oral communication in the English Language has emerged because of the ICT Revolution which has turned the whole world into a global village. It is used all over the world not out of any obligation but for its richness, progressiveness, dynamism and flexibility. A large chunk of children speak English as their first language. English symbolizes in Indian minds, better education, better culture and higher intellect. In present times, English is the most preferred language. The Indians and the Indian English language press uses many words derived from Indian language. Although Indian accent is sometimes difficult for non-Indians to understand but English has co-existed in the Indian sub-continent alongside thousands of local languages. It has remained at the heart of the Indian society. Since independence from the British rule, English continues to expand its empire. English is virtually the mother-tongue for many educated South Asian, but for the vast majority, it remains second language. So English, spoken by such speakers is heavily influenced by speech patterns of their ethnic language. But the gap still remains like those of the haves and have-nots, developed and developing, urban and the rural. Why the teachers of English are still being encountered with problems in teaching English in rural classrooms of other states in general and in Assam in particular. Being an English teacher in a rural college, many a time have to take the help of local language in the classroom to make the students better understand the topic taken for discussion. Besides, the very basics of grammar appear to be unfamiliar to the learners of higher section as well as to those who even offer English as their major subject. Who is mainly responsible for this in today's context? Whether blaming either the teachers of primary section or the students in the present Degree classrooms will bring about any solution? Or the syllabus designing authority should take into consideration the ground reality of such rural learners to make them compatible for the present-day situation? The paper aims at all these problems and tries to bring forward some suggestions in order to overcome such difficulties in imparting lessons to the English teaching classrooms. Much is required to be done by the linguists, the polyglots, the scholars and the teachers to bridge the gap between them and we have to go into the details of the English language and simplify the methodology for a better understanding of the rural classroom learners.

Rural Learners Outline in Assam

Assam is a land of 78,438 sq. km. with diverse culture and tribes. 2.64 crores of population situated in NE Region of India. Eighty-nine per cent of the total population in Assam is living in rural areas and 74% depend on agriculture. The Assamese language has been recognized as the official language in Assam but English has been given equal importance in case of communication and correspondences. Though higher education is a latecomer in the North-East region, Assam occupies a distinct place in the field of higher education among the other states of North-East. Assam has an overall literacy rate of 73.18% (2011 census). Huge numbers of educational institutes are established here for imparting education to the aspiring students. In terms of higher education, Assam has developed into top educational destination in entire North-East region. Large number of Govt. and private Higher Educational Institutes are now being set up in the state. It is seen that there has been a remarkable growth of higher education institutions in Assam in recent years resulting in about 20 university level institutions including IITs and private universities. There are about 517 affiliated colleges under Gauhati University, Dibrugarh University and Assam University. About 94% higher education students in Assam are in the affiliated colleges. But the college education has come under severe stress and in Assam it presents a gloomy and dismal picture. In spite of the phenomenal growth of higher education in Assam, it is a paradoxical to us whether the present education system has been succeeded or not in gratifying the needs and aspirations of the students of this land. Students who can't afford to go far away from home for financial constraints are accommodated in the rural based colleges and colleges are bound to admit them with poor marks. Same is the case with the Government feeder schools (High Schools and Higher Secondary Schools) of vernacular medium who admit students belonging to Below Poverty Line (BPL) category as well as those who have very poor educational background. So, except a very few, majority of those students fail to secure qualifying marks for admission into the institutions of higher education. The rate of progression to higher studies from these schools and colleges is very low.

On the other hand, most of the students (2000 and after) now studying in Degree in colleges are of first generation students. They came to Primary Schools and then to Colleges from those families the heads of which are either illiterate or are hardly educated. These learners did not receive proper educational support either from their parents or from their tutors in schools. It's because, the government schools were not equipped with teaching tools and proper infrastructure and qualified teachers were not adequate a couple of decade back. Like today, there had not been such mushroom growth of English medium schools and so Convent Educated Teachers (CET) at that time was limited. Resultantly, they remained deprived from getting sufficient support services for their capacity building. Teaching through regional languages has undoubtedly increased their potentialities to express them in their mother tongue, but the English language learning couldn't be made possible by them and with that skimpy aptitude they have now been admitted in rural degree colleges. As a result, they are deprived of sufficient support services for their capacity building.

Teachers-Students' Monologue

There may be many contributing factors for this situation. Firstly, the students of rural and semi-urban areas in Assam face speaking problems because English is not their mother-tongue. It is neither instinctive nor intuitive. Language acquisition seems to be a process of both of analogy and application, nature and nurture. Teaching becomes successful only when the learners understand the deliberations better. But because of the lack of basic grammatical and structural knowledge in English among these learners, the teachers have to take the help of the regional languages and provide ready-made notes in order to make their teaching or its purpose successful. This surely helps the learners in scoring good marks and led them to pass from one semester to the other, but the knowledge in English remains as it was and can't be developed in them. Secondly, the semester syllabuses of degree classes are designed in such a way that there is less scope for the teachers to impart language skill as he or she has to complete the prescribed syllabus within a very short stipulated time. Hence, the sole objective of the teacher and the learner turn into to clear the exams. The students never realize the importance of learning English as a language. In the past, in rural areas, English was introduced to students in the fifth class. But now there is no dearth of English medium schools in such area yet the standards of English are falling rapidly. If we compare a graduate of present time with a graduate of the past, the result is shockingly amazing. The emphasis on passing the exams lies so heavy on the students that they opt for the cramming method. Such an approach helps unscrupulous elements to flourish and it only helps the students in achieving their goals of passing the exams.

It is true that a student of a high school standard today can speak and write English better than the students studying in Degree Standard in rural areas today and the same is sometimes pertinent to the case of the teachers too. Although this level of standard may contrast in case of the stakeholders of the institutions in an urban set-up but the problems of the students and the teachers are inter-related. What can minimize the gap are the experience of the teacher and his level of English mastery? The inter-disciplinary relation of teaching and learning process brings home the fact that the problems of the teachers as well as the students can be understood better if we compare the teaching learning of the present day with that of the past.

The Past and the Present Level

Today even in the rural and semi-Urban areas, study of English language begins at an early age—at the KG level and it continues up to Senior Secondary or first Degree level. Even in the Professional Courses, the teaching of English as a communication skill is an integral part of the curriculum or the course obligations. But earlier, English was introduced in the Fifth standard as a subject, not as a language to learn. Students of the rural areas did not realize the importance of English as a language of communication whereas this is the most important aspect of this global language today. They lacked the confidence to speak in English and expression in the language was weak. The primary reason is that they have been taught English through Grammar-Translation Method. This method makes them dependent on their mother tongue. Whatever they read, they translated it into their own vernacular language. During the time of exams, they crammed the expected questions because they could not write one original sentence of their own. Because of this Translation Method, they have no vocabulary of English words. While writing, they depend on the cheap material from the Model Books. Although nowadays, the rural areas have been facilitated with some of the tools because of the rapidly increasing web of Educational facilities but it has neither helped in raising the level of the students, nor made them learn English as a language. It stays there and the teaching learning stagnates. The process of teaching is not updated even after the passage of years. So much so as the experience shows in many cases, the teachers have no idea of good dictionaries meant for the students or for themselves.

Further, the hackneyed, stereotyped and traditional pattern of examinations also aimed at clearing English not as a language but as a subject. The students, therefore, were guided to practice "pick and choose" method from the sub-standard material available in the market so that students merely pass the subject far from learning any level of the Language. It is more shocking to learn that even the questions that students were supposed to answer are told to learn through translation from English to their own vernacular. In rural areas, the students (of 90's studying at present in Degree Colleges) tend to choose the literal way of translating the sentences from Assamese into English. Some examples need consideration here:

Standard English	Translation Method
1. Never employ a person of unknown antecedent.	Do not use unknown wood as pestle.
2. Too many choices make one choice less	Heron turns blind with plenty of fishes.
3. I have fed him with ₹ 10	He ate my ten rupees.
4. A cock and bull story	Cow climbing a tree

Students make errors while translating the above sentences. Such problems arise because of translating each word of English into Assamese and *vice versa*. Whereas today's students of English medium background know that it is not possible to find an exact equivalent for every English word. They also know how the use of idioms makes the expression better. Hence, poor performance in translation, lack of proper vocabulary, no knowledge proverbs—all result a casual approach and so even after reading English for 14 or 15 years, English language learning level of the students remains as it was.

Suggestions

It is observed from the above discussion that students of the rural colleges face a number of problems. English is their second language and learning a second language means acquiring a system of rules, but just as a very little of which is known to the rural learners and so they find themselves unable to express in English. They have no idea of proper sentence structure. They do not know proper pronunciation, spellings and grammatical rules. To tackle with such problem, the teacher has to keep in mind the age of the student, his native language, his cultural background and his previous experience with English. The teachers should aim at teaching primarily, not knowledge but skill—the different skills required for good Listening-Speaking-Reading-Writing (LSRW). Teachers should find some way of helping pupils to enjoy their language activities, and of building their confidence. But in doing so, the challenge lies with the teacher is that, to achieve the desired effects, the goal of a course must be kept in mind that it is not aimed at reading, fluency in speech, inculcating translation skill but to complete the prescribed syllabus so that they can successfully appear in their next semester exam. All these objects shape methodology of teaching on the one hand and the course structure of English on the other. As such, the syllabuses are to be designed in such a way that there must be ample scope for developing the language skill of the students. The suggestions from the rural English teachers are to be sought and students' problems should be taken into considerations before prescribing them their syllabuses so that English should be taught as a language not as a subject even at present day degree standard.

Conclusion

We are now in the 21st century which is a century of challenges and opportunities. India is dreaming to be a developed and leading nation of the world by 2030 for which the right type of higher education is a must. The college sector accounts for over 88% of the total enrolment in higher education in India. Quality and effectiveness of higher education entirely depends on the collegiate education. Quality and relevance is becoming a challenge in the era of globalization. Although we have 517 colleges in Assam, but all colleges are still not eligible for the UGC financial grants as only 259 colleges have so far been recognized by the UGC under Section 2f and 12b. A considerable number of colleges are running without government assistance. The conditions of most of such colleges are deplorable. Under such circumstances, how can one expect quality language skill in classrooms as colleges are not able to provide opportunity for teachers to work in a productive way?

It is true that the changing times have witnessed the growing importance of English language in all walks of life. It does not seem that we are using English language as non-native speakers or as a second language. Knowingly or unknowingly, we use English of our own in every facet of life. Even the English illiterates in the rural areas use English words effortlessly and that may positively results in the flexibility of English language to shape and enrich it. But the above discussion shows that making

English study effective from Primary to Degree levels needs a lot of inputs and resources like trained teachers, communicative teaching material, financial, infra-structural and management facilities. These resources are not equally available or favorable for learning English in all the educational institutions of the country. In some urban elite institutions, these inputs are mostly available and the school or college learners can use English, more or less, in their further study or in jobs that they choose. But most of the rural schools and colleges lack in some or almost all these resources.

Teaching-learning English in the rural colleges cannot be done in the way it should be done. In most cases, learning English means rote learning of grammar rules and textbook contents even without understanding. But unfortunately there is discrimination between urban and rural primary school students' English language learning which ultimately have an effect on the grown-up learners in colleges. Students from urban areas show better proficiency in comparison with the students from rural areas and so more research based studies are immensely required to bridge the gap and develop the English language teaching in the rural classrooms.

References

Brown, D.H. (2001). *Teaching by Principles: An Interactive Approach to Language Pedagogy*. New York: Longman.

Burg, L. (2006). *Language Learning: Problems and Prospect*. London: Jackinson Publisher.

Deka, Pranabjyoti (2007). *Student's Own Bilingual Dictionary*. Assam Book Depot, Panbazar, Guwahati.

Edward M. Anthony's '*Approach, Method & Technique English as a Second Language*' by Allen & Campbell. T.M.H. Edition.

Hasan, M.K. (2004). *A Lingustic Study of English Language Curriculum at the Secondary Level in Bangladesh—A Communicative Approach to Curriculum Development*.

J.A. Bright and G.P. McGregor. '*Teaching of English As a second language*, English Language Books Society and Longman Group Limited, 6.

Krishanaswamy, N. and Sri Raman, T. (1984). *English Teaching in India*. Madras: T.R. Publications.

Sadek, M.A. (2002). "*The Problems of English Language Teaching at Primary Level in Rural School of Bangladesh*". Unpublished Master's Thesis, IER, University of Dhaka.

Walder, Dennis. '*Post colonial Literatures in English—History Language Theory*', Blackwell Publishing, 48.

20

Setting Learning Outcome Standards for Undergraduate Learners for English as a Language of Oral Communication

T. Kranthi

Learning outcomes are statements that describe significant and essential learning that learners have achieved, and can reliably demonstrate at the end of a course. This is to identify what the learner will know and be able to do by the end of the course.

Possessing effective communication skills has become the prime necessity for the undergraduate learners pursuing an ESP course. The engineering learners too, who generally wish to join an MNC or visit abroad for further studies should be equipped with good communication skills. This paper analyses the importance of adopting a procedural approach while enabling the learners develop their communication skills. As their facilitators and mentors, we first help them conquer their inhibitions of talking to an "English teacher" in English and make them speak in English atleast in the English class. They then start talking in English with their peer group members, participate in group discussions, debates etc., and finally face a group of audience. This is a gradual process and hence importance of appropriacy, accuracy and fluency is stressed in this paper while developing their skills.

Of the four language skills, speaking is more complex because of two reasons: first it is a productive skill and hence needs to be executed with care as there is every chance of misconception during the communicating process. Secondly, the feedback would be immediate as the conversations would be face to face. This paves a way to form an opinion about the person who is speaking, which can be either positive or negative depending on various factors like the language used, the situation, use of non-verbal communication, enunciation of the language and behaviour of the person who is speaking.

While enabling the learners to develop professional skills in an ESP context, it is advisable to adapt a procedural approach because any skill can be mastered gradually. We generally stress the importance of fluency and accuracy while teaching speaking skills, but tend to overlook the third aspect which is very vital in social context, that is, appropriacy. One should know what to speak when and how.

The (future) engineers are not generally accustomed to speaking in English because till +2 the assessment is based on written examinations. Hence, though the learners have good knowledge of the language, at the graduation level it is not very easy for the teacher to help them break their shell of fear and speak with confidence. They can be gradually motivated and trained to make them master the communication skills. The researcher recommends the following procedure to help the learners devolop their speaking skills and then their communication skills.

For this purpose the learning objectives should first be framed, the method or procedure should be followed to attain the learning outcomes.

The researcher has listed the learning objectives for developing oral communication skills, and has framed learning outcomes based on the objectives and the course conducted. The objectives and outcomes are then matched in the form of a tabular column.

Details of the Study

No. of learners: 30

Venue: English language laboratory.

No. of sessions:

- Role play – 2 Hrs.

- Debate – 2 Hrs.
- Group Discussions (2 + 2 + 2 = 6 Hrs.)
- Team Presentations (2 + 2 + 2 = 6 Hrs.)
- Interview Skills (2 + 2 = 4 Hrs.)

Stage 1: Motivating the Learners to Speak

Objectives:

(a) To motivate the learners overcome their inhibitions and self-consciousness while speaking in English.

(b) To make the learners *think* in English.

(c) To make them share their viewpoint with others.

Procedure:

The teacher can provide various opportunities to help the learners conquer their stage fear first. The learners are encouraged to talk to the peer group members first and share their hobbies, interests, etc., they are asked to share the common interests being one among the group. They are not asked to stand on the stage or even at their place during this first stage. Instead, they are encouraged to sit at their place and respond.

The question that could be raised at this point is whether code switching and code mixing can be encouraged during the initial activities of speaking. In EFL situations code switching/mixing has become a natural outcome even when the communication is between educated Indian bilinguals. As the class consists of learners from vernacular medium till their +2, code mixing can be encouraged only at this initial stage.

Outcomes:

1. Identify the importance of effective communication skills.
2. Interact effectively and spontaneously.
3. Apply interpersonal skills in real life situations.
4. Articulate his/her viewpoint clearly and confidently.

Matching Objectives to the Outcomes

	Outcomes			
Objectives	1.	2.	3.	4.
(a)	✓	✓		✓
(b)	✓	✓		
(c)		✓	✓	✓

Pairing and Grouping Students

Advantages of Pair work and Group work

- It dramatically increases the amount of speaking time any one student gets in the class.
- It allows students work and interact without necessary guidance from the teacher, thus promoting learner independence.
- As in other speaking tasks, a conversation requires the speaker to face temporal constraints and the social pressures of face-to-face-interaction (Chafe, 16). So the learners also learn behavioral skills.
- It allows the teacher to focus on individual learners and motivate them accordingly.
- The students learn sharing the responsibility.
- It creates an amiable atmosphere and promotes brainstorming of ideas.
- The slow learners get motivated to speak when they are allowed to interact with peer group members.
- It promotes learner autonomy by allowing students to make their own decisions. (Adapted from Jeremy Harmer)

Stage 2: Pair work

Objectives:

(a) To understand what to speak, when to speak and how to speak during a given situation.

(b) To familiarise students with formal, semi-formal and informal language expressions.

(c) To make the learners proficient in verbal and non-verbal communication.

(d) To make the learners understand the importance of Intonation while speaking.

Procedure:

The learners are explained the difference between the formal and informal situations and the language phrases that could be used during those situations.

The Functional Aspect of English

Ordering: Telling someone to do something

Ex: Get away from her

Warning: Telling someone of the possible danger

Ex: Look out!

Cautioning: Advising about the possible danger

Ex: Don't eat so fast or you'll be sick.

Inviting: Ex: Why don't you come and dine with me?

Ex: Please take my seat/ Would you like to have a cup of tea?

Suggesting: Ex: Let's go for a walk./ Shall I open the window?

Requesting: Ex: Open the window please.

Instructing: Telling someone how to do something

Ex: First draw a straight line, then draw a line of equal length parallel to it.

Exhorting: Giving strong support and encouragement

Ex: Come on Dhoni!

Prohibiting: Telling someone not to do something.

Ex: No smoking.

Seeking permission

Ex: May I come in?

Could I talk to Mr. Prakash? (on the telephone)

The importance of using modal auxiliary verbs like can, could, will, would, may, shall is stressed at this point. They are made to listen to some sample conversations. They are then asked to enact informal role plays like introducing a new friend to the members of the family, convincing a friend to attend a birthday party etc., it has been observed by the researcher that the learners take interest in informal role-plays. They are then asked to role-play formal situations like requesting a teacher to explain a problem, selling a product to a customer etc., they are allowed to choose their partner at this stage.

Outcomes:

1. Identify the importance of effective communication skills.
2. Interact effectively and spontaneously.
3. Recognize the importance of purposeful communication.
4. Understand the importance of polite expressions.
5. Speak intelligibly with necessary pauses.

Matching Objectives to the Outcomes

	Outcomes				
Objectives	1	2	3	4	5
A	✓		✓		
B			✓	✓	
C		✓			
D				✓	
E					✓

Stage 3: Debates

Objectives

(1) To make the learners proficient in verbal and non-verbal communication.

(2) To impart interpersonal skills during small group communication.

(3) To evaluate the effectiveness of an argument logically and critically.

(4) To understand the importance of persuasion skills.

Procedure:

They are now asked to participate in a debate. The importance of logical reasoning and negotiation/persuasion skills is stressed at this point. This time the learners are selected randomly. (Appendix A—Topics for Debate.)

Outcomes:

1. Interact effectively and spontaneously.
2. Apply interpersonal skills in real life situations.
3. Articulate his/her viewpoint clearly and confidently.
4. Identify the importance of effective communication skills.
5. Be assertive in conveying the point of view.

Matching Objectives to the Outcomes

	Outcomes				
Objectives	1	2	3	4	5
A	✓				
B		✓	✓		
C					✓
D				✓	

Stage 4: Groupwork

Objectives:

(a) To make the learners proficient in verbal and non-verbal communication.

(b) To impart interpersonal skills during small group communication.

(c) To make them know the characteristics of a successful GD.

(d) Know the importance of GDs during selection process.

(e) Know how to initiate, participate and lead the discussion further.

(f) To evaluate the effectiveness of an argument logically and critically.

(g) To understand the importance of negotiation skills.

Procedure:

They are explained the importance of participating in a group discussion. The importance of group behaviour and team spirit is stressed at this point. They are then given some topics for both informal and formal group discussions. They would have developed some rapport with the peer group members and so they start speaking without any inhibitions. They are explained the importance of brainstorming and the difference between the three styles of communication, i.e., passive, aggressive and assertive communication:

Passive Communication

Passive communication is based on compliance and hopes to avoid confrontation at all costs. In this mode where one doesn't talk much, questions even less, and actually does very little. A passive communicator feels that it is safer not to react and better to disappear than to stand up and be noticed.

Aggressive Communication

Aggressive communication always involves manipulation. We may attempt to make people do what we want by inducing guilt (hurt) or by using intimidation and control tactics (anger). Covert or overt, we simply want our needs met.

Assertive Communication

The most effective and healthiest form of communication is the assertive style. It's how we naturally express ourselves when our self-esteem is intact, giving us the confidence to communicate without games and manipulation.

When we are being assertive, we work hard to create mutually satisfying solutions. We communicate our needs clearly and forthrightly. We care about the relationship and strive for a win/win situation. We know our limits and refuse to be pushed beyond them just because someone else wants or needs something from us. Surprisingly, assertive is the style most people use least.

They are asked to listen to a group discussion (How to prepare for a Group Discussion and Interviews by Hari Mohan Prasad) and identify the candidates who are likely to be selected based on the style of communication they adopt. The learners identify the speakers who are assertive in their argument, the speakers who sound aggressive and the candidates who don't prefer to share their views at all (passive). This helps the learners to understand the difference between the three styles of communication. They are then asked to watch a group discussion.

This time they are explained the importance of positive body language during the discussion.

The learners are given some language phrases that could be used for initiating, intervening while discussing and concluding a group discussion.

Function	Language Phrases	Pronunciation	Gestures
Starting a Conversation	Let's get the ball rolling... Friends, we are given a very interesting topic... Good morning, everybody, it's time to start the discussion...		
Helping somebody to begin to speak	I wonder if Sirish has something to speak about this... What is your opinion, Hari?	Stress Sirish and Hari Raises the voice at the end. (Question)	Inviting, friendly smile, eyes wide open.
Supporting the previous speaker	I think Soumya has made a good point which is worth considering... I agree with Smitha...	Stress good and worth Raising the voice a little, after Smitha	Eye contact with Soumya Pointing towards Smitha or Soumya with the hand (palm) NOT FINGER.
Disagreeing with the previous speaker	I'm sorry, but i can't agree with you...	Stress the negative	Eye contact with the listener
Interrupting for obtaining more information	Could you explain further?	Raising voice at further Stress on uncertain term	Leans forward
Concluding	Friends, it's time to sum up... So in conclusion we agree that...	Stress Sum up	Has eye contact with all the group members

They are then given some topics for group discussion. (Appendix B—Topics for group discussion.)

Outcomes:

1. Use effective negotiation skills during GDs.
2. Apply interpersonal skills in real life situations.
3. Articulate his/her viewpoint clearly and confidently.

4. Recognize the importance of purposeful communication.
5. Analyze the language expressions used in a GD.

Matching Objectives to the Outcomes

	Outcomes				
Objectives	1	2	3	4	5
A			✓		
B	✓	✓			
C					✓
D				✓	
E					✓
F					
G					✓

Stage 5: Team Presentations

Objectives:

(a) To impart interpersonal skills during small group communication.

(b) To make the learners proficient in verbal and non-verbal communication.

(c) Respond to audience queries.

(d) To deliver an effective technical presentation.

(e) To develop team spirit.

(f) To understand the concept of division of labour and unity in diversity.

Procedure:

During this stage the students are asked to give team presentations. They are asked to give a presentation about a company pertaining to their branch. The importance of field work, division of labour and unity in diversity is stressed at this point.

The following sub headings are given to them to help them in collecting information about an industry or an MNC:

Introduction

Location

Finance/Capital

Employee hierarchy

Facilities Provided

Awards/Achievements

Conclusion—Future Prospects.

Outcomes:

1. Identify the importance of effective communication skills.
2. Gather information on a given topic.
3. Organize the given information.
4. Plan organize, and prepare effective multimedia aids.
5. Identify the difference between a group and a team.
6. Identify the innards of team work.
7. Make effective power-point presentations.
8. Interact effectively and spontaneously.
9. Respond to the queries confidently and logically.

Matching Objectives to the Outcomes

	Outcomes								
Objectives	1	2	3	4	5	6	7	8	9
A								✓	
B								✓	
C									
D		✓	✓	✓			✓		✓
E					✓	✓			
F					✓	✓			✓

Stage 6: Interview Skills

Objectives:

(a) To make them understand the purpose behind an interview.

(b) To impart interpersonal skills during small group communication.

(c) To make the learners proficient in verbal and non-verbal communication.

(d) To train them in listening skills.

(e) To prepare them for facing an interview.

Procedure:

They are explained the importance of interview skills. The importance of being spontaneous and confident is stressed at this point. They are given a set of interview questions and are asked to draft a convincing response for them.

In this manner, the learners can be tuned in a proper way to develop both their communication and professional skills (Appendix C).

Outcomes:

1. Recognize the importance of purposeful communication.
2. Plan organize, and prepare for an interview.
3. Interact effectively and spontaneously.
4. Apply interpersonal skills in real life situations.
5. Listen properly and respond accordingly.

Matching Objectives to the Outcomes

	Outcomes				
Objectives	1	2	3	4	5
A	✓				
B		✓	✓	✓	
C				✓	
D					
E		✓			

In the above-mentioned manner teaching can become more effective if learning outcomes can be gauged along with the objectives of teaching.

Appendix A

Topics for Debate

1. Should morals be taught to engineering students?
2. Should there be a dress code for engineering students?
3. Is peer pressure always beneficial?
4. Should undergraduate students be required to take a physical education course?

5. Is the opening of global markets good for the average Indian?

6. The internet brings more harm than good.

7. It is sometimes right for the government to restrict freedom of speech.

8. Should colleges focus on core technical subjects exclude less fundamental subjects like art, music, and sports?

9. Is a technical course like engineering becoming a question of just obtaining a degree?

10. Is internet producing copy cats?

Appendix B

List of Group Discussion Topics

1. Which job you prefer? A lucrative private job or a secured Govt. job?

2. Man or Machine?

3. City life Vs Rural life.

4. Are daughters are more caring than sons?

5. Money makes as well as mars many things.

6. Nuclear family Vs Joint family.

7. Love marriages Vs arranged marriages.

8. Is science a boon or a bane?

9. Is cricket eclipsing other sports in India?

10. Is India a soft Nation?

Appendix C

Interview Questions

1. What are your strengths and weaknesses?

2. Tell me about yourself.

3. What are your team-player qualities? Give examples.

4. Of the courses you have had at college which courses have you enjoyed the most?

5. How have your educational and work experiences prepared you for this position?

6. What work experiences have been most valuable to you and why?

7. What have the experiences on your resume taught you about managing and working with people?

8. Of the hobbies and interests listed on your resume what is your favorite and tell me why?

9. Where do you see yourself in five years?

10. To what do you owe your present success?

11. Why should I hire you?

12. What is your most significant accomplishment to-date?

13. Why do you want to work here?

14. Describe a leadership role of yours and tell why you committed your time to it.

15. In a particular leadership role you had, what was your greatest challenge?

16. Give me an example of a creative idea that has come to you and what you did with it?

17. Give me an example of a problem you solved and the process you used?

18. Give me an example of the most creative project that you have worked on.

19. Since attending college, what is the toughest decision that you have had to make?

20. Tell me about your most difficult decision and how did you go about making it?

21. What types of situations put you under pressure, and how do you deal with pressure?

22. If I asked the people who know you well to describe you, what three words would they use?

23. If I asked the people who know you for one reason why I shouldn't hire you what would they say?

24. When you take on a project do you like to attack the project in a group or individually?

25. Describe a situation where you had to work with someone who was difficult, how did you handle it?

26. Why did you choose this college and how did you arrive at this decision?

27. Since you have been at college, what is it that you are proudest of?

28. How have you changed personally since starting college?

29. If you could change a decision you made while at college what would you change and why?

30. Why did you choose the campus involvements you did? What did you gain? What did you contribute?

References

Chafe, W. (1986). Writing in the Perspective of Speaking. In C.R. Cooper and S. Greenbaum (Eds.), *Studying Writing: Linguistic Approaches*. London: Sage Publications.

Assertiveness and Diversity-Anni Townend, Palgrave Macmillan, New York, 2007.

Christopher Brumfit (1984). Communicative Methodology in Language Teaching—The Roles of Fluency and Accuracy, Cambridge: CUP.

Jeremy Harmer (2001). *The Practice of Teaching English*. England: Pearson Education Ltd.

21

Trends, Approaches and Techniques in Error Correction

Muhammed Ali Chalikandy

Abstract

Just as everyone makes mistakes in their life and in their first language learning, EFL/ESL learners make mistakes when they learn a foreign or second language. The learners learn when they don't make mistakes, but they learn better when they make mistakes. Furthermore, the learners' mistakes will tell us more about the learners, their current level, competence, their need, and their lacks. However, everyone worries about learners' mistakes. Teachers of English often ask why students go on making the same mistakes that have been corrected frequently. There is no unanimous view on error correction. Theorists view differently from practitioners. The current trend in error correction is to know learners' perception of error correction and to include it in the classroom practice. This paper discusses the trend, approaches and techniques in dealing with error correction both in accuracy and fluency based activities.

Keywords: Errors, Correction, Views, Trends, Techniques.

Introduction

Learning is a life long process. It starts as soon as we are born and lasts till the end. However, L2 learning is different from L1 learning since it happens in a very formal set up like a classroom. A person cannot learn anything from anyone else. No one else can make a learner understood or acquire a skill except the learners themselves. Scrivener (2005) claims that "learning is the result of learners' personal effort" (17). We learn by trail and error by testing what works and what does not. "By a gradual process of trial and error and hypothesis testing, learners slowly and tediously succeeded in establishing closer and closer approximations to the system used by native speakers of the language" (Brown 2007: 256). As a result, errors are inevitable byproduct of the process of learning.

What are Errors?

The term error has been defined differently by different scholars based on their views on learning and the learner. "An error is a noticeable deviation from the adult grammar of a native speaker and reflects the competence of the learner" (Brown 2007: 259). Edge (1989) divides mistakes into three broad categories such as slips, errors, and attempts. Corder (1974) calls this a deviation from the accepted form and has grouped deviant language into three kinds: lapses, mistakes, and errors. Both slips and lapses are errors of performance due to memory lapses, exhaustion and stress. Attempts and mistakes are those which mismatch the utterances with the situations and are inappropriate utterances in that context. Such errors occur due to ignorance of a particular usage in a specific context and the learners' lack of knowledge of the target language. Students can correct slips, lapses and mistakes as soon as they make them, whereas they cannot correct errors by themselves because they are unaware of them. As a result, learners need guidance and help to identify and correct errors. Moreover, errors need special consideration because they occur because of learners' language incompetence.

Current View on Errors

Errors are no longer considered as a sin. They are part of learning a language, which go along with the learning. Errors indicate learners' progress because they tell us whether the learners are "experimenting with language, trying out ideas, taking risks and attempting to communicate" (Scrivener 2005: 298). Errors reveal the learners' competence—the transitional competence. Second language learners' errors are important because they are "the researcher evidence of how language is learned or acquired, what strategies or procedures the learner is employing in the discovery of the language" (Corder 1967: 167) and he claims that errors show that the learner's current language level. In fact, errors are learners' tools that they use to acquire the target language. According to James (1998) analysis of learners errors will help us to understand the process of second language acquisition. Brown (2007) aptly said, "Mistakes misjudgments, miscalculations, and erroneous assumptions form an important aspect of learning virtually any skill or acquiring information" (257).

Correct Errors or Not?

There is no definite answer because although a number of studies have been carried out, there is no unanimous view among scholars. For instance, Krashen (1981), Schwartz (1993), Terrell (1977) and Truscott (1999) view that explicit focus on linguistic structure is unnecessary and corrective feedback is ineffective. Krashen (1982) argues that error correction is "a serious mistake" (74) because "error correction has the immediate effect of putting the student on the defensive" (75) and he adds that error correction only help learning not the acquisition of language. Similarly Mory (2004) points out that feedback has no effect on learning. In contrast, many researchers consider feedback is vital in the learning process because it increases knowledge and develop skills (Azevedo and Bernard, 1995; Corbett and Anderson, 1989; Moreno, 2004). Feedback has impact on learners' success; furthermore, it motivates learners (Lepper and Chabay, 1985; Narciss and Huth, 2004). Cohen (1985) claims that feedback "is one of the more instructionally powerful and least understood features in instructional design" (33). It has been suggested that feedback facilitate learning and accelerates learners' performance (Bandura 1991; Fedor 1991). Furthermore, Canadian immersion programs (Swain 1985) and Swedish immersion programs (Skutnabb-Kangas 1976) show us that second language learners still produce grammatically inaccurate utterance even though they have had many years of target language exposure.

Children make a lot of mistakes when they learn L1. However, gradually they produce acceptable language using the feedback that they get. Similarly L2 learners will make mistakes and they have to learn from their mistakes because language learning is "a process in which success comes by profiting from mistakes, by using mistakes to obtain feedback from the environment, and with that feedback to make new attempts that successively approximate desired goals" (Brown 2007: 257).

Trends and Techniques in Error Correction

The current trend in language teaching is to understand learners' perception so that the teachers will be able to adapt their strategies and classroom activities to the learners. Beliefs influence and play key roles in language learning and teaching. For instance, there is a correlation between beliefs and the strategy that are used in the class, learner motivation and language proficiency (Mori 1999; Yang 1999). Beliefs influence teachers in classroom decisions and actions (Borg 2003; Burgess and Etherington 2002). Sawir (2002) found that unrealistic beliefs and wrong concept about learning a language hinder the learning process. Kern (1995) argues that teachers' and learners' beliefs are very important for understanding the learning process because they help us to avoid learners' frustration, deal with their anxiety, and motivate learners.

Extensive research has been done on beliefs and found that beliefs influence teachers and their attitudes about learning, teaching, learners' behavior and their classroom practice. Casciani and Rapallino (1991) conducted a study and found that students believed that error correction was necessary. Bang (1999) carried out a study and discovered that students felt that oral correction was imperative for language learning. Lee (2005) did a study to find out learners' beliefs and attitudes about teacher correction and found that the learners wanted their teachers to correct their errors. Students are eager to get teachers feedback and they believe that it is useful (Leki 1991; Radacki and Swales 1998). Chalikandy (2014) conducted a study and found that undergraduate students believed correction was useful to them because it helped them to learn better and they preferred teacher correction to peer correction.

Understanding learners' perception of error correction will help the teachers to decide who to correct, when to correct what to correct and how to correct.

Who Should Correct Errors?

One of the most important things in error correction is to decide the person who corrects the mistake. Now that we have moved from traditional classroom to learner centered approach in language learning, teachers have comparatively no active role in correcting a mistake. Teachers should not be the first person to correct a mistake in a language classroom; on the other hand, he should be the last person to correct the mistake when all the other options fail. According to Scrivener (2005) teachers can use any one of these: self correction, student to student correction, small group correction, whole class correction and course book or reference book. The teacher can give chance to correct the mistakes to the student who has made it. If he can't, get another student to correct the mistake and so on. Sometimes mistake can be corrected in a small group. When the small group fails, get the whole class work together to correct the mistake. It is psychologically sound to get the students to self discover by referring the course book or a source book.

Time of Correction

The second issue is when to correct: immediately or later. Many studies have been done to see the effect of timing of feedback (Clariana 1999; Jurma and Froelich 1984). Although there is no clear conclusion about timing, some favour immediate feedback because it prevents errors going into the memory and others argues for delayed feedback because it reduces the interference. According to Clariana (1999) immediate feedback is useful for difficult tasks whereas delayed feedback is suitable for easy tasks. Gaynor (1981) argues that immediate feedback is beneficial to low-achieving students whereas delayed feedback will be more suitable for high-achieving students. Mathan and Koedinger (2002) examined a number of studies on the timing of feedback and concluded that the effectiveness of feedback depends not on the timing but on the nature and type of the activity and the learners' ability.

Teachers, generally, prefer to correct the mistakes soon after they occur. The question is when to correct if not immediately. There are number things to be considered before choosing the time. The teacher should see the aim and type of the activity, the impact of correction on the learners: whether it would help them in learning or prevent them from learning. Teachers also should consider whether the students have already learned the items or not. If they do not know what is corrected, it is worthless spending time on correction. Learners' attitudes towards correction and teachers' intention of correcting mistakes should also be considered. After seeing these the teachers can correct "immediately; after a few minutes; at the end of the activity; in the next lesson; later in the course; never" (Scrivener 2005: 299).

The Type of Activity: Accuracy and Fluency

It is necessary to distinguish an activity as accuracy based or fluency based. According to Harmer (1998) while a teacher can correct during an accuracy activity, he should not indulge in a fluency activity unless the situation require so. There are a number of factors that affect the effectiveness of corrective feedback in the oral classroom. To illustrate this, according to Havranek and Cesnik (2001) the error type, characteristics of learners like verbal intelligence, proficiency, level, and learners' attitude towards correction and even the format of feedback influence its success in the classroom.

Teachers tend to correct students' mistakes during an oral activity since they are evident in their production. The teachers should control their temptation however strong it is because "the immediate and constant correction of all errors is not necessarily an effective way of helping learners improve their English" (Harmer 1998: 104). Indiscriminate correction will have adverse effect on learners. Therefore, teachers should not deal with all oral production in the same way. They should see the stages of the lesson, the type of activity, the type of mistakes and the student who is making mistakes.

Correction during an Accuracy Activity

What is the classroom procedure for correcting errors if the teacher has decided to deal with them? Scrivener (2005) says that there are two steps in dealing with the correction. First of all the teacher has to signal the students that they have made a mistake and the kind of mistake that they have made. The teacher can use a number of techniques to show that there is an error. For example, teachers can directly tell the learners that they have made an error, use gestures and facial expression to indicate the mistake, repeat up to the mistake, echo mistake with exaggerated tone, ask questions, use board to indicate that there is a mistake or even use humour to show that there is a mistake. The second step is to help the learner to correct the mistake. The first step and second step are not separate but they are integrated.

Correction during a Fluency Activity

Errors during a fluency activity need a special attention. Correction technique during a fluency activity can be divided into two categories: during the activity and after the lesson. According to Scrivener (2005) the feedback during fluency activity should focus on the content, but not on the form. The teachers can correct the activity gently if there is a complete breakdown of the message. For instance, a teacher can observe the classroom activity and makes a list of mistakes to be used as a material for classroom discussion. Recording students' performance using a recorder unobtrusively is very useful because this recording can be played to the students who watch and discuss the mistakes in the group and finally report to the class. An effective correction technique is scaffolding. Hartman (2002) states that scaffolding consists of models, cues, prompt, hints, partial solutions, and even direct instruction from the teacher. It is a sort of support given by the teacher to help the learners to complete the task. It is the spontaneous way of correcting a mistake during fluency activity. According to Scrivener (2005) scaffolding is the "way a competent speaker helps a less competent one to communicate by both encouraging and providing possible elements of conversation" (162). In other words, it is correcting mistakes through which a teacher offers feedback to the students without interrupting the flow of the conversation.

Correction can be even carried out after the session and the tolerance of errors is greater than during the activity. The teacher has a lot to do after the fluency activity. He can even use the mistakes as the resource for the future lesson.

Conclusion

Traditionally, errors were treated as hindrance to learning. However, the concept has been changed. Now mistakes mean learning is taking place. When the students are making mistakes, they are learning and improving. Therefore look for the mistakes which tell the teachers about the level of the students and the stage that they have reached, which in turn help the teacher to make a future plan. Instant correction may be useful during an accuracy activity, but it is inappropriate during a fluency activity. However, an occasion may occur during a fluency activity where teachers' intervention and correction is necessary. Then the teacher has to take the class forward without affecting the flow of the lesson and breaking down the message and without intimidating the learners.

References

Azevedo, R., and Bernard, R.M. (1995). A meta-analysis of the effects of feedback in computer-based instruction. *Journal of Educational Computing Research*, 13(2): 111-27.

Bandura, A. (1991). Social theory of self-regulation. *Organizational Behavior and Human Decision Processes*, 50: 248-87.

Bang, Y. (1999). Reactions of EFL students to oral error correction. *Journal of Pan-Pacific Association of Applied Linguistics*, 3: 39-51.

Borg, S. (2003). Teacher cognition in grammar teaching: A literature review. *Language Awareness*, 12: 96-108. Burgess, J., and Etherington, S. (2002). Focus on grammatical form: Explicit or implicit? *System*, 30: 433-58.

Brown, D.H. (2007). *Principles of Language Learning and Teaching*. New York: Person Education.

Burgess, J., and Etherington, S. (2002). Focus on grammatical form: Explicit or implicit? *System*, 30: 433-58.

Casciani, S., and Rapallino, L. (1991). "Pronouns in the oven," or the correction of errors in teaching Italian. *Italica,* 68: 457-72.

Chalikandy, M.A. (2014, May). *Correction: Myth and Reality.* Paper presented at Oman 14th International ELT Conference.

Clariana, R.B. (1999, February). *Differential memory effects for immediate and delayed feedback: A delta rule explanation of feedback timing effects.* Paper presented at the Association of Educational Communications and Technology annual convention, Houston, TX.

Cohen, V.B. (1985). A re-examination of feedback in computer-based instruction: Implications for instructional design. *Educational Technology, 25*(1): 33-37.

Corbett, A.T., and Anderson, J.R. (1989). Feedback timing and student control in the LISP intelligent tutoring system. In D. Bierman, J. Brueker, and J. Sandberg (Eds.), *Proceedings of the Fourth International Conference on Artificial Intelligence and Education* (64-72). Amsterdam, Netherlands: IOS Press.

Corder, S.P. (1967). The Significance of Learners' Errors. *International Journal of Applied Linguistics,* 5: 161-70.

Corder, S.P. (1974). Error Analysis. In J.P.B. Allen and S. Pit Corder (eds.), *Techniques in Applied Linguistics* (122-54) London: Oxford University.

Edge, J. (1989). *Mistakes and Correction.* Harlow: Longman.

Fedor, D.B. (1991). Recipient responses to performance feedback: A proposed model and its implications. *Research in Personnel and Human Resources Management,* 9: 73-120.

Gaynor, P. (1981). The effect of feedback delay on retention of computer-based mathematical material. *Journal of Computer-Based Instruction,* 8(2): 28-34.

Harmer, J. (1998). *The Practice of English Language Teaching.* England: Longman.

Hartman, H. (2002). Scaffolding and cooperative learning. In *Human learning and instruction* (23-69). New York: City College, University of New York.

Havranek, G. and Cesnik, H. (2001). *Factors Affecting the Success of Corrective Feedback* (Vol. 1). Amsterdam: John Benjamins.

James, C. (1998). *Errors in language learning and use: Exploring error analysis.* Harlow, UK: Addison Wesley Longman.

Jurma, W.E., and Froelich, D.L. (1984). Effects of immediate instructor feedback on group discussion participants. *Central States Speech Journal,* 35(3): 178-86.

Kern, R.G. (1995). Students' and teachers' beliefs about language learning. *Foreign Language Annals* 28: 71-92.

Krashen, S. (1981). *Second Language Acquisition and Second Language Learning*. Oxford: Pergamon.

Krashen, S. (1982). *Principles and practice in second language acquisition*. Oxford: Pergamon.

Leki, I. (1991). The preferences of ESL students for error correction in college-level writing classes. *Foreign Language Annals*, 24: 203-18.

Lepper, M.R., and Chabay, R.W. (1985). Intrinsic motivation and instruction: Conflicting views on the role of motivational processes in computer-based education. *Educational Psychologist,* 20(4): 217-30.

Mathan, S.A., and Koedinger, K.R. (2002). An empirical assessment of comprehensionfostering features in an intelligent tutoring system. In S.A. Cerri, G. Gouarderes, and F. Paraguacu (Eds.), *Intelligent Tutoring Systems, 6th International Conference, ITS 2002* (Vol. 2363: 330-43). New York: Springer-Verlag.

Moreno, R. (2004). Decreasing cognitive load for novice students: Effects of explanatory versus corrective feedback in discovery-based multimedia. *Instructional Science,* 32: 99-113.

Mori, Y. (1999). Epistemological beliefs and language learning beliefs: What do language learners believe about their learning? *Language Learning,* 49: 377-415.

Mory, E.H. (2004). Feedback research review. In D. Jonassen (Ed.), *Handbook of research on educational communications and technology* (745-83). Mahwah, NJ: Lawrence Erlbaum.

Narciss, S., and Huth, K. (2004). How to design informative tutoring feedback for multimedia learning. In H.M. Niegemann, D. Leutner, and R. Brunken (Ed.), *Instructional design for multimedia learning* (181-95). Munster, NY: Waxmann.

Radecki, P., and Swales, J. (1988). ESL student reaction to written comments on their written work. *System*, 16: 355-65.

Sawir, E. (2002). Beliefs about language learning: Indonesian learners' perspectives and some implications for classroom practices. *Australian Journal of Education,* 46: 323-37.

Schwartz, B. (1993). On explicit and negative data effecting and affecting competence and linguistic behavior. *Studies in Second Language Acquisition,* 15: 165-75.

Scrivener, Jim (2005). *Learning Teaching*. Oxford: Macmillan Education.

Skutnabb-Kangas, T. (1976). Bilingualism, semilingualism and school achievement *Linguistische Berichte,* 45: 55-64.

Swain, M. (1985). Communicative competence: Some roles of comprehensible input and comprehensible output in its development. In S. Gass and C. Madden (Eds.), *Input in second language acquisition* (235-52). Rowley, MA: Newbury House.

Terrell, T. (1977). A natural approach to second language acquisition and learning. *Modern Language Journal,* 61: 325-37.

Truscott, J. (1999). What's wrong with oral grammar correction? *Canadian Modern Language Review/LaRevue canadienne des languesvivantes,* 55: 437-56.

Yang, N. (1999). The relationship between EFL learners' beliefs and learning strategy use. *System,* 27: 515-35.

22

Setting Standards for English Language Teaching through Teachers' Continuous Professional Development

Nizara Hazarika

Introduction

Continuing Professional Development (CPD) has become a buzz word for the teaching fraternity. It has been defined as "a planned, continuous and lifelong process whereby teachers try to develop their personal and professional qualities, and to improve their knowledge, skills and practice, leading to their empowerment, the improvement of their agency and the development of their organisation and their pupils" (Padwad and Dixit 2011: 10). This definition brings to the fore the importance of CPD for a teacher who can contribute towards the development of English Language Teaching scenario. CPD is a lifelong process that extends from the early training to continuous professional development activities that take place throughout one's career. It has been a given fact that learners' improvement depends on teaching quality and to enhance the quality of teaching, the teachers need to be aware of their own professional development. As lifelong learners, the teachers need to engage in various activities that develop their individual skills, knowledge, and expertise throughout their teaching career. To achieve the goal of this personal as well professional development, the teachers need to reflect on their teaching, improve and update on their professional competencies, update on their skills, approaches and knowledge of the subject in the light of newer development in the concerned area. This knowledge will be translated to the teaching context which will develop their students and the institutions. They need to take part in various CPD activities to keep pace with the learners' growing demands. Christopher Day has stressed on the CPD as both natural and conscious and planned activities undertaken by teachers which contribute to the quality of education in the classroom. He opined that

> It is the process by which, alone and with others, teachers review, renew and extend their commitment as change agents to the moral purpose of teaching; and by which they acquire and develop critically the knowledge, skills and emotional intelligence essential to good professional thinking, planning and practice with children, young people and colleagues throughout each phase of their teaching lives. (Day 1999: 4)

What comes out is the role of teachers to enhance the educational scenario through their own PD activities.

Need of CPD: Teachers all over the world have faced certain barriers that comes on their professional development like heavy workload, lack of time, lack of support from the management, financial constraints and so on. It is observed that pursuing CPD is not much followed in the ELT fraternity due to various reasons. One of the main reasons is teachers' lack of awareness of the need of their own personal as well as professional growth through various CPD strategies. Moreover, the institutions and Policy-makers too exhibit a total lack of awareness regarding the need of teachers' CPD. In most cases, CPD is controlled by school/college administration and hence, there is reluctance on the part of the administration to provide their teachers the opportunity to go for their own PD. For a long time, the teachers' training sessions and courses were regarded to be the main element of teachers' professional development. However, that narrow definition have been replaced by a more broader perspective where "CPD embraces a number of activities, such as mentoring, self-evaluation, action research, peer coaching and learning, as legitimate and effective forms of CPD. Training is just one stop on the CPD journey towards quality teaching and learning..." (Hayes 2014: 21). Though CPD is an autonomous activity undertaken by a teacher for her professional growth,

CPD takes place in collaborative activities where teachers can share and learn together and grow together. These CPD activities can empower the teachers with new knowledge and skills which leads to the improvement of the teaching-learning scenario. But the pertinent questions here are: Are the teachers aware of their own CPD? How much do they give importance to their own CPD?

Over the years, the CPD scenario has gained a new momentum. The teachers training as a top down strategy has been replaced by CPD activities as a bottom up strategy where the teachers have the major role to play. In the traditional top-down strategy the teachers did not have any decisive role to play. But in the various CPD activities, it is the teachers who have to be active all along. The teachers gain a lot from the various CPD activities. PD activities enhance the interest of the teachers in their teaching and motivate them. There lies its need. The in-service and pre-service training are not enough for their professional growth. They are provided at fixed timeframe. So, the follow up does not take place most of the time. The teachers are not aware of their PD opportunities and hence they need the various avenues open before them for their growth. With their participation in the PD activities, there will be positive changes in them which will be percolated to their teaching contexts and the ELT scenario as a whole will improve.

An awareness of the positive impact of the CPD activities can enhance teachers' enthusiasm towards the various CPD activities. Harland and Kinder (1997) suggest nine outcomes of the CPD avenues which are non-hierarchical and teachers gain a unique "outcome profile" from each CPD. According to them the outcomes are material and resources for teaching, gaining fact-based information, new awareness towards new ideas and values, value congruence, affective outcomes, motivation and attitude, knowledge and skills, institutional outcomes and finally impact on practice. Harland and Kinder are of the opinion that though the outcomes of CPD are different and varied, certain outcomes may have knock-on effects on other outcomes. Taking a different approach to Harland and Kinder's outcome profile approach, Joyce and Showers (1980) takes on a linear model of CPD outcomes. Their model moves in a linear way from one outcome to the other. The first outcome, for them is awareness, i.e., recognizing the importance of the chosen area of CPD which is followed by concepts and organised knowledge, i.e., an awareness of the processes of knowledge acquisition. The third outcome is principles and skills, i.e., acquiring the tools needed for the teaching of the learners and finally the fourth outcome is application and problem-solving, i.e., transferring the knowledge and skills to the classroom teaching. For Joyce and Showers, the outcomes are linear in nature and one outcome leads to the other.

Thus, CPD activities can enhance the motivation level of the teachers and update them on the various roles that they need to engage in. The teachers can keep themselves abreast with the new knowledge in their own domain and by application of which they can bring positive changes to their teaching contexts. But how far are the teachers aware of the CPD activities? Do they have enough resources or networking to take part in the various CPD activities?

Some Continuing Professional Development Activities for Teachers

Though CPD is accepted as crucial in ELT, a large number of teachers are yet to gather knowledge about meaningful and effective measures for their own professional growth. A detailed exploration of the various individual and collaborative CPD opportunities has been provided for the benefit of the teacher fraternity who can choose their own CPD strategies. One of the main thrust for teachers going for CPD is reflecting on one's teaching. Through Reflective teaching, teachers can think about their teaching strategies, ask questions and develop greater awareness about teaching. Farrell (1998) opines that reflective teaching helps free teachers from impulsive behaviour or, on the other extreme, from monotony in their teaching; it also allows teachers to develop their own educational perspectives. Teachers can even benefit by sharing their reflective teaching experiences with their peers. In the words of Alice Murray:

> One way to take control of one's own learning is through cooperation with other teachers. Collegial cooperation can help teachers become more assertive and decisive about their personal learning; it can also boost their confidence and empower them to find solutions to challenges they face in their teaching. (English Language Forum 2010: 4)

Thus, keeping in mind the teaching-learning contexts, teachers can take part in various CPD strategies that are beneficial for them. The CPD activities could be individual and informal as well as collaborative and formal. The teachers need to have knowledge about the various CPD opportunities that they can take part. Some of the CPD strategies can be,

- Individual and Informal
- Keeping Teaching Journal
- Making Self Observation
- Making Self-Appraisal
- Attending Online Conferences, webinars
- Taking help from online resources: portals, websites, blogs, Courses
- Reading
- Publishing articles
- Participating in workshops and conferences
- Holding positions of responsibility.

Collective and Structured

- Taking part in Peer Observation and Mentoring
- Joining a Teacher support Network
- Forming or joining local and national teachers' associations
- Participating in workshops and conferences
- Forming local CPD Groups
- Forming Idea Sharing Groups—local and online
- Participating in Community of Practices.

Contextualizing CPD

In India, CPD has not been given enough importance till recently. In-service training (INSET) was almost the only avenue open before the teachers for their professional development. Most of the teachers do not possess a teaching diploma or degree. Under such situations, motivating the teachers was almost a herculean task, as neither the topdown strategy nor the bottom up strategy was adequate. Both for the teachers as well as the Policy-makers, CPD means nothing but in-service training. Bolitho and Padwad, in their introduction to Continuing Professional Development: Lessons from India, talk about CPD in Indian context. They opine,

> The CPD scenario in India seems to suffer from a dual handicap—there is little top-down support from state policies and programmes or from administrators and school management for CPD beyond INSET, while there are also few instances of bottom-up initiatives and efforts by teachers to take responsibility for their own CPD and to explore the full range of alternatives options for CPD rather than simply being content with INSET designed and delivered by state agencies.(Bolitho and Padwad 2013: 8)

Studies reveal that in many schools CPD of teachers are decided by the school authorities, and teachers are the passive recipients of those dictums. Teachers too lack the enthusiasm in taking part in the various CPD activities. They simply take part in the programs that are made mandatory by the authority or the Government. Under such situation, the CPD environment will surely suffer. Padwad and Dixit opine that teachers are supposed to work as 'just teachers' who should do what others like experts, principals, and educational authorities say. In other words, teachers function in a climate of very limited autonomy and agency. Therefore, teachers seem to be unaware of their potential to develop professionally (Bolitho and Padwad 2013: 12). On the other hand there seems to be a gap between the policy-makers, the administrators and the teachers who will take part in the CPD activities. The Policy-makers, till very recently thought that mere INSET was enough for the teachers to cope with the new trends of teaching. Therefore, the teachers would not receive any encouragement and support to take part in activities like attending conferences or acquiring additional professional qualification. Moreover, the varied needs and interests of the teachers were not recognized by the authorities.

However, with the passage of time, there has been a total overhauling of the CPD of teachers. But again the important point here is how far the teachers, school authorities, the policy makers are aware of these avenues?

In Assam, to enter into a teaching job, the Pre-service training, the Professional Teaching Degrees like B.Ed. or D.Ed. is not required. Pre-service training is not a requirement. The early stage teachers do not need to go for INSET. Only after teaching for a certain period, they are required to go for the INSET. Teachers lack the basic awareness about the need of their own PD. The topdown strategy is at work. The State or the Institution is equally responsible in the professional stagnation of the teachers. The institution is the mediator as whatever comes from up (State/Policy-makers) must go to teachers through it. But the institutions, most of the time, do not encourage such activities. The Govt. policy of initiating teacher training through Sarva Shiksha Abhiyan (Universal Primary Education) and Rastriya Madhyamik Shiksha Abhiyan (National Secondary Education Mission) is a welcome move, but still there are miles to go. The Cascade Method has been adopted by the Government of India and as a part of it, the Resource persons will be oriented first at the District level and then they will train the teachers. This training by the RPs will be inclusive of motivational training, recent trends in pedagogy, classroom interaction and so on. The teachers' progress or performance will be observed and further training will be provided.

The Study

A small study was undertaken where 26 Higher Secondary teachers from Assam, who came for a Workshop was made to respond to a small questionnaire. They were asked to express their ideas about CPD, whether they take part in CPD activities and if not the reasons and what are some of the challenges that they have faced. They are also asked how they rate themselves as a teacher and whether they are satisfied with their competency. Finally they were also asked how frequently they engage themselves in CPD activities.

The Data

- A 20% (5) of the teachers are aware of the concept of CPD and they are eager to take part in them. But their institutes don't provide them the required time and space to attend them.
- Thirty per cent (8) of Higher Secondary teachers are aware of the various CPD opportunities available for them.
- Another 30% (8) has the opinion that though they know about some of the CPD opportunities, they are too busy with their work time schedule and cannot manage time to take part in the PD activities.
- A 20% (5) of the teachers expressed their disinterest in such PD activities as they feel that there is no need of it as they are qualified to do justice to their job.

In response to the query regarding their participation in the CPD activities, it came out that the teachers were sharing with colleagues, reading journal articles and taking part in the workshops organised by Assam Higher Secondary Council or ELTI. The challenges faced by them were from the side of the authorities. They do not get enough opportunity to take part in the CPD activities due to lack of time and sometimes interest as well. Moreover, they are not properly aware of the various CPD activities. For some of them, the term CPD means sometime unattainable, which requires a lot of finance, time and energy. For them publishing in books and journals are not meant for the College teachers and not for them. Same is with attending various Seminars and Conferences.

Some of the challenges faced by teachers are lack of time, lack of resources, large class, lack of support from the institution, lack of support from Government, lack of peer support, poor quality of learners demotivate some of the teachers. At times, the junior teachers are not given enough opportunity by the senior teachers.

Findings

The study brings to the fore the lack of awareness of a section of the teachers regarding the CPD strategies for their own development. Without being aware of CPD, a teacher cannot contribute to the development of the teaching-learning situation. While another section teachers are very much interested in taking part in the CPD activities. Another section expressed their disinterest in the CPD activities. But, for each and every teacher CPD is a must. Once they enter in the profession of teaching, they have to update themselves on the current trends of knowledge. In the words of Bolitho,"CPD is the process of teachers' development after joining the profession, a process of lifelong learning, both formal and informal, and involves both voluntary teacher initiatives and programmes externally planned and mandated by authorities" (Bolitho and Padwad, 2013: 13). The various stakeholders have an important role to play for the overall improvement of the teaching scenario. The teachers are not solely responsible for not taking part in the CPD activities. The institution has a crucial role to play in encouraging and motivating the teachers to take part in the CPD activities. The bottom up strategy is the need of the hour. The teachers need to reflect on their teaching, to plan and execute their professional development activities. Teachers' perception regarding their own CPD varies a great deal and hence teachers' awareness of their professional growth will direct them towards the opening of a new horizon where they will participate in the various activities that will develop and improve the ELT scenario in their own contexts.

Conclusion

Professional development is a continuous and ongoing process. There is no single way for the professional growth of a teacher. Each teacher has to go for her/his own CPD as their teaching contexts demand. Teachers need to work in collaboration with their students, peers, authorities, government and so on to attain a position where their CPD can take place without any hurdle. But for this, they need to reflect, renew and reframe their knowledge and skills to suit their purpose. CPD is a lifelong process and teachers need to refresh and enhance their knowledge and skills throughout their professional career. To evolve as a teacher and to set a standard for teaching in the context of modern day education, the teachers' participation in the CPD is highly warranted. They have to be ready to face challenges that come on their way. The teachers need to accept the newer pedagogical developments with a free mind. Once they accept them and realise the need to take part in the PD activities, change will surely come to the ELT context. The teachers can be agents to change the ELT scenario through their CPD activities. The process leading to one's professional development empowers the teachers and with this sense of empowerment, the teachers can certainly improve the ELT scenario.

References

Bolitho, R. and A. Padwad (eds). (2013). Continuing Professional Development: Lessons from India. New Delhi: British Council.

Day, C. (1999). *Developing Teachers: The Challenges of Lifelong Learning*. London: Falmer Press

Drago-Severson, E. (2004). *Helping teachers learn: Principal leadership for adult growth and development*. Thousand Oaks, CA: Corwin Press.

Farrell, T. (1998). Reflective teaching: The principles and practices. *English Teaching Forum* 36(4): 10-17.

Harland, J. and Kinder, K. (1997). Teachers' continuing professional develop development: Framing a model of outcomes. *British Journal of In-Service Education*, 23(1): 71-84.

Hayes, D. (ed). (2014). Innovations in the Continuing Professional Development of English Teachers. London: British Council.

Joyce, B. and Showers, B. (1980). Improving in-service training: The messages of research. Educational Leadership, 37: 379-85.

Kathleen M. Bailey, Andy Curtis, and David Nunan (2001). *Pursuing Professional Development: The Self as Source*. Boston: Teacher Source.

Murray, A. (2010). "Empowering Teachers Through Professional Development". *English Teaching forum*, no. 1: 2-11.

Padwad, A. and K.K. Dixit. "Multiple Stakeholders Views of Continuing Professional Development". *Continuing Professional Development: Lessons from India*. Eds. R. Bolitho, and A. Padwad. New Delhi: British Council, 2013: 11-22.

Continuing Professional Development: An annotated bibliography. New Delhi: British Council, India.

Prince, Emma-Sue and Alison Barrett. "Continuing Professional Development in Action: an Indian Experience". *Innovations in the Continuing Professional Development of English Teachers*. Ed. David Hayes. London: British Council, 2014: 19-44.

23

A Study on the English Method Teacher Educators' Attitude Towards and Perception of Critical Thinking in B.Ed. Teacher Education Course in West Bengal

Piku Chowdhury

Abstract

The teacher education field has recently undergone dramatic changes leading to a shift of focus from transmission models towards alternative approaches and theories that emerged in the post-transmission era addressing sociocultural, political, ideological, and critical issues. Despite worldwide changes in teacher education programs, it seems that alternative theories and ideas have had little or no impact on teacher education [B.Ed.] for English language teaching Method in West Bengal. This study investigates the applicability of the post-transmission perspectives and theories to the teacher education in West Bengal, in addition to the concerns and challenges faced by teacher educators working in that context. To this end, the views and beliefs of 150 experienced English teacher educators of both private and Govt. as well as Govt. aided colleges were collected using three methods of data collection: questionnaire; reflexive narrative; and, interviews. The questionnaire was developed to find the attitude and perception of the teacher educators towards significance of critical thinking in English method. The data were analysed to identify emerging themes relating to the current status of teacher education in the state, including impediments, constraints, and concerns in case of any change. The study found that participants were not very favourably inclined to the concept of critical thinking, especially in the rural regions due to cultural influences that set a great premium upon courtesy and silence in the place of open criticism.The study showed that policy makers, educators, and teachers needed to adopt alternative theories and approaches in order to improve pre-service and in-service ELT teacher education in the state.

Keywords: Teacher Education, Critical Thinking, English Method, Attitude, Perception.

Introduction

Teacher education programs are generally viewed as the most crucial stages in teachers' educational lives through which they can gain skills, expertise, knowledge, and preparation for teaching. For years, the central job of English language teacher education has been to prepare teachers to teach through the transmission of knowledge and information to students (Johnson 2006). However, the field of English language teaching (ELT) has recently undergone dramatic changes in its conceptualisation (Izadinia 2012), with a move towards addressing critical, social, and educational issues. These changes, influenced by socio-cultural and critical theories, have altered the focus of language teacher education. Teacher educators have been encouraged to operate as transformative agents considering issues like social transformation, teachers' agency, subjectivity, self, identity, values and beliefs (Kumaravadivelu 2012). Their mission is to empower teachers and transform them into reflective practitioners' confident to cope with language classroom challenges. Teachers' aims are not solely the improvement of students' communicative and linguistic competencies but to create social space and opportunities for them to interrogate, criticise, and analyse the status quo (Safari and Pourhashemi 2012). Critical thinking is thus significant and needs to be developed among the trainee teachers. The trainees must also be taught how to develop critical thinking among the school students. However the perception and attitude of teacher educators teaching English method in various teacher education colleges must come under the scanner. The teacher educators are recruited as per NCTE norms that calls for Master's degree in their subject which in most cases is Masters degree in English Literature under present circumstances. Additional Degrees of B.Ed. and M.Ed. are required which means that these teacher educators are supposed to have mastered the skill of critical thinking in their B.Ed. and M.Ed. courses. However, how far they themselves are well equipped in this area remains a grey area to be explored. Their perception in tandem with attitude towards critical thinking among students in the English class needs to be explored to detect the status of English teacher education in B.Ed. colleges today, preparing thousands of Pre- and in-service English teachers , who in their turn would develop thousands of students in the state.

Unfortunately, the term "critical thinking" has been used and understood in several different ways (Garrison 1991: 288-92). For example, Norris and Ennis (1990) associate both inductive and deductive forms of thinking with decisions about belief and action. On the other hand, Brookfield (1987) sees critical thinking in a less scientific sense. To him critical thinking is practically synonymous with "reflection". The debating of issues in the area of study known as "critical thinking", therefore, has been complicated because of the coexistence of differing meanings and perspectives used by contemporary scholars in the field. There has been much debate on the question 'what is critical thinking?' (Kennedy et al. 1991: 13-14, 26). While there are still disagreements about matters of detail, considerable agreement has been achieved that critical thinking is a combination of abilities and dispositions. The most influential characterisation of critical thinking is due to Ennis (1987). According to Ennis, good thinking is critical thinking which he defines as follows:

> Critical Thinking is reasonable reflective thinking that is focused on deciding what to believe or do.

As Ennis elaborates it, critical thinking includes both dispositions and abilities. He lists 14 dispositions (e.g. seek reasons, use and mention credible sources, look for alternatives) and 12 abilities (e.g., focusing on a question, making and judging observations, identifying assumptions). The latest account includes 12 dispositions and 16 abilities, in Ennis

(1991). According to Ennis, to think critically in some discipline or subject is to display these dispositions and abilities within that discipline or subject, i.e. the dispositions and abilities are general. Again, Edward Glaser (1941), identifies a list of 12 abilities as basic for critical thinking:

To recognize problems

To find workable means for meeting those problems

To gather and marshal pertinent information

To recognize unstated assumptions and values

To comprehend and use language with accuracy, clarity and discrimination

To interpret data

To appraise evidence and evaluate statements

To recognize the existence of logical relationships between propositions

To draw warranted conclusions and generalisations

To put to test the generalisations and conclusions at which one arrives

To reconstruct one's patterns of beliefs on the basis of wider experience

To render accurate judgements about specific things and qualities in everyday life

How far the English Method teacher educators inculcate these in their classes remains a hitherto unexplored territory. Their attitude towards the emerging significance of these abilities and more importantly, their knowledge about these basic abilities as crucial for critical thinking remain largely obscure.

A Review of Related Literature

Over the past century, teacher education has been affected by different views of language learning and teaching. For decades, teacher education programs aimed at providing student teachers with instructional programs, pedagogical strategies and specific methods to build security and stability for novice teachers (Mann 2005). To improve student performance on critical thinking tests, schools of education must improve teacher training. They must teach cognitive skills to preservice teachers before training them to teach these skills in the classroom (Ashton 1980: 2). They must integrate critical thinking skills into all aspects of teacher preparation and train future teachers to be models of effective thinking strategies (Walsh and Paul 1988: 49).

Historically, teacher education was predicated on the notion that knowledge about teaching and learning could be transmitted to teachers by educators, through theoretical readings, lectures, and workshops occurring external to classrooms (Johnson 2009). The positivist paradigm actually focused on the notion of transfer to show how knowledge and ideas travelled from one context to another. Kumaravadivelu (2012) believes that transmission models of EFL teacher education have several features. First, teacher educators' role is restricted to that of conduits passing on digestible bits and pieces of pre-selected, pre-determined, and pre-sequenced bodies of information to student teachers. Second, there is a master-pupil relationship between educators and student teachers by which teachers absorb the pedagogic knowledge and skills. Third, these models rarely allow for teachers' autonomy to develop and to construct visions and versions of their own teaching. Fourth, they are based on a topdown hierarchy relying on externally generated professional knowledge. Finally, they create a dichotomy between student teachers and educators; educators are considered the producers of knowledge whereas student teachers are the consumers of knowledge.

The transmission approaches do not give teachers the chance to exhibit any agency or subjectivity except the absorption of pedagogic principles, theories, strategies, techniques, and skills handed down from an expert. Thus, teachers are expected to operate like robots, with no role in developing students' capacity to learn how to learn. Learning as a means of promoting liberatory autonomy, in Freire's (1972) sense, and as the ultimate goal of education, is given little or no consideration.

In the mid-1970s, as a reaction to Positivism, an interpretive epistemological paradigm drawn from ethnographic research in anthropology and sociology began to emerge (Stenhouse 1975). This interpretive perspective was based on an assumption that knowledge is socially constructed and emerges from people's participation in social practices (Johnson 2009). This approach constructs teachers as decision makers rather than doers. Teachers' prior knowledge has a crucial role in their current thinking and educational practices, which in turn shapes their professional knowledge (Freeman 2002).

Johnson (2009) argues the interpretive stance requires a shift from observational investigations towards ethnographic descriptions based on observation, description and interviews with teachers about why they do what they do, and how they make sense of their own practices. However, despite an acknowledgement of the significance of teachers' mental lives in their formation as reflective and skilled practitioners, many believed this perspective gave too much emphasis to teachers' beliefs, prior knowledge and skills, and paid insufficient attention to students' learning (Izadinia 2012). It was, therefore, at risk of failing to establish a firm connection between teachers' prior knowledge and students' learning (Cochran-Smith 2004).

From 1990 to 2000, the interpretive epistemological perspective gave way to a post-modern perspective suggesting a new understanding of the self and the status of knowledge. Kumaravadivelu (2012) claims that teachers are confronted with the challenge of adjusting their teaching selves to the demands of existing realities, while at the same time attempting to go beyond the artificial boundaries imposed on them. As Martin (2007) states, the teacher's self is not characterised by passivity and conformity, but by a socially constructed reactivity that includes agency as an essential characteristic.

Another characteristic of the post-modern perspective is the different way that knowledge is envisioned. Whereas modernism attempts to find a coherent, overarching truth and incorporate all forms of knowledge into a grand narrative, post-modernism acknowledges diversity, difference, a multitude of narratives, and alternative forms of expression and interpretation (Kumaravadivelu 2012). Thus, regarding the post-modern perspective, one expects a multiplicity of voices and narratives reflecting marginalised people's multiple worlds and experiences in educational settings. The emergence of different voices and diverse views results from the liberatory autonomy that the post-modern perspective bestows on teachers which empowers them to become critical thinkers (Kumaravadivelu 2003).

The emphasis of post-modern perspective on issues outlined above led to critical approaches to teacher education (Hawkins and Norton 2009) referred to as 'critical pedagogy'. The advent of critical pedagogy has influenced teacher education in a number of ways such as creation of new opportunities, roles, and responsibilities for the people working in educational settings. Educators and teachers were no longer seen as the transmitters of taken-for-granted knowledge and information. Rather, they were assumed to operate as transformative intellectuals (Giroux 1989) and critical practitioners. This role gave them the opportunity to liberate themselves from oppressive systems in society by working for educational and professional progress through transformative actions.

Kumaravadivelu (2012) stated that teacher education could transcend the constraints of transmission models by moving beyond the concept of method. That is, in order to transform teacher education and educational settings into social institutions, teachers are required to refuse to become the slaves of methods that demand a rigid application of techniques. According to Pennycook (1989), method characterises a specific vision of the world which is based on the unequal power relations between an expert and teachers. However, the post-method condition calls for the development of an alternative approach, rather than the adoption of yet another method which reproduces the top-down nature of teacher education (Kumaravadivelu 2012). The post-method pedagogy takes teachers' autonomy into account. That is, it recognizes the teacher's potential and capability to know how to know and how to operate autonomously within the restrictions imposed by textbooks, curricula, and institutions (Kumaravadivelu 1994).

Objectives of the Study

- To find out whether the English Language teachers of various teacher education colleges are aware of the importance of critical thinking as a part of teacher development.

- To find out whether the English Language teachers of various teacher education colleges are aware of the basic skills that are to developed for critical thinking.
- To find out whether the English Language teachers of various teacher education colleges possess a favourable attitude towards critical thinking as a part of teacher development.
- To find out whether there is any significant difference between English Language teachers of various teacher education colleges with M.Ed. or B.Ed. with M.A. in Education in awareness about the importance of critical thinking as a part of teacher development.
- To find out whether majority of the English Language teachers of various teacher education colleges look upon critical thinking as distinct from decision-making abilities of the students
- To find out whether there is any significant difference in attitude towards critical thinking in the English class between educators with M.Ed. and those with M.A. in education.
- To find out whether there is any significant difference in attitude towards critical thinking in the English class between educators with M.A. in English Literature and those with M.A. in Linguistics.
- To find out whether there is any significant difference in attitude towards critical thinking in the English class between male and female educators.

To find out whether there is any significant difference in attitude towards critical thinking in the English class between urban and rural educators.

Sample

One hundred and fifty teacher educators, both male and female, from different private and government teacher education colleges of Kolkata and districts of Purulia, Howrah, North and South 24 Parganas, Midnapore and Siliguri were randomly selected for the study.

Tool

A questionnaire was prepared with 20 items. The tool had the following dimensions:

t Test was applied on the scores obtained by teachers under the following classifications:

Case 1: Male vs. Female

Case 2: Rural vs. Urban

Case 3: Literature vs. Linguistic

Case 4: M.Ed. vs. M.A.

In each of the above cases, we compute the value of t statistics as follows:

Let x1 and x2 denote the scores of the two sets.

x1(mean) and x2(mean) are sample means from the two sets. n1 and n2 are the sample sizes of the two sets.

t statistic is computed as follows:

t = (x1(mean) – x2(mean)) / (sXN)

N = square root (1/n1 + 1/n2)

s = square root ((X1 + X2) /(n1 + n2 – 2))

$X1 = \Sigma \times 12 - n1\ (x1(mean))^2$

$X2 = \Sigma \times 22 - n2\ (x2(mean))^2$

Tabulated value of t at 5% confidence level = 1.645

Values of t statistic (rounded off to 3 decimal places) and corresponding inferences are summarized in the table below:

Case	x1	X2	x1(mean)	x2(mean)	n1	n1	X1	X2	t	Inference
1	Female	Male	30.73	30.56	55	95	2168.909	3431.432	0.163	Insignificant
2	Urban	Rural	31.19	29.4	98	52	3379.316	684.28	1.995	Significant
3	Literature	Linguistic	30.02	29.06	134	16	5330.933	538.9375	0.576	Insignificant
4	M.Ed.	M.A.	29.41	29.36	86	64	3070.756	2250.734	0.048	Insignificant

For Case 2, computed value of t statistic is greater than the one-sided tabulated value, i.e. 1.960. Hence it may be concluded that based on the sample, we have sufficient reason to infer that urban teachers have more favourable attitude than their rural counterparts. In other three cases, namely case 1, 3 and 4, the computed value of t statistic is less than the tabulated value and thus it may be concluded that there is no significant difference in attitude between male and female, Teachers with Masters degree in Literature and Linguistics and teachers with M.Ed. and those with M.A. in Education.

Discussion

In recent years, teacher education college teachers are coming to realize that efforts to develop critical thinking skills must be included in language learning. However, in India, especially in rural areas, where teacher educators have grown up engaged with passive learning, cultivating critical thinking is one of the most difficult tasks in class. Educators agree that understanding the differences in thinking dispositions between different cultures will help students to develop critical thinking. Hall (1969) in his book *The Hidden Dimension* makes the point that one cannot shed one's own culture, and that it can penetrate at the very roots of one's nervous system. Culture determines not only the specific verbal and non-verbal behaviour that represents or symbolizes specific thought, feeling, but also when it is appropriate to display or communicate various thoughts, feelings, or internal states. Educators agree that it is important to understand the role of culture and its characteristics and potential impact on thinking dispositions in a variety of ways. In fact, some Indian cultural dimensions have become barriers to the development of good critical thinking skills. As Indian agrarian culture emphasizes respect for and obedience to the authority, language teachers usually dominate the class and do most of the talking, while most students are busy taking notes. In this way, students become passive receivers instead of active thinkers. And face-to-face conversations between teachers and students contain many emollient expressions of respect and courtesy, while directness and especially criticism are much disliked. Even if it is a conversation between peers, students are reserved when criticizing others because they think it will make others lose face. Indians regard compliance with norms as a primary value and unique individual beliefs as a secondary value. We emphasize goals, needs, and views of the group over individual outcomes. Therefore, it is not surprising that, students show more synchrony in their opinions. While Westerners are perceived as assertive, Indians are not. Submissiveness and the maintenance of pleasant social relations are valued more. That is why, in English language learning, students are shy of expressing their ideas, because they are afraid of being hurt. They tend to be more active when having a group discussion, but there are few students volunteer to present their ideas individually.

Success in most professions requires good critical thinking skills. Most of our everyday activities require us to make use of some of the basic skills involved in critical thinking, such as: taking steps to find out whether something is likely to be true; arguing our own case if someone doesn't believe us. However, just because we can think critically this doesn't mean we always do, or that we do it well. This is to be expected, as we don't need to employ the same level of critical thinking for everything we do (Cottrell 2005). Critical thinking is broadly seen as the kind of logical thinking that helps us to analyze and make sense of, or interpret, all forms of situations or information so that the conclusions we draw from our interpretations are sound. The etymology of the English word shows that thinking and knowledge are derived from the same root. Therefore, if teachers wish to cultivate students' critical thinking in language class, they should both introduce culture-based knowledge and apply new teaching methods. The question which arises next is how to do it. Here are some suggested procedures: One important step in helping students to develop critical thinking is having an understanding of the target culture itself. It emphasizes informational aspects of learning. Teachers could teach common parts of the target culture, so that students will recognize them and understand them when they encounter them. One way is to assign readings including different thinking dispositions. The priority might be to teach verbal codes that have negative meanings in the target culture. Understanding different thinking disposition in reading assignments will increase the students' understanding of the text.

While providing information about different cultures, teachers should be trained how to ask questions appropriately and effectively (Shen 2012). At the heart of teaching critical and creative thought is the ability to ask the right questions to students. The method of teaching critical thinking skills requires students to engage in independent thinking such as problem-solving, analysing and evaluating information. While the students answer the questions, teachers should give explicit instruction in it by praising or criticizing certain ways of thinking and responding. But the most significant aspect of developing critical thinking may be conveyed implicitly, not by lesson but through brainstorming, which calls for a teacher educator with a positive frame of mind and the enthusiasm to encourage critical response. Discussion about the cultural differences is one of the most effective ways to reinforce the individual for producing behavioural patterns which are likely to develop critical thinking. Assessment can also provide an additional, important incentive for critical thinking. The assessment's emphasis on open-ended possibility reinforces the opportunities inherent in critical thinking. Using this form of assessment encourages students to execute what is being asked of them actively (Mendelman 2007).

References

Cottrell, Stella (2005). *Critical Thinking Skills: Developing Effective Analysis and Argument*. New York: Palgrave Macmillan.

Finn, Patrick (2011). Critical thinking: knowledge and skills for evidence-based practice. *Language, speech, and hearing services in schools* Vol. 42: 69-72.

Geertz, C. (1973). *The Interpretation of Cultures*. New York: Basic Books.

Hall, E.T. (1976). *Beyond Culture*. Garden City, N.Y.: Anchor Books.

Henrik Bohlin. (2009). Perspective-dependence and Critical Thinking. *Argumentation* 23: 189-203.

Hofstede, G. (1982). *Culture's Consequences*. Newbury Park, Calif.: Sage Publications.

Mendelman, Lisa. (2007). Critical thinking and reading. *Journal of adolescent & adult literacy* 51(5): 300-02.

Nickerson, R.S. (2008). *Aspects of rationality: Reflections on what it means to be rational and whether we are*. New York, NY: Psychology Press.

Phung, Thanh Ha (2010). A Pilot Comprehensive Critical Thinking Education Framework in TESOL. In Azadeh Shafaei (eds.), *Frontiers of Language and Teaching: Proceedings of the 2010 International Online Language Conference* (IOLC 2010). Florida: Universal Publishers.

Ramsey, Eric Ramsey (2011). Somehow, Learning to Live: On Being Critical. *Communication and Critical/Cultural Studies* Vol. 8, No. 1: 88-92.

Samovar, Larry A. and Richard E. Porter (1994). *Intercultural Communication.* California: Wadsworth Publishing Company.

Shen, Ping (2012). A Case Study of teacher's Questioning and Students' Critical thinking in College EFL Reading Classroom. *International Journal of English Linguistics* Vol. 2 No. 1.

Stanovich, K.E. (2009). *What intelligence tests miss: The psychology of rational thought.* New Haven, CT: Yale University Press.

Wade, C. and Tavris, C. (2008). *Psychology* (9th ed.). Upper Saddle River, NJ: Prentice-Hall.

24

Teaching English in Government Schools of Delhi

Manju Gautam

Abstract

English is widely read, written and spoken in Delhi. Almost all the official work is done in this language only. In government schools of Delhi, English is taught as second or third language. In teaching a language, a teacher's objective is to develop four skills in his students: reading, writing, understanding and speaking, but in spite of teaching for years, in most of the cases, teachers are not able to develop all the four skills in their students.

Let's have a look at the challenges faced by English teachers of Delhi. Students in government schools come from very low strata of society. They are children of slum-dwellers or labourers. They are first generation learners. Their parents are illiterate or semi-literate who cannot help their kids in their studies. Large size of class, poor span of concentration, no detention policy etc. are some more reasons which make the teaching a challenging task for teachers, but if problems are there, solutions are also there. Group discussion, role play, activity-based teaching, learner centered teaching, proper feedback and motivating words of teachers can do wonders.

Introduction

English is one of the most popular languages in the world today. "There is no Royal Academy of English Language. The language belongs to no one...and everyone. It generates culture (books, films, plays with virulence. It is the language of trade and commerce." If we talk about India, English is deep-rooted in this country. Today it has become the language of educated people. Studying in English medium school has not only become a status symbol today, but it is also considered essential for securing a bright future. This belief is so strong among common masses that even parents belonging to economically weaker section leave no stone unturned to send their ward to a good public school.

This desire of sending child to an English medium school can well be seen at the time of Nursery admissions, when each parent applies at least in 15 to 20 schools and sometimes even in more than 25 schools in the hope of securing a place for the child in a convent or public school.

"Language acquisition around the world is increasingly being seen as a skill for personal as well as national development. Governments are implementing English language policies grounded partly in an economic rationale, propelled by a focus on building the proficiency of the population in part to boost a country's competitiveness in a globally integrated marketplace."

In order to help the poor, our government has reserved 25% seats for economically weaker section and disadvantaged groups. Hundreds of forms are filled for a few seats available in these schools and when the names of successful applicants are announced, the remaining hundreds of left out parents sink in the darkness of despair feeling uncertain for the future of their children. Seeing this increasing demand for English medium schools and quality education, Delhi government has brought about some changes in education system in the past few years.

- The decision of starting English from class 1 in MCD schools has improved the quality of education in these schools.
- Not only this, even the senior secondary schools coming under Delhi Administration have been converted into Sarvodaya Vidyalaya which now start from K.G. and the medium of instruction from K.G. to class V is mostly English.

Every school whether Sarvodaya Vidyalaya or any Senior Secondary school should have at least one English medium section. There may be more depending on the requirement of the students but having at least one English medium section is must.

These are some of the changes which are slowly but surely improving the quality of education in government schools of Delhi.

Delhi government has launched many schemes to increase literacy rate, to reduce drop out rate and to promote the education of girl child but improving the quality of education in government schools is not as easy as it is considered. Most of the students in government schools lack the aptitude required to be in that particular class. There are many reasons for this undesirable situation. Let's have a look why it is not easy to raise the standard of education and bring about noticeable changes in these schools.

If we talk from beginning, students in MCD schools come from a very low strata of society. These children are mostly from slum clusters or resettlement colonies. They do not have social atmosphere conducive to learning. Their parents are unable to help their children as they themselves are illiterate. The destiny of these students entirely depend on how well they perform in school but unfortunately atmosphere of school also does not help them much in their personality development. Although standard of education has improved with the introduction of English from class 1 but since the medium of instruction is purely Hindi, these children lack understanding of English.

Not only in primary schools but in senior secondary schools also, background of students set challenges for teachers to get desired results. The parents of these children are mostly construction labourers, vendors, sweepers, domestic servants etc. Education for them is secondary as their main concern is earning money for survival.

Most of these students are First Generation Learners. If any portion of chapter is not clear to them or if they misses out any exercise, it cannot be completed at home as there is nobody in their families to teach them. Their parents are uneducated rustics who cannot help their child in his homework. It is because of this reason that their home assignments are mostly incomplete or not done at all.

Another problem that teachers face in these schools is that these students have a very poor span of concentration. The reason being that most of these children come from slum clusters or resettlement colonies where in small cavernous rooms live two to three generations. Not only parents, uncle and aunts and grandparents but many a times newly married couples also sleep in the same room. Such unhealthy, disturbing and distracting atmosphere leave little space for these children to concentrate on their studies. Their minds keeps wandering in those adult erotic realms which squeeze the innocence out of these teenagers. They become premature adults with mind obsessed with sexual matters. Not only this, lack of basic amenities and non-fulfillment of even simple desires leave their minds running helter skelter from poverty to desire and from desire to despair. In such an atmosphere, it is very difficult for these teenagers to cope up with academic challenges.

Child labour is another bitter reality that these students live with. Most of them come to school in morning and work at tea stalls or food stalls in evening or *vice versa*. Girls also work as maids in other people's houses and if not in others houses, they have to look after all the household work in their own houses as mothers are mostly out on work. This hectic schedule drain energy out of these children leaving little or no time at all for them to study at home.

Most of the government schools have large number of students leading to overcrowded classes. It becomes difficult for a teacher to maintain discipline in a class of 60 to 70 students. In many densely populated colonies this number reaches between 80 to 100. Teaching so much overcrowded classes and getting desired outcome is really a difficult task which needs a lot of pre-planning, extra energy, management skill, aptitude, command and most of all patience. In the face of these problems, a teacher sometimes loses hope of improving quality of education.

Now the question arises how can we teach students and get desired result even if all these problems are there?

Problems are there and will always be, but finding solution is there in our hands. Where there is a will, there is a way.

In primary schools, children are at an age when they learn by doing, observing and experimenting. They observe their teacher minutely and try to copy their mannerism, speaking style and their way of dealing with class. Therefore, teachers of primary students should take extra care of what they speak and how they speak as children are learning every moment from them. This is an age of their social, mental and emotional development. They make new friends learn from them, gain skills which enable them to become independent and develop their personality.

At this stage, lessons should be taught by including fun filled activities in them. Students should be taught through games, drama, rhymes, songs, role play etc. These activities will not only create interest in them but also will keep them involved in class.

In order to give them practice in picture composition or story writing, divide your class in four or five equal groups. Give them 15 to 20 words. Ask each group to make a story based on these words. After the given time, group leaders from each group will stand one by one and read the story. Listen to their stories and see how lovely and new stories come out.

While designing activities, age and level of learner must be kept in mind otherwise results of these activities may be destructive rather than constructive. If activities are not designed properly, students may not be able to do it confidently and suffer from inferiority complex or despair. Properly designed activities not only develop their speaking skills but also their grammar.

Here is an activity by which children can be taught the use of 'have'.

Divide your class into 4 or 5 groups with minimum 6 or 7 children in each group. Each group will stand in a circle. First child will throw ball to other child saying aloud "I have a dog". Then second child will throw ball to some other child saying, "I have a pen" and so on. The ball should be passed on to each child so that everyone gets a chance to speak and throw the ball.

In the second round of this game, use of 'doing words' can be taught. First child will throw the ball to other child saying, "I play with my dog". Then second child will throw ball to some other child saying, "I write with my pen" and so on. Thus each child will throw the ball at least once speaking aloud what he does i.e. play, write, read, eat etc. In this activity, teacher's role is to monitor the game. He should check that no student is left or that ball should not be thrown and caught among same children again and again. If any child does not know what to speak or how to make a sentence, teacher's duty is to help him. Grammar, thus learnt last long in the memory of child and he can use it in his day-to-day life also outside his class.

Students' projects should be designed in a manner which provide them opportunity to use their knowledge of English that they have learnt in their previous chapters. Their communication skills can be developed through pair work and group discussions.

- Group discussions are one of the most challenging methods of teaching when you have to build a rapport with your students and when you have to act as an organizer, observer and a monitor. Group Discussions stimulate critical thinking of students and give them a chance to express their ideas more clearly. Critical analysis of one group by other groups leads to even deeper thinking and develop an ability to view the same thing from all the different possible angles. Group Discussion also helps in developing leadership qualities as each group has to be represented by a group leader. While organizing Group Discussions in class, a teacher should keep the following things in mind.
- Discussion among groups should always be positive.
- Controversial topics must always be avoided in order to maintain discipline and order in class and most important, to keep the atmosphere of class conducive to learning.
- If a participant challenges the ideas of other participant, he should be asked to prove it with appropriate logic and also to justify his point of view with real life examples.

- Encourage students by repeating their comments, and writing their answers on board.
- If anywhere you do not know something or make a mistake, it is better to accept your confusion rather than imparting students wrong information.

If you do not know anything, students can be asked to find the answer of the same or it can be given as homework to be discussed the next day. Meanwhile try your best to get information about the same so that answers from the students can be checked.

This method can be used in all the classes i.e. from primary level to senior secondary level but teacher should be careful in choosing topic according to the level and knowledge of students.. Advance planning is necessary for conducting group discussion.

At middle and secondary level, students are in their teenage which is a period of transformation from childhood to youth, from fairy tale dream world to real world. At this age, children love movies, music, mobile, internet etc. Therefore their activities should be designed keeping in mind their capabilities, creativity and curiosity. In beginning, topics covering music and movies or sports can be taken for activities in order to create interest among them and to ensure their 100% participation .When they are confident and comfortable about these activities, lessons can be converted into role play or any social issue addressed in their chapter can be taken as a topic for group discussion.

For making the revision interesting, the teacher can read a few lines from a chapter. Students can be asked which chapter he just read from. Then students can be asked to frame questions related to those lines. Ask the students to read the question framed by them. Third round of this activity will comprise of the answers. Students will answer the questions framed by other students. This activity can also be done in groups also. In this activity, teacher's role is that of a manager and guide. He should conduct the whole activity in such a way that students do not lose interest in it at any stage. If any student frames wrong question, teacher can ask other student to find error in it. If he finds the error and replaces it with correct word, give your feedback and encourage that child but if students are not able to correct it, correct it yourself.

Role play is an interesting method to teach drama and chapters with dialogues. Students can be assigned roles of different characters. Drama can be played in front of class by the students who prepared it. After that, divide class in 5 or 6 groups. Ask each group to write negative and positive traits of any two characters as depicted in the chapter. After they have done, group leaders from each group will stand up and read out one by one personality traits of different characters given to them. When a group leader reads out the traits written by his group, other groups can be asked for more personality traits. Student will never forget the character sketches done by this play way method. Active participation in these activities boost up their confidence and deepen their insight into literature.

These are some of the methods that can be used to teach chapters in a play way and interesting manner ensuring 100% participation of students. Although in beginning, teachers may find it difficult to conduct these activities due to the problem of sufficient time and space or students may not respond or they may go out of control but again, I will say, "Where there is a will, there is a way." Problems are there and will always be. Finding solution with positive and constructive outlook is in our hands.

Let's bring a change so what if it is difficult.

References

The Auto-English Teachers' Book by Bob Wilson from autoenglish.org published in 2009, Robert Clifford McNair Wilson.

BBC, English in Latin America, an examination of policy and priorities in seven countries...submitted by Ellenpd on 9 June, 2015. 18:27

25

Creative Writing in the ELT Classroom

Vinita Dhondiyal Bhatnagar

Abstract

This paper will argue that creative writing has an important role to play in the ELT classroom. Creative writing is normally considered the domain of the native speaker and ELT focuses on equipping the learners with the linguistic tools with which to communicate.

I suggest that creative writing offers an imaginative input into the teaching/learning session. It liberates the learner and empowers him/her. It creates an inspiration and a motivation for learners to expand their vocabulary and grammatical range.

The role of motivation in enhancing language-learning competence cannot be denied. This paper will argue that creative writing may offer a valuable tool in the ELT classroom and may create an avalanche of learning experiences that can benefit the language learner. It can also equip the learner to become a creative reader by drawing attention to the way that writers craft their poems and their stories.

Case studies will be discussed where creative writing has been introduced into the ELT classroom and suggestions/ conclusions/further directions will be suggested.

Introduction: The Story as a Metaphor for Life

As a creative writer who was often called upon to write poems on demand for important school occasions I can vouch for the empowering and liberating effect of Creative writing on a language learner. Creative writing brings the whole learner into the classroom: experiences, feelings, memories, beliefs.

Once upon a time, man relied on philosophy, science, religion and the arts to make meaning of his life. Today, in the words of that great writing guru, Robert McKee "the story arts have become humanity's prime source of inspiration, as it seeks to order chaos and gain insight into life" (1). In the words of the dramatist Jean Anouilh "Fiction gives form to life."

A culture cannot evolve without honest powerful story telling. The writer digs deep into life and emerges with insights into what's worth living for and what's worth dying for—what are the central values and meanings of lived experience.

When learners engage with powerful stories in the classroom, their entire being is involved as they wrestle with the central problems of their own time. Reading *The Great Gatsby* is still a powerful experience for an Indian adolescent in Bhopal. Stories travel across time and across space. They speak to us.

When a learner learns to design stories, he brings to the class his knowledge of society, nature and the human heart. Story demands vivid imagination and powerful analytic thought.

To quote McKee again: "A storyteller is a life poet, an artist who transforms day-to-day living, inner life and outer life, dream and actuality into a poem whose rhyme scheme is events rather than words."

Story Building in the Language Classroom

In her book *Storybuilding* Jane Spiro explores the ways in which stories can be used in the ELT classroom to practise speaking and writing skills in a context which is deeply engaging and personalized. Story writing can be used:

- to encourage group sharing, team-building, and co-operative text-making
- as opportunities to develop oral fluency and confidence
- for specific language practice of tenses, descriptive adjectives, reporting verbs, and punctuation for direct speech

- for specific language practice of functions such as giving advice, describing, and instructing
- for development of extensive writing that includes narrative, description, dialogue, and character development
- to provide an incentive for learners to write, edit, and reformulate their writing so it can be shared with others
- to prepare students for the written narrative components of exams such as First Certificate, Proficiency, and IELTS
- to encourage learners to read more appreciatively, and to understand the processes of story writing for themselves.

The Outcome of Story Activities

- students can share stories orally in class
- the stories can be developed into short sketches or pieces of 'mini theatre'
- stories can be written during the lesson, then displayed around the walls
- stories can be edited and corrected after the lesson, typed up and included in a class collection
- stories from one class can be used as readings for another class
- students can explain why they wrote a story, or what they would like readers/listeners to notice about their story.

Why We Should Include Creative Writing in the Language Classroom

In an article entitled "Creative writing for language learners (and teachers)" Alan Maley lists the benefits of creative writing for learners:

> CW aids language development at all levels: grammar, vocabulary, phonology and discourse. It requires learners to manipulate the language in interesting and demanding ways in attempting to express uniquely

personal meanings. In doing so, they necessarily engage with the language at a deeper level of processing than with most expository texts (Craik and Lockhart 1972). The gains in grammatical accuracy and range, in the appropriacy and originality of lexical choice, in sensitivity to rhyme, rhythm, stress and intonation, and in the way texts hang together are significant.

As mentioned above, a key characteristic of CW is a willingness to play with the language. In recent years there has been a resurgence of interest in the role of play in language acquisition. (Carter 2004, Cook 2000, Crystal 1998) In some ways, the sunami of the Communicative Approach has done a disservice to language teaching by its insistence on the purely communicative functions of language. Proponents of 'play' point out, rightly, that in L1 acquisition, much of the language encountered by and used by children is in the form of rhythmical chants and rhymes, word games, jokes and the like. Furthermore, such playfulness survives into adulthood, so that many social encounters are characterized by language play (punning, spontaneous jokes, 'funny voices', metathesis, and a discourse which is shaped by quasi-poetic repetition (Tannen 1989)). These are precisely the kinds of things L2 learners are encouraged to do in CW activities. This playful element encourages them to play creatively with the language, and in so doing, to take the risks without which learning cannot take place in any profound sense. As Crystal (1998) states, 'Reading and writing do not have to be a prison house. Release is possible. And maybe language play can provide the key.'

Much of the teaching we do tends to focus on the left side of the brain, where our logical faculties are said to reside. CW puts the emphasis on the right side of the brain, with a focus on feelings, physical sensations, intuition and musicality. This is a healthy restoration of the balance between logical and intuitive faculties. It also affords scope for learners whose hemisphere dominance

> or learning-style preferences may not be intellectual or left brain dominant, and who, in the normal process of teaching are therefore at a disadvantage.

(https://www.teachingenglish.org.uk/article/creative-writing-language-learners-teachers)na

The four modes of writing are summarised in the table 1:

Table 1: Modes of Writing (Richards, Jack C. and Schmidt R. 2010: 371)

Descriptive writing	Narrative writing	Expository writing	Argumentative writing
Provides a verbal picture or account of a person, place or thing	Reports an event or tells the story of something that happened	Provides information about and explains a particular subject (giving examples, describing a process of doing or making something, etc.)	Attempts to support a controversial point or defend a position on which there is a difference of opinion

Where would we place creative writing?

It could be placed under the category of narrative writing. However I would argue that Creative Writing could be considered as a fifth mode of writing with great potential for catalysing language learning. Alan Maley comments “In fact, the line between creative writing (CW) and expository writing (ER) is not carved in stone. In general, however CW texts draw more heavily on intuition, close observation, imagination, and personal memories than ER texts.”

Ken Hyland (2002) defines creative writing as “any writing, fiction or non-fiction that occurs outside of everyday professional, journalistic, academic and technical forms of writing. Most typically we think of novels, short stories and poems in this category, but it can also include screenwriting and playwriting, which are texts to be performed, and creative non-fiction such as personal and journalistic essays” (229).

The focus of creative writing is on self-expression.

What are the potential benefits of creative writing?

- It entertains students,
- Fosters their artistic expression,
- Explores the functions and values of writing,
- Clarifies thinking,

- Stimulates their imagination,
- It enables them to learn to read and write (Tompkins 1982: 718-21).

Creative writing is an empowering and liberating force in the English Language Teaching and Learning classroom. Alan Maley has done a tremendous amount of work in this field. In his article "Creative writing for students and teachers" (2012) he compares the main characteristics of creative writing with expository writing and proposes the following chart.

Chart: Contrasting modes of writing (Maley 2012)

Expository writing	Creative writing
Instrumental	Aesthetic
Facts	Imagination
External control	Internal discipline
Conventions	Stretching rules
Logical	Intuitive
Analytical	Associative
Impersonal	Personal
Thinking mode	Feeling mode (plus thinking!)
Appeal to the intellect	Appeal to the senses
Avoidance of ambiguity	Creation of multiple meanings

Maley explains that expository writing is mainly instrumental, focused on providing facts, it "rests on a framework of externally imposed rules and conventions. These range from grammatical and lexical accuracy and appropriacy to specific genre constraints. The aim of expository writing is to be logical, consistent and impersonal and to convey the content as unambiguously as possible to the reader" (Maley 2012). Creative writing focuses on the aesthetic function. Creative writing "often proceeds by stretching the rules of the language to breaking point, testing how far it can go before the language breaks down under the strain of innovation" (Maley 2012). This can be especially helpful in terms of practising grammatical structures, exploring new ways of expressing oneself and exploring vocabulary. The unique combination of feelings and thoughts present during creative writing can definitely enrich every student taking part in it.

Elsewhere Maley posits "[p]erhaps most notable is the dramatic increase in self-confidence and self-esteem which CW tends to develop among learners. Learners also tend to discover things for themselves about the language...and about themselves too, thus promoting personal as well as linguistic growth. Inevitably, these gains are reflected in a corresponding growth in positive motivation" (Maley 2009).

A set of key conditions of a motivating classroom which are met by the well run creative writing class shown in Table 2 (borrowing from Dornyei)

Table 2: Key conditions which should be met in a well-run creative writing class (Dörnyei, 2001: 138-44; Maley 2012)

5	Create a pleasant and supportive atmosphere in the classroom
6	Promote the development of group cohesiveness.
13	Increase the students' expectancy of success in particular tasks and in learning in general.
17	Make learning more stimulating and enjoyable by breaking the monotony of classroom events.
18	Make learning stimulating and enjoyable for the learner by increasing the attractiveness of tasks.
19	Make learning stimulating and enjoyable for the learners by enlisting them as active task participants.
20	Present and administer tasks in a motivating way.
23	Provide students with regular experiences of success.
24	Build your learners' confidence by providing regular encouragement.
28	Increase student motivation by promoting cooperation among the learners.
29	Increase student motivation by actively promoting learner autonomy.
33	Increase learner satisfaction.
34	Offer rewards in a motivational manner.

Maley conducted a survey among 50 leading ELT professionals in order to "justify the inclusion of creative writing, in addition to aesthetic reading, in our language teaching practices" (Maley 2009). The questionnaire survey took place in 2006 and from its results he states the following areas, which are positively affected by using creative writing in teaching English. For a good arrangement, I put them into table 3.

Table 3: Areas which are Positively affected by using Creative Writing in Teaching English (Maley 2009)

(a)	Grammar, vocabulary, phonology, discourse	Significant gains in grammatical accuracy, appropriacy and originality of lexical choice, and sensitivity to rhythm, rhyme, stress and intonation
(b)	Playfulness	Playing with language
(c)	Development of a 'second language personality'	Taking risks with the language, exploring it without a fear of reproof
(d)	Focus on the right side of the brain	Feelings, physical sensations, intuition
(e)	Increase in self-confidence and self-esteem	Which creative writing tends to develop among learners; It leads to a corresponding increase in motivation
(f)	Creative reading	The development of aesthetic reading skills provides the learner with a better understanding of textual construction, and this feeds into their writing
(g)	Improve of expository writing	By helping learners to develop an individual voice, it makes their factual writing more genuinely expressive

What Kind of Creative Writing Activities Can Be Used in the Classroom?

Teachers have experimented with Haiku poems, stem poems, acrostics as well as stories and plays in the English Language Teaching classroom.

Jane Spiro offers a range of activities that can be tried in her books: *Creative Poetry Writing* and *Creative Story-building*.

Patrick T. Doungherty and Aya Dougherty have demonstrated how effective these kind of creative writing activities can be in the South Asian context http://jalt-publications.org/archive/proceedings/2007/E059.pdf

Some examples for creative writing activities in the classroom are available at: http://www.englisch-hilfen.de/en/words/topics_creative_writing.htm

Assessing Creative Writing

Special care has to be taken in assessing creative writing. The teacher may need to overlook inaccuracies if they do not interfere with the creative communication. A creative piece is deeply personal and perhaps it may be a good idea to personalize assessment and look for ways in which learners have challenged themselves. Inaccuracies are gaps in the learner's knowledge which they try to fill up creatively.

Rubrics developed by the teacher maybe shared to facilitate peer assessment.

It is important to recognize that the goals of a creative writing session should govern the assessment and feedback mechanism. Spiro offers the following rubruc:

Ideas of evaluating creative writing (Spiro 2007: 11).

Goal	How to evaluate it
To encourage oral fluency	Make a note of some of the key errors that disturb comprehension, report back on these.
A precise linguistic goal (i.e. correct use of past tenses)	Ask learners to self-correct just this aspect, then check the work again yourself.
To encourage writing fluency	Invite learners to read one another's stories to check for clarity and comprehensibility. Ask them to check with you if there are any parts that they cannot correct or improve for themselves.

Conclusion

Creative writing offers an exciting new terrain for language teaching and learning. In conclusion I would like to draw attention to two projects. The First Story Project links creativity, literacy and self-confidence and offers creative writing classes for state run schools in UK.

This is how they describe their mission:

> "First Story changes lives through writing.
>
> We believe that writing can transform lives, and that there is dignity and power in every young person's story.

> First Story brings talented, professional writers into secondary schools serving low-income communities to work with teachers and students to foster creativity and communication skills.
>
> By helping students find their voices through intensive, fun programmes, First Story raises aspirations and gives students the skills and confidence to achieve them."

(http://www.firststory.org.uk/description/)

First Story is based on the premise that writing can liberate and strengthen young people's sense of themselves as nothing else can. Thus the motto is not just writing for pleasure but writing for power. One of the stories written by a young participant is called "The Single Mother":

> Play with your dolls in the collapsed doll house. The one your father gave you for your seventh birthday. Detangle her knotted hair and apply her strawberry-scented lip balm. Push her arms around in unrealistic angles. Make her dance. Look at your photographs. In the corner there's the photo of you and Father last Christmas. It's alone in its bed of broken glass. Don't lean on the walls. The white paint hasn't dried yet. Don't worry, Father will come home and finish it. I promise you he will finish it. I know it's been six years, he's coming.

(http://www.firststory.org.uk/2015/02/08/writing-can-be-a-source-not-just-of-pleasure-but-of-power-william-fiennes-in-the-sunday-times/)

> Another interesting project of importance to the Non Native Speakers teaching English in Asia is: The Asia Teacher-Writers Project"

The following rationale underpins the activities of the group:

- A belief in the value of creative writing in English both for teachers and for students.
- A belief in the ability of teachers in the region to produce their own English teaching materials.

- A belief that these materials will provide useful input for promoting reading (and other activities) in English.
- A belief in the value for professional and personal development of forming a closely-knit, Asia-wide, mutually-supportive learning community of teacher/ writers.

The objectives are:

- To produce poetry and stories appropriate in level and content for use by Asian students of English at secondary level.
- To publish and promote these as widely as possible, thus creating a wider awareness of the value of CW.
- To develop materials and activities for the teaching of creative writing.
- To run creative writing conferences and workshops for the wider teaching community wherever possible.

These projects give an exciting glimpse of where the future of creative writing in ELT may lie.

References

Brown, H. Douglas (2000). *Teaching By Principles: An Interactive Approach to Language Pedagogy*. White Plains, NY: Longman, 2nd ed.

Can creative writing boost pupils confidence? (2015, January 5). Retrieved from http://www.yorkshirepost.co.uk/news/features/can-creative-writing-boost-pupils-confidence-1-7033883/

Chastain, K. (1988). *Developing second-language skills: Theory and practice*. San Diego: Harcourt Brace Jovanovich, 3rd ed.

Crusan, D. (2010). *Assessment in the second language writing classroom*. Retrieved from http://eds.b.ebscohost.com/eds/ebookviewer/ebook/bmxlYmtfXzU3

MjcwNl9fQU41?sid=c2dbda4e-aa83-49ae-bc01a122561089d8@ sessionmgr 114&vid=3&format=EB&rid=17

Crystal, D. (1998). *Language play*. Harmondsworth, UK: Penguin.

Davies, G. (2015, March 16). *The Writing Paradox*. Retrieved from http://oupeltglobalblog.com/2015/03/16/the-writing-paradox/

Dell, W.C. (1964). Creative Writing in the English Classroom. *The English Journal*, 53(7): 500-03. Retrieved from http://www.jstor.org/stable/810594

Dörnyei, Z. (2001). *Motivational strategies in the language classroom*. Cambridge: Cambridge University Press.

Dörnyei, Z. (2003). *Questionnaires in second language research: Construction, administration, and processing*. Mahwah, NJ: Lawrence Erlbaum Associates.

First Story (2015). *About Us*. Retrieved from http://www.firststory.org.uk/description/

Google Trends (2015). *Creative Writing*. Retrieved from Feb. 14, 2015 http://www.google.com/trends/explore#q=%22creative%20writing%22&cmpt=q&tz=

Harmer, J. (2007). *How to Teach English*. New Edition. Harlow: Pearson Education Ltd.

Hyland, K. (2002). *Teaching and Researching Writing*. Harlow: Longman.

James, G. (2006). *Writing Creatively in Another Language*. Retrieved from http://www.tefl.net/esl-articles/creative-writing.htm/

Maley, A. (2009, December 16). *Creative writing for language learners (and teachers)*. Retrieved from http://www.teachingenglish.org.uk/article/creative-writing-language-learners-teachers/

Maley, A. (2012). *Creative Writing for Students and Teachers*. Humanising Language Teaching, 14(3). Retrieved from http://www.hltmag.co.uk/jun12/mart01.htm

Mueller, L. (1972). *Stealing Apples: Creative Writing for All Students. The English Journal*, 61(7): 1020-25. Retrieved from http://www.jstor.org/stable/813712

Petri, H.L. (2014, September 3). *Motivation*. Retrieved from http://www.britannica.com/EBchecked/topic/394212/motivation/

Pintrich, P.R., & Schunk, D.H. (1996). *Motivation in Education. Theory, Research and Applications*. Englewood Cliffs, NJ: Prentice Hall Merrill, 2nd ed.

Richards, Jack C. & Schmidt R. (2010). *Dictionary of Language Teaching and Applied Linguistics*. London: Longman, 4th ed.

Routman, R. (2000). Kids' poems: Teaching Third and Fourth Graders to love writing poetry. New York: Scholastic.

Scrivener, J. (2011). *Learning Teaching: The Essential Guide to English Language Teaching*. Oxford, UK: Macmillan, 3rd ed.

Sharples, M. (1999). *How We Write: Writing as Creative Design*. London: Routledge.

Spiro, J. (2004). *Creative Poetry Writing*. Oxford, UK: Oxford University Press.

Spiro, J. (2007). *Storybuilding*. Oxford, UK: Oxford University Press.

Tompkins, G.E. (1982). Seven Reasons Why Children Should Write Stories. *Language Arts*, 59(7): 718-21. Retrieved from http://www.jstor.org/stable/41405103

Warren, A. (2013, February 14). *10 creative ways to teach English that deliver outstanding results*. Retrieved from http://www.theguardian.com/teacher-network/teacher-blog/2013/feb/14/teaching-english-creatively-outstanding-results

26

Teaching the Students of Mixed Ethnicities

Shyam Ji Dubey

An appropriate style will adapt itself to the emotions of the hearers....

It is in cohesion with the above statement of Aristotle that this paper forms the basis for. The aim of this paper is to help the teachers of different disciplines to master a plain and effective speaking/writing style so that they can convey the messages as quickly and clearly as possible. The suggestions and recommendations in this paper characterize the type of style a teacher of whatsoever subject should adopt in a class of mixed ethnicities, where English is the medium of instruction. The suggestions are the outcome of intensive qualitative research of a number of institutions, national and international and the special training programs designed by different companies to get their employees meet the expectations of international relations.

Language, in general, is a medium of imparting and sharing information in the form of certain codes. It functions in a reciprocal system where the idea in a speaker's mind is translated into a meaningful message; the message is transferred via a channel and conversely the sounds or the meaningful messages are translated into meanings in the listener's mind. The process is generally referred as 'encoding' and 'decoding'. This can be represented in a better way through the following diagram:

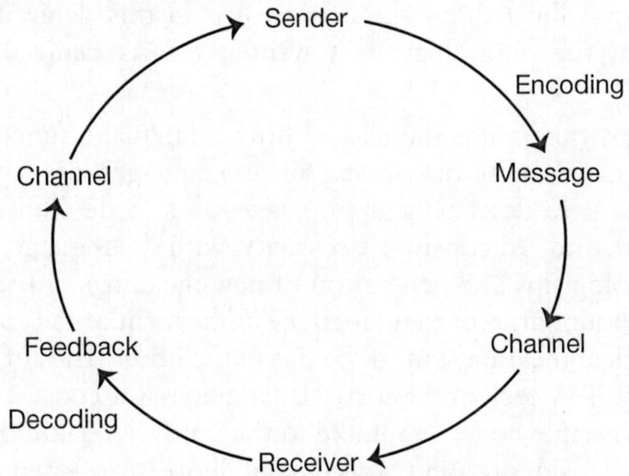

The process in a spoken or a written discourse involves Semantics (the study of relationship between words and meanings), Syntax (lexico-grammatical choices—choices of words and grammatical choices involved in forming a sentence), and Phonology (sound patterns of a language represented by phonemes, stress, rhythm, intonation, etc.). In addition to these, a fourth level of linguistic organization, Graphology (an alternative way of realization to phonology in a written system), also plays a prominent role in written communication. Leech and Short, through the following diagram, give a pictorial representation to show the difference between the ways a language operates in a written and in a spoken discourse:

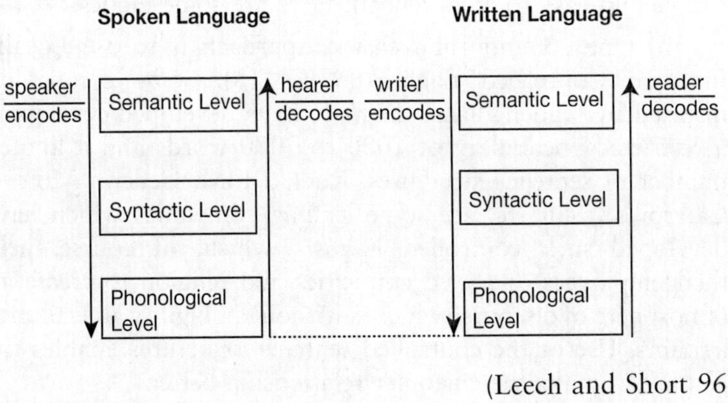

(Leech and Short 96)

Leech and Short draw the broken line in this diagram to indicate that the phonology in a written text is realized 'by implication'.

However, this is not the end of how a language functions in spoken or written discourse. Since languages are open-ended in nature, describing a language as a code limits its functionality and practicality. Creativity with a language, for example neologisms and generation of new meanings, infringes the defined boundaries of that language in the form of the codes. A metaphorical meaning cannot be put in the boundaries of this code system. To Leech and Short, "If language is a code, it is a complexly variable code, adaptable to the innovative skill of its users" (97). This quotation by Leech and Short is the essence of making the appropriate style for a classroom. Teachers have to use their innovative skills, complexly variable from classroom to classroom. A teacher's job is not to show his/her linguistic competence to the students but to make them comprehend the message easily by his/her situationally and contextually conditioned innovative skills. To achieve the target, following suggestions can be incorporated in one's teaching methodology:

(i) Teaching students who use English as their second language must be unusually simple, unambiguous, and literal. One should always keep in mind the acronym, KISS: Keep it simple and short. Simplified discourse reduces the burden on the audience. There are many approaches to make one's English simple and easy to comprehend. Here are some tactics:

(ii) One common and easiest approach is to use Locally Invented Controlled English (Weiss 18). Some companies, inspired by Ogden's *Basic English*, have developed/developing a restricted vocabulary of 1000 to 3000 words and a limited number of sentence structures. Kodak, IBM, General Motors, Caterpillar, Sun etc. are some leading companies which have developed such controlled English, which, of course, help their employees of mixed ethnicities and religion to create an atmosphere of discourse which is without ambiguity and cultural irritants. Use of the controlled sentence structures enables the employees make the customer relationship better.

(iii) The same approach can be used by subject experts in their classrooms. Using limited and subject specific vocabulary certainly make the message easily comprehensible to the students, provided that the students are given to use that vocabulary before the beginning of the theoretical part of that subject. For example, for a student who has done his/her 12th from a Hindi medium school, and now has taken admission in B.Tech. course in a college where the medium of instruction is English (This is one of the most serious problems in Engineering colleges across India), the following subject (Engineering Physics) specific vocabulary may be of utmost help to such students to understand and comprehend the lectures of that particular subject. The students should be encouraged to use the given vocabulary in his/her discussion in the classroom.

Engineering Physics

S.No.	Words	S.No.	Words	S.No.	Words
1.	Mechanics məˈkæn.ɪks,	42.	Fractional ˈfræk.ʃᵊn.ᵊl	83.	Converge kənˈvɜːdʒ
2.	Circular Motion ˈsɜː.kjə.ləʳ ˈməʊ.ʃᵊn	43.	Excitation ek.sɪˈteɪ.ʃᵊn	84.	Diverge daɪˈvɜːdʒ
3.	Inversion ɪnˈvɜː.ʃᵊn, -ʒᵊn	44.	Radiation ˌreɪ.diˈeɪ.ʃᵊn	85.	Infinitesimally ˌɪn.fɪ.nɪˈtes.ɪ.mᵊli
4.	Relativistic ˌrel.ə.tɪˈvɪs.tɪk	45.	Maxima / Minima ˈmæk.sɪ.mə / ˈmɪn.ɪ.mə	86.	Electric/magnetic Flux ɪˈlek.trɪk / mægˈnet.ɪk flʌks
5.	Momentum məʊˈmen.təm	46.	Deviation ˌdiː.viˈeɪ.ʃᵊn	87.	Orientation ˌɔː.ri.enˈteɪ.ʃᵊn
6.	Inertial ɪˈnɜː.ʃi.əl	47.	Differentiate ˌdɪf.ᵊˈren.tʃi.eɪt	88.	Resolution power ˌrez.ᵊlˈuː.ʃᵊn paʊəʳ
7.	Transformation ˌtræn s.fəˈmeɪ.ʃᵊ	48.	Decay dɪˈkeɪ	89.	Permeability ˌpɜː.mi.əˈbɪl.ə.ti
8.	Postulates ˈpɒs.tjə.ləts	49.	Comparison kəmˈpær.ɪ.sᵊn	90.	Permittivity
9.	Hypothesis haɪˈpɒθ.ə.sɪs	50.	Ellipsoidal ˌel.ɪpˈsɔɪ.dᵊl	91.	Fluid ˈfluː.ɪd
10.	Contraction kənˈtræk.ʃᵊn	51.	Projectile prəʊˈdʒek.taɪl	92.	Dispersive power dɪˈspɜː.sɪv paʊəʳ
11.	Dilation daɪˈleɪ.ʃᵊn	52.	Aberration ˌæb.əˈreɪ.ʃᵊn	93.	Identity aɪˈden.tə.t|i
12.	Variation ˌveə.riˈeɪ.ʃᵊn	53.	Horizontal ˌhɒr.ɪˈzɒn.tᵊl	94.	Cylindrical səˈlɪn.drɪkᵊl

13.	Equivalence ɪˈkwɪv.əl.əns	54.	Angular ˈæŋ.gjʊ.ləʳ	95.	Spherical ˈsfer.ɪkəl
14.	Reference point ˈref.ər.ənt s pɔɪnt	55.	Deflection dɪˈflek.ʃən	96.	Coherence kəʊ ˈhɪə.rənt|s
15.	Recapitulation ˌriː.kəˌpɪt.jəˈleɪ.ʃən	56.	Linearly ˈlɪn.i.əʳli	97.	Spatial/temporal ˈspeɪ.ʃəl/ˈtem.pər.əl
16.	Paradox ˈpær.ə.dɒks	57.	Arbitrary ˈɑː.bɪ.trər.i	98.	Classification ˌklæs.ɪ.fɪˈkeɪ.ʃən
17.	Simultaneity ˌsɪm.əl.təˈneɪ.ə.ti	58.	Quadratically kwɒdˈræt.ɪkəl.i	99.	Diffraction dɪˈfræk.ʃən
18.	Conservation ˌkɒnt .səˈveɪ.ʃən	59.	Propagation ˌprɒp.əˈgeɪ.ʃən	100.	Dielectric ˌdaɪ.ɪˈlek.trɪk
19.	Event ɪˈvent	60.	Existence ɪgˈzɪs.tənt s	101.	Homogeneous ˌhɒm.əˈdʒiː.ni.əs
20.	Instant ˈɪnt .stənt	61.	Reflection/ refraction rɪˈflek.ʃən / rɪˈfræk.ʃən	102.	Heterogeneous ˌhet.ər.əʊ ˈdʒiː.ni.əs
21.	Apparent əˈpær.ənt	62.	Barrier ˈbær.i.əʳ	103.	Intensity ɪnˈtent .sə.t|i
22.	Significant sɪgˈnɪf.ɪ.kənt	63.	Displacement dɪˈspleɪs.mənt	104.	Induced ɪnˈdjuːst
23.	Polarized ˈpəʊ.lər.aɪzd	64.	Longitudinal ˌlɒn.dʒɪˈtjuː.dɪ.nəl	105.	Alignment əˈlaɪn.mənt
24.	Coordinate system kəʊˈɔː.dɪ.nət ˈsɪs.təm	65.	Conservative kənˈsɜː.və.tɪv	106.	Oscillation ˌɒs.ɪˈleɪ.ʃən
25.	Accelerated əkˈsel.ə|.reɪtɪd	66.	Isolated ˈaɪ.sə|.leɪtɪd -leɪ.t̬ɚz	107.	Function ˈfʌŋk .ʃən
26.	Rectilinear ˌrek.tɪˈlɪn.i|.əlәʳ	67.	Solenoidal ˈsəʊ.lə.nɔɪdəl	108.	Electromotive force ɪˌlek.trəʊ ˈməʊ.tɪv fɔːs
27.	Electromagnetism ɪˌlek.trəʊ ˈmæg. nɪtɪ.zəm	68.	Superimposed ˌsuː.pər.ɪmˈpəʊzd	109.	Continuity ˌkɒn.tɪˈnjuː.ə.ti
28.	Hypothetical ˌhaɪ.pəʊ ˈθet.ɪkəl	69.	Gradient ˈgreɪ.di.ənt	110.	Curvature ˈkɜː.və.ʧəʳ
29.	Imaginary ɪˈmædʒ.ɪ.nər|.i	70.	Divergence daɪˈvɜː.dʒən s	111.	Correlation ˌkɒr.əˈleɪ.ʃən,
30.	Absolute ˌæb.səˈluːt	71.	Curl kɜː	112.	Tangential tænˈdʒen.tʃəl
31.	Dragging drægɪŋ	72.	Coplanar	113.	Surrounding səˈraʊndɪŋ
32.	Intrinsic/extrinsic ɪnˈtrɪnt .sɪk / ekˈstrɪnt .sɪk	73.	Transmission trænzˈmɪʃ.ən	114.	Inherent ɪnˈher.ənt

33.	Contradiction ˌkɒn.trəˈdɪk.ʃən	74.	Electric Field ɪˈlek.trɪk ˈfiːld	115.	Slope / tangent sləʊp / ˈtæn.dʒənt
34.	Normalization ˌnɔː.məl.aɪˈzeɪ.ʃən	75.	Equipotential	116.	Dextrorotatory
35.	Cavity ˈkæv.ə.t|i	76.	Integration ˌɪn.tɪˈgreɪ.ʃən	117.	Specific rotation spəˈsɪf.ɪk rəʊˈteɪ.ʃən
36.	Sustained səˈsteɪnd	77.	Orthogonal ɔːˈθɒg.ən.əl	118.	Demonstration ˌdem.ənˈstreɪ.ʃən
37.	Annihilation əˌnaɪ.ɪˈleɪ.ʃən	78.	Respectively rɪˈspek.tɪvli	119.	Isotropic ˌaɪ.səˈtrɒp.ɪk
38.	Propagation ˌprɒp.əˈgeɪ.ʃən	79.	Magnitude ˈmæg.nɪ.tjuːd	120.	Stimulated ˈstɪm.jəleɪ.tɪd
39.	Inclined ɪnˈklaɪnd	80.	Cartesian kɑːˈtiː.zi.ən	121.	Collimated ˈkɒl.ɪ-meɪ.tɪd -
40.	Vertical ˈvɜː.tɪ.k|əl	81.	Operator ˈɒp.əreɪ.təʳ	122.	Transition trænˈzɪʃ.ən
41.	Invariant ɪnˈveə.ri.ənt	82.	Characterization ˌkær.ək.tər.aɪˈzeɪ.ʃən		

*The list is suggestive only. Depending on the needs, words can be included or excluded.

Besides the subject specific lexicon, a list of common words, applicable to all the subjects, should be prepared separately. The institutions should work on the controlled permissible sentence patterns as well. Guidelines like this seem to be difficult to work on, but they will undoubtedly lessen the burden on students.

- Besides, there are many other small tactics, if used eclectically, may certainly be helping to the students:
- Maintaining cohesion, coherence and grammatical consistency. Avoiding ambiguous words or phrases. For the purpose one may be selective of using words with one or few meanings.
- Loosely connected words, phrases or sentences like '*After eating my lunch, the project director reassigned me.*' may be avoided.
- One should be careful while using confused terms like *fourth/forth, foreword/forward, their/there/they're* etc. Words that can have opposite meanings may create ambiguity unnecessarily. For example, the word *Sanction* may either mean to authorize or to punish. Acronyms

and abbreviations should also be avoided as they may mean differently in different contexts and on different locations.

- Figurative language, literary and cultural allusions may create unnecessary burden on the students. Words with regional meanings or translations with regional touch may create ambiguity.
- Utmost care should be taken while using verbs. Phrasal verbs or verbs with two or three words may be replaced with simple and one word verbs e.g. *make clear vs. explain*. Nominalizations increase the level of difficulty e.g. *reaching to a decision vs. decided*.

Above suggestions will certainly decrease the average sentence length. Additionally one should prefer simple sentences and active voices, but not on the risk of meaning loss.

- A teacher who is preparing study material may take help of the statistical tools to maximize the readability. The first step is to come out with 'Average sentence length' and 'Average word length' and then to any one of the following readability tests, depending on the needs:
- **Gunning Fog Index** is often used in the health care and insurance industries for analysing business publications.
- **Coleman-Liau Grade** is an approximate U.S. grade level needed to comprehend the text.
- **Flesch-Kincaid Grade Level** relates to a U.S. grade level, or the number of years of education required for understanding the text. This test is considered most reliable when used on materials that are for upper elementary school and secondary level education.
- **Flesch Reading Ease** is used to assess adult reading materials. It is also used by some United States government agencies and the United States Department of Defence as an indicator of readability.
- **SMOG** is used to come out with an estimate of the number of years of United States education needed to fully comprehend the text.

The above-mentioned tools are objective, quantitative tools for estimating the difficulty level of a written material. Depending on the needs, one may google these tools on Internet and they are available for free. In minutes one can apply any one of these readability tests.

Conclusion

The suggestions given in this paper are just abstract generalizations. They may be fruitful in most of the classroom situations but these curatives may be avoided in certain situations, if they are hampering meaning or they are becoming obstacle in maintaining the rhythm of the classroom, for on occasions these suggestive measures may make the class atmosphere dull and boring, for a teacher is an entertainer as well.

References

Leech, Geoffrey N. and Mick Short. *Style in Fiction: A Linguistic Introduction to English Fictional Prose*. London: Longman, 2007. Print.

Weiss, Edmond H. *The Elements of International English Style*. New Delhi: PHI, 2005. Print.

Sharma Sangeeta and Binod Mishra. *Communication Skills for Engineers and Scientists*. New Delhi: PHI, 2009. Print.

27

ELT and Nativism: A Pedagogical Perspective

Ravi Bhushan

Abstract

The issue of relevance of English *vis-à-vis* regional languages has been under discussion at political, pedagogical and social levels. Due to politics of convenience, English is presented as rival to local languages, and a monster ready to decimate vernacular languages and cultures. In fact even people of academic merit describe English as a "killer language". Is English relevant or not? The learner has been left completely confused and helpless in this tug of war between the nativists and the real job market.

The question on English should not be "to have it or not to have it"; rather we shall debate on how to make teaching of English effective without jeopardizing indigenous languages. There is an urgent need to contextualize and integrate ELT with the idea of nativism. This paper is an attempt to discuss the rationale, strategies and possible suggestions for indigenizing ELT and as a result making English more relevant and interesting for the disillusioned Indian learner.

Keywords: ELT, Nativism, Indigenous Languages.

Introduction

The importance of English in the 21st century is undisputable, in fact English and globalization have come to be understood as synonyms. But can globalization succeed in the absence of localization. This point is upheld by Google India's estimate that next 300 million users from India will not use English in future.

That simply means Indians' own languages will become the mode of communication and information. There is an urgent need to explore and incorporate the vast reservoir of Indian languages in ELT. If English for masses is the target, then the pedagogy and material shall be pro masses. The context and texts lying in oral-rural traditions of India can be the best resource for making ELT effective. The indigenous narratives are not only learner friendly but also strengthen cultural, social and critical thinking traits of learners. One should not forget that in this age of globalization and digitalization, learners' linguistic and communicative competence will not be adequate in the absence of their inter-cultural communicative competence.

Linguistic Identity

Each language provides a new perspective on how the human mind works and how it expresses itself in linguistic categories. "Language embodies the intellectual wealth of the people who use it" (Hale 1992). The value of knowing other languages is immense. Ezra Pound said, "the sum of human wisdom is not contained in any one language, and no single language is capable of expressing all forms and degrees of human comprehension" (Ezra Pound 1960). One way of increasing our stock of human wisdom is to learn more languages and to learn more about languages. Negative attitude towards one's own language is common and very dangerous. It is said "the decision to abandon one's own language always occurs from a change in the self-esteem of the speech community" (Brenzinzer, Heine and Somner 1991). So how can a community boost its confidence in its own language? To quote David Crystal, "there is little hope for a language unless its speakers feel that it is worth continuing with, in spite of its erosion by years of contempt. There is need to remove linguistic apathy or despair. Multilingual situation is always better than a monolingual situation" (Crystal 2010).

Assumptions on ELT

In the context of polyphonic and geographically diverse India and English hegemony, ELT in Indian context is governed by a few false assumptions; discourage use of L1 or mother tongue, treating language learning as a habit (repetitive practice) leaving no scope for contrastive thinking, using the given standard material neglecting the local/indigenous content, emphasis on native standard variety of English excluding Indian varieties, discouraging other Indian languages. These assumptions are in conflict with the research findings on second language acquisition and bilingual education (Kapoor 2013).

Language Pedagogy

Notwithstanding the prolonged debate on teaching methods, a more deliberate interpretation of second language teaching (English in Indian context) in terms of educational theory is needed. The model developed by Dunkin and Biddle (1974) for the study of classroom teaching distinguishes four main categories of variables; presage, context, process and product. In their seminal book *The Study of Teaching*, Dunkin and Biddle critically examine classroom teaching in terms of these essential factors (relationships). Moreover this model identifies two principal actors; the language teacher and the language learner. The teacher like the learner brings to language teaching certain characteristics which have bearing on educational treatment; age, sex, previous education, personal qualities and social context.

Talking about the use of indigenous methods in language teaching and learning, Wolf and Simo Bobda (2000) assert that the model of teaching English is one of the most hotly debated issues in the field of English as a second/foreign language. They believe it is misguided to think that L1 varieties are inappropriate for a broader international communicative purpose because they are "culturally and geo-politically specific in orientation". The conceptual diversity, which is realised lexically, enriches the English language, and learners profit most if indigenous cultural elements occur alongside native English elements.

ESL

Teaching English as a Second Language (ESL) in the globalized scenario should have learner's communicative competence (use of English in a variety of situations, social contexts and professional areas) as the primary objective.

Unfortunately our learners are limited to producing formal, curriculum-confined utterances. They never get to know how to exploit and particularly use in their day-to-day life situations what they have learnt through their knowledge of formal grammar and exposure to literature.

Functions of Native Literature

The mother tongue (L1) helps a great deal in second language acquisition, indigenous literature plays an important role in teaching referential and representational functions of communication in target language. It helps in:

(a) providing meaningful and memorable contexts for new vocabulary and structures, thus encouraging language acquisition and expanding students' language awareness.

(b) developing students' procedural abilities to interpret discourse.

(c) providing access to new socio-cultural meanings, offering opportunities for the development of cultural awareness.

(d) stimulating the imagination as well as critical and personal response.

Oral Literature: Pedagogical Tool

Indigenous literature especially in oral tradition (folk narratives, folk tales, myths, legends and fables) like *The Ramayana, The Mahabharta, Panchtantra, Jataka Kathaye, Shilpadigaram, Manimekalai* etc. can be used as teaching resources in ELT classrooms for enhancing communicative competence of our learners. The literature used in ESL classrooms should no longer be restricted to canonical texts from certain English speaking countries, rather it should include the oral works of poets like Andal, Lal Ded, Kabir, Shah Hussain, Mirabai etc. The works of non-native writers in English are unique in revealing local sensibilities. Mallikarjun (2003) asserts that folk literature which is studied for its intrinsic merit and enjoyment is a powerful educational tool to imbibe values, style of language, and many other important learning items in the minds of learners. We are yet to recognize the pedagogical potential, folk literature offers for creative language curriculum, rhetoric and communication skills. Folk literature in terms of language pedagogy uses spoken form of language, lexicon and sentence patterns that are more frequently used in daily life and natural form of presentation. The curriculum that prepares teachers for the teaching profession does not include a methodology that helps the teachers to exploit folk literature as an important pedagogical tool. Potential of linguistic aspects of folk literature as pedagogical tool is yet to be exploited.

Indigenous literature provides authenticity to the teaching material. The learners take language samples from their own life. It acts as a means of cultural enrichment and acquaints the learner with understanding how communication takes place in their set up. Indigenous literature is representational rather than referential because it involves learners mentally and physically. That makes language learning more interesting and exciting. It acquaints learners with a wide range of language varieties used in different situations, the subtlety and imaginative force of the language and encourages the scrupulous use of words. Besides improving all the four communication skills, it also improves language areas such as vocabulary, grammar, pronunciation etc. They learn about the syntax and discourse functions of sentences, the variety of possible structures, and the different ways of connecting ideas.

Learners' Motivation

Learner's motivation plays an important role in learning and using a second language like English. It is possible to orient a learner's motivation in positive direction by using certain pedagogical methods. L2 motivation is always influenced by sociocultural aspect and is never static, it passes through generation, maintenance and retrospection phase. Effective and personalized strategies can increase the learners' linguistic self-confidence and generate sustainable motivation. Motivation to learn a second language is very different from the motivation to learn any other subject. This is because an L2 is not only a communication code, but also a representative of the L2 culture. Learning a second language therefore always entails learning a second culture to some degree. As Williams (1994) argues that learning of a foreign language involves far more than simply learning skills, or a system of rules, or a grammar; it involves an alteration in self-image, the adoption of new social and cultural behaviors and ways of being, and therefore has a significant impact on the social nature of the learner. As a consequence, L2 motivation will always have a strong sociocultural component. That is why some people will be able to communicate with 100 words while others will not be able to communicate even with 1000 words. The learners' initial belief about L2 learning affects motivation.

L1: Teaching Resource

In order to allow learners think without inhibition and express with clarity and precision, use of mother tongue could be the best option. To quote the National Integration Council (1962), "the change of medium of instruction from English to regional languages is justified not so much by cultural or political sentiments as on the very important academic consideration of facilitating grasp and understanding of the subject matter. University men would be unable to make their maximum possible contribution to the advancement of learning unless there is a continuous means of communication in the shape of regional languages between its masses, artisans and technicians and its university men." The elite have always debunked the idea of mother tongue, arguing that imparting education in regional languages will restrict interstate and global mobility of students. Evidence however suggests that language has never been a bottleneck for brilliant scholars wishing to go global.

Indigenous Languages

According to the People's Linguistic Survey of India (PLSI) there are 780 living languages in India. "These Indian languages are crucial for the effective development of fragile communities and for stemming the erosion of India's diverse multilingual and composite heritage", says Dr Ganesh Devi (Devi 2013). The Indian languages which are a very good teaching-learning resource for ELT can be strengthened by adopting a proactive approach in the following ways:

(i) recognizing the prestige of speakers of indigenous languages.
(ii) strengthening the financial position of indigenous language speakers.
(iii) consolidating legitimate power of the speakers of indigenous languages.
(iv) increasing presence of Indigenous languages in educational system.
(v) the written system of indigenous languages must be strengthened.
(vi) use of technology in devising parallel and alternate tools for using indigenous languages.

Conclusion

It is said in our oral traditions that knowledge is neither a privileged discourse nor a discourse of the privileged. There is an urgent need to integrate Indian multilingual and multicultural context in TESL so that English (which is now an Indian language with its own varieties) becomes an instrument of empowerment for the rural learner. ELT in India must incorporate indigenous oral narratives. Having known that 70% of India lives in villages, majority of the potential workforce comes from rural areas. It becomes imperative that students from such areas are given opportunities to use English as a tool for empowerment. The dream of taking English to masses can only be realized by contextualizing the whole process of ELT in oral-rural traditions of *Bharat* (India).

References

Devi, Ganesh (2013). *We are Talking More Using Fewer Words*. Interview by Chitra Padmanabhan, published in 'The Hindu': New Delhi. September 03, 2013.

Hale, Ken (1992). *On Endangered Languages and the Safeguarding of Diversity*. Languages. 68: 1-3.

Kapoor, Kapil (2013). *Culture and Literature in ESL Context* (draft paper).

Krystal, David (2010). *Language Death*. New Delhi: Cambridge University Press.

Mallikarjun, B. (2003). *Use of Folk Literature from a Pedagogical Perspective.* Language in India. Volume 3: 12 December 2003. http://www.languageinindia.com/dec2003/folklorepedagogical.html

Pound, Ezra (1960). *The ABC of Reading.* New York: Laughlin.

Williams, M. (1994). *Motivation in Foreign and Second Language Learning: An Interactive Perspective.* Educational and Child Psychology, 11, 77-84.

Wolf, H-G. and A. Simo Bobda (2000). *The Use of an Indigenous Cultural model in English Language Instruction in Cameroon.* Essen: Laud Linguistic Agency. Series A: General and Theoretical Papers No. 514.

28

Enjambment as One of the Stylistic Features in the Poetry of Lord Alfred Tennyson

Sonia Gouri

Stylistics studies the use of language in literature and those linguistic devices which enhance the expressive resource and charm of the language in literature. This approach helps to develop the skill to use that particular device on any work of literature as required. As we know that there exists a relationship between syntactic units and verse lines. Commonly a distinction is drawn between 'end-stopped lines', in which the last syllable coincides with an important grammatical break, and 'run-on lines' in which there is no congruity of this kind. For the second case, in which there is a grammatical overflow from one line to the next, we may use the term ENJAMBMENT.[1] Enjambment is therefore like metrical variation in setting up a tension between the expected pattern and the pattern actually occurring. Enjambment is most frequently discussed in connection with heroic couplets and blank verse. By using this striking device which has been acknowledged as enjambment, L.A. Tennyson has successfully become obtrusive not only in creating foregrounding and desired literary effect but also in encouraging the deviant and stylistic use of language at the graphic level of language.

In the poetry of Tennyson we find that he has used this linguistic feature quite often in order to create foregrounding effects on the graphic level of poetry. See this example:

> Myself? Is it thus? Myself? Had I
> So little love for thee? But why

Prevail'd not thy pure prayers? Why pray
To one who heeds not, who can save
But will not? Great in faith, and strong
Against the grief of circumstance
Wert thou, and yet unheard. What if
Thou pleadest still, and seest me drive
Thro' utter dark a full-sail'd skiff,
Unpiloted i' the echoing dance
Of reboant whirlwinds, stooping low
Unto the death, not sunk; I know
At matins and at evensong,
That thou, if thou wert yet alive,
In deep and daily prayers wouldst strive
To reconcile me with thy God.

('Supposed Confessions' 87)

If one read these lines by Tennyson's poem 'Supposed Confessions' in a regular way, with silent stresses (pauses) at the end of each line, this would definitely create a conflict between the metrical system (which demand a pause) and the grammatical system (which resists one). Here Tennyson flouts the norms of grammatical break and metrical pauses and has foregrounded his poetic language with the help of this device.

Moreover Tennyson does not to have a major grammatical break (e.g. between clauses) every few words, so that where enjambment occurs, such breaks are almost bound to occur either in the preceding line, or in the following line, or in both. These breaks require pauses, making up for the silent stress omitted at the end of the line. One disturbance of the metrical movement therefore tends to rectify the other: a reader is held up by an un-metrical break before the end of one line, but makes up for it by a headlong swoop into the next.

"When enjambment becomes more than an occasional device, it becomes almost impossible for a listener to follow the line-division of blank verse without a text in front of him."[2] Enjambment is really a matter of the degree of grammatical cohesion between the end of the line and the beginning of the next. The most common and least startling form of enjambment is that in which the end of one line and the beginning of the following one belong to different phrases, but are part of the same clause.[3]

As in the following example from Tennyson's Poem 'Supposed Confessions' we are not able to find the smallest grammatical unit to which the end of one line and the start of next line belong. See the example in which Tennyson has started almost all the grammatical units (sentences) from the middle of the line:

Why not believe than? Why not yet
Anchor thy frailty there, where man
Hath moor'd and rested? Ask the sea
At midnight, when the crisp slope waves
After a tempest rib and fret
The broad-imbased beach, why the
Slumbers not like a mountain tarn?

('Supposed Confession' 123)

We may describe enjambment as the placing of a line boundary where a deliberate pause, according to grammatical and phonological considerations, would be abnormal; that is, at a point where a break between intonation patterns is not ordinarily permitted. Such a break most frequently coincides with a clause boundary or sentence boundary. As punctuation marks generally indicate places where a pause is allowable, the identification of enjambment is a rule-of-thumb good enough for most purposes.[4]

One of the important functions of enjambment is its role in building up expensive structure known as verse paragraphs. The term has been applied to succession of blank verse lines which seem cemented into one long monumental unit of expression. The verse-paragraph is neither a unit of syntax nor a unit of verse: it is rather a structure which arises from the interrelation of the two.[5]

To analyze this feature in Tennyson's poetry we should examine this stanza:

With earliest light of Spring,
And in the glow of sallow Summertide,

And in red Autumn when the winds are wild
With gambols, and when full-voiced Winter roofs.
The headland with inviolate white snow,
I play about his heart a thousand ways,
Visit his eyes with visions, and his ears
With harmonies of wind and wave and wood,—
Of winds which tell of waters, and of waters
Betraying the close kisses of the wind—
And win him into me: and few there be
So gross of heart who have not felt and known
A higher than they see: They with dim eyes
Behold me darkling.

('Timbuctoo', 97)

1. In this verse there is also a metrical finality of line division. The essence of verse paragraph is an avoidance of finality (end of phrase, end of clause, etc.), leading up to the absolute finality of the end of a sentence.

2. Perhaps we may refer to the various kind of medical stopping place as 'points of arrest', reserving the term 'point of release' for the ultimate point of rest: the coincidence of line-end and sentence-end.[6]

What is remarkable about these lines from Tennyson's famous poem 'Timbuctoo' is first of all length of the verse (paragraph) does the unit extended far enough to make the term 'paragraph' applicable from the graphalogical point of view. The piece quoted is evidently only an excision from the middle of one of these units of expression for although it constitutes a complete sentence; it begins and ends at point of metrical incompleteness - i.e. in the middle of a line. Thus when the metre bids the reader pause, the syntax urges him on, and *vice versa*. In blank verse, a point of complete rest is only reached when a sentence boundary and a line boundary coincide. If either occurs without the other, some structural expectation is still unfulfilled; the reader has, as it were, arrived at a halting-place, not to a destination.[7]

Thus, we find that enjambment is one of the most stylistic features in the poetry of Tennyson; he uses to create for grounding by halting the readers.

Notes

1. Geoffrey N. Leech. *A Linguistic Guide to English Poetry* (London: Longman, 1988), 123.
2. *Id.* at 124.
3. *Id.* at 125.
4. Supra note 1, at 125, see Halliday and Strevence, *op. cit.*, 51.
5. *Ibid.*
6. *Id.* at 126.
7. *Ibid.*

29

Demand of Communication Skills in the Present Era

Kartikey

Abstract

This paper deals with the new trends in communication skills, i.e. the place of communication and its importance in today's era. Communication Skill has evidently become an essential essence in the human personality. The corporate today seeks specifically well communicated people as they represent the companies globally. In order to transform the students into an individual which fulfill the necessities of corporate world, a teacher has to have a strategic plan and set of innovative methodologies. This paper also highlights the change in communication system and its adaptability in present time, which has drastically changed the whole picture of world of work.

Our former Prime Minister Pandit Jawaharlal Nehru rightly said "The Destiny of a nation is shaped in her classrooms". This was a prophetic statement and castes the reality of the learners as the young are the inheritors of tomorrow. We need to be extra careful with our students who are standing at the threshold of adulthood, where the world of work is beckoning them to participate and contribute through effective communication. Core competence in engineering and science education as well as study of human values and philanthropic philosophy need to be synthesized to eliminate any kind of mental insufficiency and this will develop confidence to excel in the work place. Employers are now looking for people who can do more than just perform a set of assigned tasks. They are increasingly searching for more than a qualified, and highlighting one's mental stability ornamented by good communication skills, it can put one at a considerable advantage over similarly qualified candidates. In fact, the ability to communicate ideas and concepts to others effectively is an absolutely essential requirement for technical, engineering and IT professionals, as the nature of the industries makes them dependent upon shared knowledge.

Till date, the learning or teaching of communication revolved round spoken and written skills—like presentations, group discussion, reports of different kind and so on. However, in regard to students doing professional courses, it extended upon project writing, thesis, etc. But a very effective communicator must have more than these skill sets. In fact, communication is to a large extent a matter of attitude, a willingness to communicate, share ideas and information and a good communicator has all these. In short, it is the right attitudinal input that helps a person to emerge as a better and effective communicator with a balance of all necessary ingredients.

The adaptability of science and technology clearly shows that today a three year old play games on computer, high school students surf the internet, dual telephone lines (fax and phones) are hooked to many Indian homes, instant world wide communication is common and communicating via satellite is the norm. All these tools recognize the changing trends in the communication skills. Present day perspective clearly reveals that technology and communication are inter-related and effective communication is the foundation of learning. Employers who communicate effectively have more productive employees, ready to represent themselves globally.

There has been such an expansion in communication that it may be called as communication revolution owing to the unprecedented information explosion. Students do confront a lot of challenges vis-a-vis the demands of corporate world. All over the world it has become an established fact that people from India while technically brilliant, lack communication skills and soft skills as well. Education systems are getting revamped to include efforts to develop communication skills and soft skills from early on and having a major part of grades dependent on them. Concentration mainly on inner strengths and verbal and vocal communication which is less than 20% of any communication, any message, will not be able to develop proper communication skill development requirement.

In today's competitive world of work the need for creating a first impression is paramount to success in personal, professional and social life. Numerous articles in newspapers and magazines highlighting the need for presenting oneself in the possible manner are now being published. The corporate culture today demands not only a very effective communication skill but a highly attractive soft skill in the shape of image management. As it is known that corporate now demands a personality comprising of all necessary contents with an ability to execute effectively and to obtain this personality, image management is a must. Image management is actually, a science and an art of projecting a powerful and attention-drawing image to create a great first impression by the optimal utilization of one's personal resources of clothing, grooming, body language, etiquette and vocal communication mingled with the dynamics of stress, tone, rhythm and modulation. Image management specializes in visual communication which is over 80% of any communication, any message. It helps in gaining and acquiring image that corporate demand.

In fact, students with effective communication skills in addition to subject knowledge have an immense advantage over others lacking similar skills and has been commonly observed. In view of this perspective, we need to put forward over our ideas, concepts, views and opinions regarding language pedagogy for the underprivileged students coming from non-English medium backgrounds to pursue higher studies. They have the necessary talent, caliber and potentialities. We need to bring them out of the Cocoon they are in; they need to be trained properly so that they can confront the challenges of the world of work. They need to have the confidence and is possible only when they develop effective communication skills.

Institutions of academic excellence should try to locate the communication needs of students vis-a-vis the requirements of the working world in different situations and to guide and equip the users to fulfill them appropriately. We should have a comprehensive view of the requirements in regard to latest game plan communication. This can be made possible with the help of modern and effective teaching tools. As discussed earlier, modern and latest technological communicative components have transformed traditional communication system. Making students aware about these components and telling them their utilization in today's scenario will help in building and boosting up their personalities. The students can also be shown the relevant videos so that they may absorb the essential elements which are needed. The interactive Communication Lab set ups also help in judging various factors which can be utilized in day to day activities. These methods can act as effective transference of communication abilities.

The ability to communicate effectively has always provided advantages to those who possess it. In fact, communication is the 'life-blood' of every organization. Ineffective messages or communication alienate customers and these are more expensive than effective ones and they also destroy good will. Such risk factors cannot be undertaken by the companies and in order to reduce risk factors they employ candidates equipped with effective and impressive communication. In multinational corporations, thousands of hours are spent daily to interviews, conferences, memos, reports, employee manuals, letters, advertising, new articles, bulletins, news letters and other messages. Time is the chief element in the overall cost of written and oral communication. For example, the time spent just in written tasks can occupy much of the working day. In a survey of four professional areas, a substantial number of respondents, none of whom was employed as a writer, indicated that they spent from 29 to more than 50% of their time in writing. Manager, technical workers, clerical staff and social service workers spent 49.4%, 40.7%, 29.1% and 51.6% of hours respectively, in writing. The ability to communicate orally and in writing affects the company's public image. Today's workplace is increasingly diverse in age, gender and national origin. Diversity has brought both problems and strengths to organizations. Management styles have also undergone several changes. Its key motive is making effective communication central to success in carrying out the organization's business. Today's managers and workers need to be flexible in the way they deal with others; problems can be avoided by keeping an open mind and being willing to make extra efforts in communication. The workforce in such sort of environment works with full efficiency and with zero communication barriers. This high potential work and endeavors helps the company to acquire a position known globally and thus facilitating globalization. The term Globalization in the business world means the company for the sake of its survival must establish markets not only in its own country but also in many foreign countries. Thus, employees become potential international communicators and they must understand and appreciate other's cultures and variables. Therefore, to communicate effectively with global companies we must be aware of our own country's ethnic diversity. In fact, there is a large mix of nationalities and people throughout the world. And central to improving and understanding one another in communication training, captured in a statement made by a scholar in South Africa: "Stress is placed upon the concept of background which we believe is necessary to an understanding of the total communication process. By background which we mean those aspects that can either impede or aid effective communication: language, culture, status, education and age". Different cultures use different communication methods. In short, knowing core characteristics of a country are basic to better international communication. Our students should therefore be exposed before the highly delicate communication pattern that keeps the pace with the complex variables resulting from confrontation with various international cultures. The faculty shall have to equip themselves with these patterns of communication and make the students aware of the same. Secondly, the faculty shall have to be extra careful about the word usage. The knowledge that a faculty imparts, should keep the vision of today's challenges; the pronunciation, vocabulary and strategic plans should meet the aforesaid necessities. Miscommunication occurs not only in business and industrial offices but also among government officials, military leaders, professionals and all of us in our everyday contacts. Therefore, to avoid communication errors we should be sure that the words we use convey the intended meaning to the recipient. Thirdly, in a world of increasing competition we seem to need more refined skills of communication than was necessary before. We need to be aware of certain norms, techniques and methods to excel. The difference is similar to knowing how to run naturally and participating in a running competition. Many know how to run but to excel; one has to have proper training. Hence there is need for training to communicate effectively and appropriately. All this can be achieved by the usage of refined techniques and best strategic plans targeting students to turn them into perfect personalities.

In view of what has been stated regarding the ever increasing and emerging domains in communication, we do need to put emphasis more on the urgent communication requirements resulting from the information explosion, business, world diversities dealing with customers, clients and the public. Students should be exposed before the practical communication requirements and they should be nurtured accordingly so that they are properly equipped to confront the communication from the world of work.

As globalization and competitiveness becomes the benchmark of any multinational organization, it is obviously important for employees to be equipped with employable skills. Considering skill based training is the need of the of the hour, one of the important parts of the training program should include workshops and guest lectures conducted by industry and language experts to help students get the right exposure and understanding of the existing and new trends of communication. Students need to be motivated to understand the efficacy of having effective language skills, for language efficiency is the key to develop self-confidence. Students come to the university with hopes and expectations and they need to be nurtured but effective nurturing is possible only when we, in the university, are aware of our responsibilities to see to it that willing-to-learn-students are given special care so that they can face the rigors of the demands of the world of work, the challenges thrown by the corporate world and the high job market competition. Our education system, are innovative techniques, our sincerest efforts shall have to be there to develop the competencies, among the students, required for the world of work.

With this sense of responsibility and modern methodologies a teacher can rectify the existing errors in the student with positive inputs meeting today's challenging boundaries. These techniques indeed propagates a student to voice out his or her opinion with more and better self confidence. Thus communication gives perfect add-ons to the personalities which are actually needed.

Works Cited

Krishna Mohanand Meera Bannerji: *Developing Communication Skills*, Macmillan India Ltd.

Friedrike Klippel: *Keep Talking*, Cambridge University Press, London, 1984.

Patricia Hayes Andrews and Richard T. Herschel: *Organizational Communication: Empowerment in a Technological Society*. Honghton Mifflin Company, U.S.A., 1998.

Andra J. Rutherford: Basic Communication Skills for Technology, Pearson Education, Inc, New Delhi.

30

Quantity versus Quality—A Dilemma for English Teaching in India

Varsha Vats

Abstract

Teaching English in India meets with enormous challenges where one of the major, most debating and inevitable challenge is to establish equilibrium between 'Quantity' and 'Quality'. These inter-reliant terms generate an impact on the overall personality of a student but the question is—Does quantity really matters?.... Or better teaching pedagogy can overcome the quantity issue. The fact remains controversial with different perspectives as the results vary region to region. Though the essential factors to bring both in decorum i.e. *Quantity and Quality* are Class-size and Teaching Methodology. A focused and preparative teaching can help the students to gain the accurate motive imparted by a teacher independent of class-size, thus results may be obtained even with exceedingly high strength. On the other hand, the issue remains entrenched for the students with less grasping power and therefore they are subjected to *quantity*; condensed strength works in unveiling the hesitation and gives better perceiving power, undeniably *quality* is needed there too. The paper outlines a dogma on the various conceptualizations of English Teaching in India.

India is a country of multilingual society and diversified cultures where teaching parameters vary to a large extent. Teaching English becomes a hardcore task as at many points just teaching isn't ample to suffice various aspects, several other factors are also indispensable to obtain desirable results and in order to achieve the goal, a teacher experiments with the curriculum and methodologies. But the proceedings take a pause when it comes to the supply of *quantity* or *quality*.

Quantity says about comparative dimensions or measurable components, on the other hand, quality is about the degree of excellence. To establish a concord between the terms becomes immensely essential when it comes to the mode of teaching and learning English. The liability for the whole set-up falls upon the shoulders of a teacher. A teacher has a critical role to play as it has the responsibility to regulate the entire scenario with an impact of positive results taking in count—teaching style, ability, skills, techniques, curriculum, etc. All this definitely helps in the betterment of quality but the question again scuffles on quantity. How can that be managed?...... Is the management really needed? ....Or the quality can diminish the issue of quantity. India faces number of complexities in stabilizing the two terms especially in English teaching in comparison with the teaching of other subjects and the major reason is adaptability of English as a Second Language. The act of practicing English as a Second Language makes Communicative Language Teaching more complicated and reduces the amount of learner's attention while the focus is diverted more towards other subjects and English understanding becomes just "subject oriented" lacking depth. This happens because teachers use regional languages and English merely for instruction and clarity is provided between the two if needed, without any translation and keep learner in pace by this sort of theory. Effective teachers imply active teaching patterns such as communicating clearly while giving directions, specifications of tasks and execution of information. They also keep a check on learner's progress and provide them with feedback. Such teachers act as mentors with a sense of efficacy ensuing quality but if quantity fluctuates then it may hinder the quality as monitoring of students becomes inflexible leading to unfavourable results.

Further, "learnability" is an attention gathering factor which requires debate, based on these two inter-reliant terms. To justify the learnability factor an example will throw a light on the subject matter:

A teacher divides a group of learners into two, viz. Group A & Group B. Group A was instructed to craft single pot out of clay and should uphold perfection. The task was to be performed by each learner of the group within 15 days for which they would get an A. Synonymously Group B was also instructed to make pots but 50 in number by each learner and perfection wasn't necessary, within same time frame, they will be awarded A. Which group would have produced better pots? Whose work would have been better the Quality Group – Group A or the Quantity Group – Group B?

Group A invested several hours on a single pot, shaping and reshaping it…yet they were unable to turn out ideal pots, Group B on the other hand made so many pots that over time they figured out the correct way of doing it and they were now more capable of designing perfect pots. Here quantity wins hence, learnability factor is observed. This also encompasses an additional set of observation, i.e. the repetition of task helps in acquiring learnability which in turn produces quality and puts forward a view 'Quantity produces Quality'.

So far, many aspects have been in inclusion but one thing that continuously strikes is…. How this argument came to the fore? How has this occupied space?

As far as India is concerned there are numerous factors, as mentioned earlier that India is a multilingual society therefore it deals with the language and articulation issue and have been found quite usual in different parts of India which hinders the quality education provided by a teacher. And talking in terms of quality, certainly Demographic Conditions cover a major portion for the answer of this question. The continual raise in population depicts a lot of serious Teaching and Learning problems. According to census 2011 India's population is 121 crore and have shown a tremendous growth in comparison with earlier years. It becomes obvious that the supply of learners in the educational institutes also increases resulting in the exceeding strength from the normal ratio. These demographic conditions points towards the ability of institutions to respond effectively as it collide with the teachers' population too which is relatively less. To overcome such troublesome circumstance more schools and colleges are opened. According to 'Seventh All India School Education Survey' held by *National Council of Educational Research & Training (NCERT), New Delhi* Primary Schools have shown a growth of 14.13% including rural and urban increment of 12.85% and 24.45% respectively. In Upper Primary Schools a growth of 50.68% has been recorded with respect to the Sixth Survey. Secondary Schools and Higher Secondary have depicted a raise of 38.40% and 85.40% respectively. In addition to these figures *The District Education Revitalization Programme (DERP)* has also opened 16,000 new schools including 84,000 alternative educational schools delivering education to approximately 3.5 million children, supported by UNICEF and other international programmes. The statistics clearly reveal drastic elevation which in turn signifies the incessant population expansion.

The above data also shows the enhancement in number of enrolment but the levels of quality remains low due to shortage of resources, lack of political will, high poor levels of teacher training and off course high pupil to teacher ratio.

At last a conclusive view that is observed is that the foundation of English Learning is laid at the primary levels of education; if the teaching quality is imparted best at the learner's initial developmental stages then it can provide better understanding and outcome as Steve Jobs quoted "Quality is more important than Quantity. One home run is much better than two doubles".

The fine and flawless English Teaching at the beginning is far better than the struggling phase later.

References

http://www.ncert.nic.in/programmes/education_survey

http://en.wikipedia.org/wiki/Education_in_India

http://educationnext.org/quantity-over-quality/

http://www.teachingenglish.org.uk/article/revising-lexis-quality-or-quantity

31

Usage-Based Approaches in Acquisition of English Language: Towards a Better Tomorrow

Neha Anand

To Survive in the Modern Society English Language Learning is as Important as Water to us

India, an all-embracing gamut of dialectal background, merges in numerous languages. English, with the fame of the official lingo, has been acknowledged as pane of success in all the walk of life. In fast paced world, where things acquire the apparels of new into the blink of an eye, where man hovers in the sky of technology and floats in the sea of communication, ascendancy of any venture hinges on the knack of unveiling the thoughts in an awe-inspiring way. With this expansion, English teaching and learning process has met with a whirlwind of translocations in its pedagogy from translation of grammar to direct method, to audiolingualism. Lamentably, the contemporary education system asserts teaching and learning of English not less than a challenge as majority of teachers and students are in habit of dealing with English in the way alike to other subject. Consequently, the standard of English has not spring up to that radius it should effectuate. To amend socio and fiscal stature of the country, to address the echelon of expertise, to cater the need of globalized epoch, the teacher should throw away concepts and techniques of bygone days classroom teaching and should cuddle the topical and novel teaching techniques as it would pave way for learning the language along with the cherry of self-reliance on the persona of learner.

Education, a modus operandi of sophistication and empowerment to bestow the individuals a sheltered, a better eminence of life, has converted into inclusive and a versatile social service, which aims at the expansion of body, mind, intellect and soul. Consequently, the need of the hour is to embrace modern knowledge planted on age old culture.

English lingo, the contemporary lingua franca of the international business, technology, aviation, diplomacy, banking, computing, medicines, engineering and tourism is spoken by 1.8 billion people all over the globe and the number still increasing by leaps and bounds.

Alexander V. Sandoval, in his essay, "The Importance of English", claims very aptly that "English is becoming the world's language of the 21st century. Most of the world's population, about 70% speak English or know it. And more than 80% of all stored information in the world is written in English or translated into it. Foreign language skills, and in particular the English are a good tool in work, school, on vacation, when building a career or promote your own business. The man who speaks fluent in English will not get lost in the world where there are people."

English owns all the right to be the tool of empowerment and estrangement, the way of bringing about rectitude and creating divisions, the apparatus of edification.

Krishnaswamy and Shriman (1994) have truly stated: "English has become an international commodity like oil and the micro ship and more than a quarter of the world's people use English; the world has become a global village. English has become necessary for mobility and social and economic success in the world today".

Below listed are the reasons that describe the importance of English.

The Language of the World

English has turned out to be the dialect of choice for communication from one corner to the other corner of the world. People are so acquainted with words of high rate of recurrence from the spoken lingo that these words have even been embraced by other languages.

The Language to Open up More Opportunities

Even the countries which have not welcomed English as an official language use it as lingua franca. The knack to verbalize English opens up lots of possibilities as professions like aviation, tourism and film industries, bring into play English as their official lingo, and many employers hailed from these sectors are liable to entail evidence of a assured echelon of expertise in English before they will deem employing anyone. Where on one hand, the applicant's ability or inability to speak glibly in English is one of the noted selection criterions, on the other to linger employable, to have career growth, the skill to use a language competently in both oral and written form is extremely obligatory. The present scenario witnesses the situation, when the mere domain information won't assure one a good job. It is English which can offer a greater number of possible careers to choose from. Howsoever adroit a job-hunter is in hard skills until and unless he has equal mastery over communication skills, he can't come off with flying colours in job. A candidate with the cherry of soft skills is many more time taken in than one who lags behind on the same ground. Whether it's engineering, science, commerce or technology, English open the road of success. A latter day review said that out of very hundred interviews, only five qualified for employability. It is not that were technically sound but they lacked is communication skills.

The Language of International Trade

On the ground of international trade and commerce, speaking a lingua franca is a key. In a situation when a denizen of country does trade with the one of which dialect he is not aware of, the arbitration and transactions come about in none but English only. The rise of globalization has given this opportunity to the domestic companies to think beyond the precincts of their nations. Language is no more a fence for populace who has it in mind to settle down in other country. To represent the company on the global stage and to deal with huckster and parochial exertion, it is big-league for acquaintances to have expertise in English.

The Language of Education and Research

Most of the world's top universities have opted English as medium of instruction and proffer copious courses and degree programs which are taught in English. The ubiquity of English, as an empyrean language, holds importance in light of the fact that more than few people leave their countries not only on the ground of business and pleasure, but also on getting studied there. People going to other country to study have the option of English as their medium of study since the individual will not be competent to become skilled at a subject in the provincial language of the country.

Maukalel (1998) states, "English as become a status symbol and a student without a reasonable command over English is perhaps not very comfortable with attainment of any educational goal. Similarly teaching of English holds the key position in the entire curriculum of education. Teachers of English, in this context, owe the responsibility to enable the learners to achieve the educational goals in general and language."

The Language of Travel

Language varies from country to country. When a person rambles in a place where English is acknowledged as the preeminent tongue, it is more than imperative to be adept in it. In most of the countries, symbols have a propensity to appear in the local tongue first and English second for the reason that globetrotter may not versed with the local vernacular of that country but they have high chance of speaking English. It can be of great relieve for speakers of not as much of broadly spoken languages to have basic English to speak with foreigners and to explore the regions that may otherwise remain unknown.

The Language of Same Country

In countries like India whose legacy in languages is one of the richest in the world, where the land is so cosmic with people of a variety of cultures, where populace put on show high degree of multiplicity in their languages and dialects, English bridges the gap and connects the people.

The Language of Wider Access to Knowledge

Knowledge of English allows tapping into far more of the world's intellectual resources since 55% of the world's web pages are in black and white in English. Subsequently command over English will not bestow only an entrée to a bigger percentage of the vast sum of information existing on the web; but also makes one able to train oneself still further by being able to read scientific books and papers.

In the epoch of globalization, English has received emancipation from the manacles of four walls of a classroom—an issue between the student and the instructor—but has been applauded, across the globe, as a link language for all the activities performed by civilization.

Language varies to teach in the regard of its outcome. Being very old language, English has undergone many forms transformation from Proto English derivative from the Latin and the German customs to the Modern English. Present day in spite of being the simple most version of a very old Language, it is no less than thorny to educate this lingo lucratively in particular to those who have accepted English as a second language.

Since English is not the first language of majority of Indians, the standard of English has not spring up to the extent, to that radius, it should effectuate. Due to the less attention paid by the education ministers, it has not come out with the marvelous results. Teaching English which is the 'language of development', 'the language of modernization', 'the language of science and technology', 'the language of opportunity', has become herculean task here and now and incontrovertibly, the reason of this is that students apprentice English alike other subjects, not as language. Communicating in English is something that is not less than a bug bear

> The English language in all an advanced and flexible one and its teaching should not be discarded

altogether. Indian cannot afford to ignore this language.
—Dr. Rajendra Prasad

"For more than two centuries of intimate contact has made English an integral part of our educational system mid this can't be changed without endangering our education in India. Moreover, English has today become one of tire internationally spoken language of the world and we Indians can't neglect its study as it will put us in backwardness but the medium of instruction must be from the very nature of the case by the mother tongue", said our late Education Minister Maulana Azad.

Problems with Current Methodologies

Till mammoth degree, teacher holds the accountability for the letdown of English in view of the fact that the way in which teachers are shaking hands with teaching of English in our colleges is not able to serve the purpose. There are scarce means to comprehend the lofty targets of English language learning and teaching. Since English is not the mother tongue of the country, students bump into a plenty of problems in handling it. The situation gives birth to the need of knowing the problems in learning English.

Psychosomatic Problem: The misunderstanding that lies in the midst of students is that it is English which deserves to be considered as the most difficult subjects they have. Through the year, what they have is prejudiced vision which results into poor performance at the end of the year.

Problem of epitomizing the soul of Idea: The teachers, having problem in personifying the abstractness, of the fiction, poesy, passage, fail to create live pictures in class rooms. Due to that novice fails to come off with flying colours in getting the abstract idea. If truth be told the teacher who possesses the mentality that it is waste of time to arouse emotions and interact with the students is, for all time, in hasten to wrap the portion.

Translation Method: Translation technique, the most trendy method of teaching English at rustic areas, enables the students to be responsive to the content of the text but creates obstacles in the path of learning the language and put the main aim of teaching the language on the back burner as it puts all the meaning on the teaching of content and theme.

Lack of Practice & Interest: Practice makes a man perfect. Language skills that comprised of Listening, Speaking, Reading, and Writing can be by mastered only by dint of hard work. But taughts look at the subject as an unavoidable hurdle and concentrate on this only for the sake of getting passing marks to cross this hurdle by hook and by crook.

Lack of Modern Teaching Tools: The lack of audio visual tools also adds fuel in the problem of lack of interest and practice. Countless teachers find themselves unable to teach English effectively as they lag behind in using modern teaching tool as part of teaching-learning process. Additionally the available tools are not sufficient in number to cater the needs of learners.

Nosiness of Mother Tongue: Meddling of mother tongue in speaking English plays a chief role in the birth of more than a few problems as the teachers and the students, having expertise and glibness in their own mother tongue; forget the heart of pure lingo and bring into play English words in the midst of the sentences exclusive of realizing that every language varies in the regard of stress, cadence and articulation.

Erroneous Selection of Learning Method: The present education system witnesses the situation where students who are intermediate or degree holder of graduation with English either as an enforced or as an optional subject are not competent enough to speak and write English properly since the prominence has always been on the conceptual content and syllabus completion. The teacher, without considering the obstacles, which the learners face in learning English, goes on teaching the syllabus. In learning the mother tongue, Direct or Natural method is used in which the used sequence follows—1. Listening, 2. Speaking, 3. Reading, 4. Writing to be precise from easiest to toughest one. But the method of learning English follows the vice versa sequence 1. Writing, 2. Reading, 3. Speaking, 4. Listening, i.e. from the difficult knack to a trouble-free one.

Divergence in Pronunciation of English: Unlike languages of the world, English is pronounced in a very different way in every region of the world where English. The confusion comes in existence when students are not competent enough to know the difference between US English, Queen's English and the entire sundry English's of the world.

Blemished Education System: Defective education system is unquestionably on the hook for the problem as students and teachers as well have been on a track of completing the syllabus by hook or by crook. They study English as subject from the examination point of view only. This blemished education system judges the students' caliber on the ground of the grades that they achieve in these examinations. The more grades, the max intelligent he will be considered. In contemplation of assimilating more grades, they mug up the topic of syllabus, reproduce them at the day of exam and make it dismissed from their mind on the same day itself. This era demands the knowledge on the ground of practical proficiency. The certificate of mastery will not be adequate to establish the fact how sharpened the skill students possess.

Over Packed Classrooms: The foremost challenge witnessed by the teachers is overcrowded classrooms where very students are at same level of proficiency. The classrooms are over packed with the students who vary in the regard of culture, language, and academia and so on. It has been troublesome for ELT teachers to figure out the level at which they should aim at in their classes. Since the class owns the students from medium and English background it becomes challenging for the teacher to meet their desire, to cater their needs. As a matter of fact the students coming from non-English background are blessed with all prerequisite caliber and potentials but here what is of utmost importance to bring them out of their cocoon in which they are. Student expresses an opinion that speaking in English is to cut down to size the importance of the mother tongue. Being phobia tic of speaking in English, this is undoubtedly a lame excuse given by them. Majority of students, especially from rural pockets take this seven letter word as magical and mystical word. The moment they see anyone communicating in English, they start to feel uneasiness. In order to remove their phobia their hesitation they should be asked to give their introduction to identify various difficulties that their parents under went through to make them.

Mistakes in English

While using English students commit mistakes inadvertently as when a mistake is committed on regular basis, it becomes habit of doing that.

Winkler (2008) pointed out, "Mistakes tells us more about what children understand about the language than the correct things that they say."

Our first Prime Minister Pt. Jawaharlal Nehru has truly state "The destiny of nation is shaped in her classrooms."

It is no one but youngsters only who are the inheritors of tomorrow. We need to be extra cautious with our students who are standing on the doorstep of adulthood, where, to participate and contribute through effective communication, is world's anticipation from them. Howsoever adroit a job-hunter is in hard skills until and unless he has equal mastery over communication skills, he can't come off with flying colours in job. A candidate with the cherry of soft skills is many more time taken in than one who lags behind on the same ground. Whether it's engineering, science, commerce or technology, English open the road of success. A latter day review said that out of very hundred interviews, only five qualified for employability.

The nitty gritty of English can be feasible no more than by going down the line of orthodox practice of showing the ropes of the alphabets, the words along with their uses of implementation. However, the teaching only the rules contribute a great deal in the hammering of interest of students who find it dreary. Even though there is no way other than the conventional one to edify the nuts and bolts of the lingo, these methods must be tune up in order to fascinate to the students.

Methods of Learning English in Present Scenario

Portraying the Tales: Stories, a very integral part of teaching a language, lend a hand in teaching as it keep posted the configuration of sentences and keep the students interest alive and appeal to the inquisitive nature in view of the fact that the culmination of the story is somewhat that every student desires to be acquainted with. Despite the fact that this process of using fables has been executed the modus operandi of teaching the language through it is by and large not correct. Since, the assessment system of testing the students on the ground of their expertise over the language is through questions based on the story, the students, more often than not, become inclined to take up the stories as a chapter A story which appeals to the ingenious part of the intellect, which it helps in being more creative, by visualizing the incidents, the emotions that are happening within the story, should teach them the language along with bestowing the sense of extracting a lesson from the story. When a student enacts the stories or the plays, he gets connected with the characters of those and metes out his own perception of the character to life by understanding them and setting into their shoes. It helps him in coming into the contact of other people's interpretation of the story and bestows him with an opportunity to have heads together about it which, indubitably, helps in acquiring the language. Enacting the stories with dialogue develops the skills of adding more lines, characters, change the ending, bring in an interesting twist, etc. leads to personality development. When great dramas and stories like Julius Caesar, Twelfth Night, Arms and the Man Christmas Carol, Harry Potter are taught in this way, student get the deep inside the character by understanding their emotions which the student would never understand if these are taught using traditional methods of questions and answers. When the student throws himself into the atmosphere of the story, every intention of the story becomes clear and enables the student able to answer questions without even preparing for it as an exam.

Edifying through Conversations

It is conversations, the most constructive ways of teaching the language, which proffers the prospect to a child to gain knowledge of mother tongue as the conversation between him and his parents, makes him competent to evaluate the meaning and learns it with ease. When a topic is given for reading, forming an opinion and doing the conversation, the students take care of sentences in it.

The chipping in, in the conversation can be analyzed by points which will also push the students to take part in the conversation. Students, when they converse on the topic of their day to day life, gain expertise in expressing themselves. This process may be time taking but in long term, it would come out as the most proficient one in teaching the language.

Innovative Coursework

Assignments require efforts of researching a lot on writing something new. But when this method is to be used in the field of a language, assignments should be given of that kind which give chance to modify something that already exists. When a basic knowledge and data are provided to students, they can modify it by dint of their creativity and this also overcomes the obstacles in the way of writing. They can complete the assignments whole heartedly and consequently complete the learning experience that can be secured from the assignment.

Multimedia Aids

Multimedia sources like songs, movies, TV series, magazines, newspapers play a very imperative role in improving our language since learning with these become fun for students. Students, during free time, can listen to songs which will teach him to use a language to express feelings. Movies, besides being common past time, are very instructional and didactic. Learners, after appealed by them, become connected with the songs and the movies which help them understand the meaning of expressions, usage of tools of the language like comparisons, personifications, etc. When traditional methods like reading newspaper and novels are mingled with some pioneering thoughts the entire learning and the teaching process is enriched and guarantees a success in efficient learning.

Nevertheless this method should be used in the final stages of learning as that is the aids like movies and songs use slang English which is grammatically incorrect.

Extra Activities Apart from Regular Classroom Teaching

Extra activities, apart from classroom teaching, like debates and elocutions, speeches, presentations, facilitate the students in acquiring the language as the facet of the competitions maintain them at the best in conversations for the reason that it fuel them to use the construction of sentences in best form with effective use of good vocabulary etc. and develops their personality by removing the phobia of public speaking. Apart from the syllabus the more emphasis should lay down on the speaking skills of students. Duos the teachers and students should put their genuine efforts to acquire adroitness is the regard of speaking. Extra classes of GDPI should be brought in as the part of the curriculum. As the demand of work of world is fluent English, these classes can be fruitful as it can produce the habit of communication in English. The sole responsibility of teacher is to make them confident by sharing the details that how they should speak on a topic. Instead of expecting them to speak for a longtime, just a minute technique can serve the purpose as it will be of much more convenience for the students to utilize this technique.

Word Games

Learning the vocabulary, the most important part of any language, is the task that appears very tedious and troublesome to students. Games which are designed for this specific purpose overcome this difficulty. The games like scrabble, housie help the students develop their vocabulary by improving the word database of the students such as simple aural test competitions, synonym competitions, words puzzles, anagrams and hangman. These games are very fruitful because when a student listens to these words, he becomes acquainted with it and learns its usage without finding it difficult anymore.

Conclusion

The languages which rally round in expressing the emotions, in clearing up wants and wishes, in communicating to the world for numerous purposes, play a very vital role in our lives. As language defines us, it is very obligatory to have command over language along with its proper utilization. In view of the fact that English is the official lingo of this cosmos, it is of utmost magnitude that this language has to be taught in such a way that it will help not merely to converse, note down and listen but to communicate, which is panacea of everything, a key to unlock the door of success. Since innovative methods help in bringing a change, it helps the students become skilled at in faster and in a well-organized, attention-grabbing and an interactive manner. The teachers should shoulder the responsibility of absconding to the conventional methods and developing a temptation for using innovative techniques for the students benefit. The teachers are expected to gear up to cater the need of the time. Being the language of International communication, higher learning and extra ordinary better options of career, English should be accessible to classes as well as masses to bridge the discrimination among rich and poor in the regard of opportunities for personal, professional and economic development. Duos the teachers and the students need to open their eyes to the fact that lingo awareness is meant neither as abolishment nor as amusement. We are in need to return to the world of Chaucer's clerk,

"Gladly would he learn and gladly teach."

Works Cited

Maicuse, T. and Panayota, M. (2000), "The Errors in the Second Language Acquisition," Universidad de Granada.

Mueen, A. (1992), "English Language Teaching in Pakistan," National Book Foundation, Islamabad.

http://iteslj.org/techniques/Kelly-Authentic.html.

www.eagleforum.com

http://www.preservearticles.com/201103034387/essay-on-importance-of-learning-english-in-india.html

https://www.oxford-royale.co.uk/articles/reasons-learn-english.html

http://www.tesl-ej.org/ej35/cf.pdf